CH00708717

Feb 2006

A Politics of Tensions

Robert W. Hoffert

A Politics of Tensions

The Articles of Confederation and American Political Ideas

University Press of Colorado

Copyright © 1992 by the University Press of Colorado
P.O. Box 849
Niwot, Colorado 80544

Material from *The Creation of the American Republic, 1776–1787* by Gordon S. Wood, reprinted by permission of the University of North Carolina Press.

The University Press of Colorado is a cooperative publishing enterprise supported, in part, by Adams State College, Colorado State University, Fort Lewis College, Mesa State College, Metropolitan State College of Denver, University of Colorado, University of Northern Colorado, University of Southern Colorado, and Western State College.

Library of Congress Cataloging-in-Publication Data

Hoffert, Robert W.
    A politics of tensions: the Articles of Confederation and American political ideas
/ Robert W. Hoffert.
       p. cm.
    Includes bibliographical references and index.
    ISBN 0-87081-254-8 (alk. paper)
    1. United States. Articles of Confederation. 2. Political science — United States
— History — 18th century. I. Title.
JK131.H64 1992
320.5'0973 — dc20
                                         92-3680
                                           CIP

The paper used in this publication meets the minimum requirements of the American National Standard for Information Sciences—Permanence of Paper for Printed Library Materials. ANSI Z39.48–1984
∞

10 9 8 7 6 5 4 3 2 1

for
Maureen

Contents

Acknowledgments

The dialogues that give coherence to a political tradition often appear to be parasitic. It can be difficult to know whose ideas are the sources of energy and whose ideas have energy simply because they have captured it from others. In my own case, I feel little ambiguity. I am overwhelmed by a sense of my dependency on the discoveries and insights of others. Paradoxically, the process of shaping my own views has shown me more clearly how profoundly indebted I am.

Nevertheless, I will be brief in my specific acknowledgments. There are teachers. I am especially grateful to David Ricci, William Muehl, and Werner Dannhauser for their distinctive political perspectives and for their generous support and encouragement. Eldon Eisenach masterfully enriched my own sense of the varied voices of American politics. As a teacher and friend, he simultaneously clarified and bewildered, inviting me to grow.

There are students. More than a decade of undergraduate students at Colorado State University were especially helpful. It was their patience and curiosity that helped me begin talking about ideas and interpretations central to this book.

There are professional colleagues and personal friends. Alan Lamborn, Wayne Peak, and John Straayer have made special efforts to nurture a supportive, yet stimulating, academic workplace. Tom Knight's rich and innovative perspectives were especially helpful in revitalizing my efforts during times of doubt. Jim Hardy, the "Brit" who never let me see simply American politics or American politics simply, strongly encouraged me to initiate this project. And thanks to Paul Stoecker for technical help, to the anonymous reviewers for the University Press of Colorado, and to Jody Berman and Gail Reitenbach for the sound judgment and thoughtfulness they brought to the editing of this book.

There is family. I am deeply grateful to my mother and father who, unknowingly but successfully, pushed me out into the world without encouraging me to reject or regret my eccentric Pennsylvania German roots. In Colorado, far from my origins in so many ways, I have found a deepening sense of attachment to a locale and have been enriched by a loving family. My children, Shoshana and Amanda, and especially, my wife, Maureen, have protected and valued my distinctive identity: that which makes me most different from them and most difficult for them. This is not only a great act of love; it is the foundation for life in community.

Introduction

Perhaps the surest way to jeopardize the future is to build on an inadequate understanding of the past. The consequences of a lost or distorted past increasingly limit or threaten America's future prospects. By starting their national story in 1787, Americans have schooled themselves on a homogenized account of their political identity focused on the U.S. Constitution and have lost a consciousness of the political richness in their colonial and revolutionary experiences. This book's examination of the Articles of Confederation is not driven by an antiquarian curiosity about the Articles or by an ideological hostility to the Constitution. Its exploration of the political ideas associated with the Articles is a device to recapture a greater awareness of the complexities and possibilities within American democracy. The value of a more complex account of America's past is that it provides a basis for greater insight into the political controversies of today and for an expansion of the range of acceptable options within the political choices that will shape the American future.

Consider one of the fundamental principles shaping the constitutional order of the United States: federalism. Although virtually no one contests the significance of federalism's influence on the organization and operation of American government and politics, what is contested endlessly is the precise meaning of federalism. Remarkably, the specific form and intentions of the Constitution of 1787 have not been able to create a settled, broadly shared meaning of the term. Not only are there substantial disagreements about the meaning of federalism as created by the Constitution, but the debate makes only the most tangential references to the 1787 document.

A feast of "federalisms" has been offered up to the American public. Dual federalism, national-supremacy federalism, marble cake federalism, new federalism, picket-fence federalism, and crazy quilt federalism are just some of the "flavors." Dual federalism is one of the better-known explanatory models. It suggests that federalism is a principle of coequal sovereignty — one sovereign nation and fifty sovereign states. The fact that this formula has no obvious congruence with Article 6 of the Constitution — the supremacy clause — poses no apparent difficulty to its supporters. Theodore Lowi, for example, explains that his version of this normative model of federalism is not based on any specific form or requirement of the Constitution, but on the interactions between the national authority imposed on the states by the Constitution and a set of alternative precedents: the diversified form of colonial experiences, the autonomy of the states under the Articles of Confederation, and the functional primacy of the states over Congress during the first 150 years of political life under the Constitution.

The case of federalism is representative of constitutional interpretations in the United States more generally. Frequently the meaning of constitutional principles and the full understanding of the operational political order associated with those principles are dependent on criteria other than those specifically provided by the Constitution of 1787. In these respects the U.S. Constitution does not constitute. This should not encourage a disregard for the Constitution's fundamental theoretical and practical significance. Rather, it should quicken an appreciation of other, largely tacit, sources that participate along with the Constitution in the defining of political principles in the United States. Those tacit sources include documents and beliefs whose concepts have influenced our understanding of constitutional principles without themselves being recognized or named.

If the constitutional order is more hybrid than purebred, marked by the tensions of diversity more than by uniformity, attention must be given to identifying and studying the alternative ingredients within this mixture. This is not likely to be an easy task. These sources, almost definitionally, lack the formal, overt, and familiar structure of the Constitution. They are largely tacit — the implicit habits and preferences of a people. This study is an attempt to give these tacit voices an explicit form by connecting them with an alternative, formal authority, the Articles of Confederation, for which they were essential. An interpretation of American politics is then possible that accounts for its customary forms of political expression, its unanticipated complexities and confusions, and the tensions between political expression and the attendant complexities.

Specifically, this exploration of America's familiar political understandings proceeds within two distinct but related contexts. First, it provides a reading of the theory of politics upon which the Articles of

Confederation and Perpetual Union's governmental plan is based. Second, it discusses the general structure and characteristics of America's constitutional order. These two contexts become joined through an argument that claims that understanding the theoretical basis of the Articles of Confederation is useful, perhaps essential, to understanding better the full range of competing and interacting principles within American democracy. The Articles — together with the political vitality it implies for state governments, institutions of local government, jury trials, and a rich variety of spontaneous political forms that lived and died as needed — gives expression to an essential component of America's functional constitution. The Articles offers an example of an explicit political form significantly shaped by the tacit dimensions of politics inherent in American life, but whose tacit dimensions often are absent from or rejected by the formal design and specific intentions of the Constitution of 1787.

In the first chapter of this book, the general structure of American democratic thinking is discussed. The theory of democracy by which American government and politics has been constituted — America's functioning constitutional order — is read as a tradition with dual sources often in conflict with each other. Both classical Lockean and more radical democratic principles are seen as contributing to the formation of America's democratic foundation. Furthermore, these dual sources have not been retained as clearly differentiated strands but have become read into each other, forming a unique hybrid theory of democracy.

At the same time as the tensions of a hybrid tradition of democratic principles have evolved, Americans have struggled to explain the principles of their politics on the basis of the essentially nonhybrid form of the Constitution of 1787. Thus, Americans are left with the frustrations caused by their attempts to make sense of a composite tradition while knowing only one of its elements. Just as the assumptions and principles that form the foundation for the Constitution of 1787 provide an essential understanding of one element in America's mixed tradition, so too, it is argued here, an understanding of the theoretical structure at the base of the Articles of Confederation provides useful insights into the other major elements in the mix of American political ideas.

Unfortunately, Americans' obsession with the Constitution of 1787 is matched only by their obliviousness to the Articles of Confederation. This is not unfortunate because of any either/or choice between the two documents' governmental plans or theories of politics. Rather, it is "unfortunate" because the one document to which Americans do turn is an incomplete source, and the document that receives little attention and even less appreciation is a source of insight for much that is needed to complete dominant constitutional interpretations and familiar political understandings.

American democracy possesses a tacit dimension that is vital in its routine expressions, but which is nearly absent or heavily masked in its most familiar, overt explanations of itself. The primary objective of this study, therefore, is to raise this tacit dimension to fuller consciousness by making it a recognizable part of the story of American democracy, not merely a largely unacknowledged aspect of American democratic experiences. The primary means for achieving this objective is articulating the theory of politics that supports the Articles of Confederation. Studies of both the Constitution of 1787 and the Articles of Confederation, in their literal forms and as political metaphors, can help to clarify the different vocabularies and grammars that have been joined together in a variety of ways to form the dynamic language of American democracy.

Fleshing out a positive democratic theory that informs the Articles' governmental plan is the work of Chapters 2 through 7. This is necessary because the Articles of Confederation has no theorist who gives it an interpretative voice as does James Madison for the Constitution of 1787. And it has no voice of focused advocacy equal to that provided by the *Federalist Papers.* Consequently, the political theory of the Articles of Confederation must be identified indirectly, as it is reflected in a variety of distinct but related contexts.

Chapter 2 launches this effort with a description of what the Articles specify and an analysis of the values, assumptions, and purposes implied by these specifications. Even this direct look at the Articles proceeds indirectly by proposing a possible answer to the following question: what is a theory of politics that would encourage supporters of the Articles' provisions to conclude that its specifications will lead to an effective and just political order for a people launching a new political experiment?

The political perspectives of the decade prior to independence are summarized in Chapter 3. The Articles of Confederation incorporated the theoretical orientations central to the dominant justifications of America's movement to political independence. Attention is focused on three dimensions of this prenatal environment: the role of country ideology, country ideology's kinship with classical republicanism during the culmination of colonial life, and the ideological and social debates between radical, democratic federalists and traditional, elitist nationalists.

Although the Declaration of Independence did not establish a governmental system, the principles by which it created the American nation contain relevant implications for the initial definition of governmental structures and processes. Chapter 4 argues that the principles that constituted the American nation in the Declaration of Independence were used to shape the Articles of Confederation's principles of government.

The thirteen-year period from 1776 to 1789 encompasses the writing, ratification, and formal implementation of the Articles of Confederation. These phases of design and expression also reveal a theoretical pattern of assumptions, ideals, and analyses consistent with the dominant political theory of the prerevolutionary era and the implicit political theory of the Declaration and the Articles. The discussion of Chapter 5, therefore, gives a picture of the Articles of Confederation's political theory as it is reflected in the Articles' writing and ratifying processes, and in the period of its formal authority.

"Unwitting Common Sense," Chapter 6, offers an unconventional experiment to clarify further a sense of the theoretical orientation of the Articles of Confederation. It suggests that Thomas Paine and Thomas Jefferson provide developed articulations of the fundamental principles and perspectives of the Articles even though this was not their intent. Both men quarreled with the specific architecture of the Articles but were influential and articulate explicators of the theoretical terrain within which the Articles and its political tradition came to life and lived. Ironically, the implicit theory of the Articles of Confederation was well known to most Americans largely because of the eloquence that Paine and Jefferson brought to their articulations of democratic politics. They gave defense and vitality to the underlying theoretical vision of the Articles of Confederation even if they never were direct and self-conscious advocates of its outer forms and conventions.

The Antifederalists seldom have been adequately studied or understood in terms of their positive political ideas. Instead, they have been described too frequently as the adversaries of a variety of conceptual and structural elements defined by the Constitution of 1787. Chapter 7 examines the Antifederalists' perspectives in relation to: (1) a political world that already had institutional form through the Articles of Confederation; (2) theoretical direction through the Articles and Declaration of Independence; and (3) established, explicit standards and procedures of legitimacy separate from those of the 1787 Constitution. In short, the Antifederalists' positive political ideas, in American constitutional terms, are discussed to show their centrality to the theoretical vitality of the Articles of Confederation.

Chapter 8 returns to the comprehensive framework of the first chapter. After restating the thesis that a mixed tradition underlies the form of America's democratic thinking, it summarizes the understanding of this tradition's tacit dimension as obtained through an attentive reading of the political theory of the Articles of Confederation. Two concluding arguments are presented that relate to the hybrid character of American democratic standards.

First, the chapter asserts that America's intellectual challenge is not to resolve the conflicts within its mixed tradition either by denying the reality of them or by insisting on the purification of the tradition through the domination of one of its two theoretical sources. Even if purification could be achieved, and that is most unlikely, the price of consistency is likely to be devastating for America. Physically and psychically isolated from the variety of political traditions in the rest of the world and void of any alternative political and cultural identity within its own history, America would be left with only the deadening power of a unified set of uncontested norms and without the positive tensions necessary for the political well-being of its people.

Second, it is argued that the unique form of America's political tensions must be better and more self-consciously understood. This requires special attentiveness to the paradoxical association of conflict and consensus in American democracy. The greatest potential impediment to the study of this mixed tradition and its paradoxes is the tacit status of one its major elements. Before the uniqueness of the hybrid can be explored effectively, there must be recognition and understanding of the differen-

tiated constituent parts, which is the preoccupation of this study. It uses the Articles of Confederation as both a literal and metaphorical representation of a major tacit element. The Articles must become a part of America's explicit political understandings not to supersede the literal and metaphorical content of the Constitution of 1787 but to clarify the remarkable variety of ways these two democratic orders can be, have been, and are mixed together in expressing the political ideas, values, and possibilities of democratic life in the United States.

A Politics of Tensions

The Tensions of a Mixed Political Tradition   1

T he political life of the United States has offered a complex and unique politics of tensions. This can be seen in attempts to explain the elements of American politics, in which discussion frequently moves from agreement, to disagreement, to confusion. Although the elements of discussion penetrate the breadth and depth of conventional national stories, more careful considerations of the elements reveal that the diversity expands, the coherence contracts, and the patterns of political life then become more interpretive than descriptive; in short, the basis for a politics of tensions becomes more manifest. Understandings of American politics become less routine and formulalike and more innovative and expressive as the continuities and discontinuities of American politics are openly and thoroughly explored.[1]

Perhaps there is no political commonplace more insightful and more misleading than that of the frequently claimed "consensual" form of American political values and principles. The assertion of an American political consensus, typically said to derive from John Locke, is based on significant, recurring patterns in American political thinking and experience but camouflages the inherently dynamic elements, mysteries, and diversities that are in tension with those patterns. In fact, America's political consensus is itself the source of a great national paradox. That consensus reflects persistent and pervasive agreements among Americans about their fundamental political values and purposes, but it simultaneously structures the most significant historical and contemporary conflicts within American politics. Thus, the American political consensus not only identifies specific agreements and provides national cohesion, it also shapes the distinctive character of America's political quarrels. It fosters both continuity and change in American national life.

The American political consensus functions in this seemingly contradictory manner, I will argue, because of its hybrid character. It is an artificial association of otherwise disparate, conflicting elements, resulting in an alloy — a compound of different political principles melded into a functioning union. The political consensus is the conceptual equivalent of the reality it models. And not surprisingly so, because it is the product of an American history that transformed purer and simpler sets of political experiences and understandings into a creation uniquely suited for the common purposes of diverse peoples in a new world. Because the basic political values broadly cherished by Americans are frequently self-contradictory, these values have been simultaneously sources for persistent political controversies as well as for integrative national purposes.

The consensus that marks politics in the United States has functioned in this two-sided manner largely because the diversity of its sources, with their countervailing implications, are neither fully examined nor consciously perceived. In fact, the dominant intellectual and psychological patterns of Americans have been to embrace this diversity as if it constituted the coherence of an ideological unity. Homogenized "founding fathers" are portrayed blessing America with an identity it need only revere and protect, and political principles and values quite at odds with the 1787 Constitution are, nevertheless, credited to it.

For example, principles of decentralization, localism, and reduction in the size and dimensions of the national government are frequently attributed to the 1787 Constitution in spite of the fact that there is no single event in the entire history of the United States more purposefully contrary to these goals. The Constitution of 1787 delivered a deadly blow to decentralization, overwhelmed localism, and expanded the size, complexity, and power of the national government beyond any political, economic, or social event of the twentieth century.

The popular rhetoric of Americans does not suggest an ongoing evolution of political principles or of national political identity. Rather, it characterizes the role of citizens and politicians alike to be the committed stewards of a preformed political identity. Consequently, there is little encouragement to analyze the inheritance of that identity, even if it is complex and diverse in its sources and content. For example, the love of both liberty and equality poses no special tensions or difficulties, both noble and base assumptions about human nature are simultaneously embraced by the same persons without any detectable sense of discontinuity, and for most Americans, the 1976 bicentennial was easily affirmed as the two hundredth anniversary of "our form of government" as though the events and principles of 1776 and of 1787 were made of whole cloth.

This preformed political identity contributes to a certain unintended spirit of intolerance. It is not an intolerance of principle and purpose. It is the peculiar consequence of this unique form of self-portrayal. "America" is already shaped. Given its prefiguration, love "it" or leave "it." No people have needed or used political cohesion as much as Americans have to establish a firm basis for nationhood. But there has been a price. Americans have found it difficult to express themselves as a people apart from the prefigured forms of their politics. They understand intuitively the nature and threat of the "un-American," the person who must be read out of "the people" because of an assumed or asserted misalliance with the inherited structure of America's political values, institutions, and processes.

Another price, of course, is that a coherence of purposes, values, and assumptions is attributed to the elements of America's political consensus that neither historical nor philosophical analysis can sustain. Historical and philosophical analyses can identify and confirm the presence and contributions of consensual elements in American politics, but they cannot provide for the degree or kind of natural harmonization among those elements that is often assumed and asserted. This does not mean that the elements of America's political consensus lack any significant cohesiveness. The most obvious and significant cohesion is the one most readily overlooked precisely because it is synonymous with American politics. The American political consensus expresses a remarkably broad-based and persistent commitment to the politics of democracy. American political life has never been a rich source for distinctly nondemocratic perspectives. Alexis de Tocqueville understood this well. He was much more curious about things distinctly democratic than about things distinctly American.

However, his perceptive judgment led him to a method of examination through which distinctly American things became the most reliable grounds for the exploration of distinctly democratic things.

Although it is extraordinarily important to know and affirm the democratic character of American political life, it is no less important to recognize the elementary nature of this knowledge. It is elementary both in the sense that it is foundational and in the sense that it is undeveloped. Knowing the democratic character of America allows a clear reading of its political foundations and of its differentiation from nondemocratic regimes in word and deed. But knowing only its general character results in a limited intelligibility of the precise nature of American democracy. Surprisingly, democratized America is not especially attuned to the considerable variety of configurations that can be given to "democracy" with theoretical coherence and integrity. For example, Americans most frequently prefer the language of a compass to that of democratic intentions: East Germany, not the German Democratic Republic; North Korea, not the Korean Democratic Republic; North Vietnam, not the Democratic Republic of Vietnam.

Acknowledging these other democracies is not an issue of endorsement, but of simple recognition. Just as Americans have not been attentive to the wide variety of ways in which other peoples have tried to give meaning to modern democracy, so too, they have not been sufficiently aware of the various forms and nuances they have given to democracy within their own democratic consensus. The habit of dealing with their own democratic character as if it were self-interpreting has fostered the development of an incoherent yet consensual American democratic ideology.

Nevertheless, it is possible to bring greater analytical coherence to the context of America's political consensus. The first step is to differentiate the separate conceptual traditions that have contributed most substantially to the consensus. In this way, a more detailed and precise knowledge of American democratic theory can be charted. This is a contrived, artificial, and potentially misleading approach because it implies a stable, rational duality of political thinking and action that has not been characteristic of U.S. politics. But it offers a process of analysis through which the different elements of a conceptual hybrid can be differentiated to discern better their implications for the whole. This is especially important because the whole has been commonly explained as if it constitutes a relatively pure unity. Organically, America's political consensus embodies a vision of democracy that is conceptually incoherent. Through an interpretive artifice this consensus can be reordered to reflect two reasonably coherent, competing visions of democratic life. Eventually, the habit of Americans to draw on both visions indiscriminately without any apparent sense of discontinuity must be reasserted. For now, however, the artificer's task is unavoidable.

Both visions of democracy base their primary assumptions on readings of nature. The one tradition claims that nature establishes the primacy of the individual, whereas the other asserts that nature reflects the primacy of human sociability or community. These traditional views require an inherent principle of purpose — a law of motion — appropriate to their distinctive forms. If individuals are to be genuinely "primary," they must be the source of their own dynamism. They must be self-regarding and move themselves in relationship to their self-defining activities. This is the self-interested character of human individuals. If membership in some sort of common human enterprise is to be genuinely "primary," however, then the dynamic principle must express shared aspirations and characteristics. Movement must be in behalf of the whole. The whole is also self-regarding and self-defining but expresses these attributes through the pursuit of the common good in community.

The consequent implications of these two sets of assumptions and dynamics are similarly diverse. A naturally fragmented landscape mobilized by each entity's self-interest engenders competition, especially in a finite world of limited resources unequally distributed. Competitive conflict among separate, self-regarding individuals whose desires are potentially insatiable is inevitable in a limited world. A community enterprise, on the other hand, which pursues shared goods, should foster a cooperative spirit among its members. Only a cooperative spirit will realize the shared goods of the whole, which, in turn, will benefit the separate members of the whole.

Quite different personal ontologies result from these simple but different readings of nature. Not only does the individualistic view give a fragmented form to external relationships (that is, I am distinguished from

you, and we are always, potentially, competitors), it also creates a fragmented structure for internal being. Individuals have no prior nature or
essence because they are self-creating. They start as a tabula rasa. There is
no prior organizing definition to their individuality. Individuals are the
sums of their experiences and the interactions engendered among those
experiences. Consequently, individuals are also fragmented internally. Our
"selves" come to have multiple interests that are often in direct tension
or conflict with one another. Thus, competitive self-interestedness shapes
not only our political relationships with other selves, it also reflects our
psychological condition. The significance of establishing an ordered and
secure place for ourselves with our neighbors is intensified by the need
to define ourselves at more intimate, personal levels as well.

The communal view of the natural state sees integrative patterns
precisely where the individualistic view finds divisions. Externally there
is an integrated cooperative community of common purposes. This public
condition creates integrative personal, or internal, conditions as well.
Persons experience themselves as rooted, confederated wholes. It does not
fall upon them to create and constantly recreate either public or private
identities. They simply must cherish and fulfill their naturally communal
beings. Personal and public identities are viewed as organic wholes, not as
negotiated artifices.

Although neither of these natural metaphors directly expresses a
theory of politics, both structure the direction and form of politics
appropriate to their respective readings of nature. In both perspectives,
politics — at least originally — is postnatural. Properly conceived, politics
must appropriately reflect the natural agenda: the possibilities nature
permits and the necessities nature requires. Because nature has been read
with such substantial differences, it is not surprising that the readings of
politics that follow from these views of nature are also different.

The view of natural individualism suggests a necessarily compensatory role for politics. That is, nature is in some respects deficient, or, as
Locke said, "inconvenient." It is deficient in providing individuals with
reliable orderliness. Individuals require an orderliness to protect the
meaningful exercise of their self-interested natures to which they are,
again by nature, entitled. By nature all individuals have equal executive
powers. But their law-enforcing powers are only powers to enforce

natural law on themselves. There is no natural authority of one individual over any other individual. Thus, nature has the inconvenience of a law that can order life only through the self-enforcing acts of competitively self-interested individuals. This creates quite insecure circumstances, especially for calculating, self-interested individuals. Even if most individuals are scrupulous in their self-enforcement of natural law, will everyone be similarly scrupulous? There is no way in nature to ensure that they will be, and there is no expectation that any individual will or should adopt a suicidal position. Yet suicide it surely would be to restrain oneself when one's chief competitors refuse to be self-limiting. In nature, individuals face a painful dilemma. The successful pursuit of their interests requires an orderly environment, but there is no prudent, self-interested commitment available in nature to ensure this requisite orderliness.

Given this dilemma, rationally self-interested individuals will freely choose to limit their natural liberty and self-governance in order to create a certain kind of common authority. This common authority will be the basis for the reliable orderliness in which nature is deficient. Now it will be possible for the competitive process to realize its full, positive vitality. Competition will be conducted within fair and uniform rules of the game, the results of competition will have legitimacy, and there will be a common authority to sanction, enforce, and protect the process and its consequences. Individuals, with less freedom and authority in principle, will have more security and self-satisfaction than is ever possible for them under the pure conditions of their natural freedom.

The movement of individuals from nature to civil society defines the primary responsibilities of politics: the establishment and maintenance of a fair and secure order in which individuals can maximally pursue their self-defining activities. Thus, not just any order will do. Merely to establish "law and order" is not to remedy the natural deficiency but to create a tyranny far worse than the limitations of nature's "inconveniences." An order must be established that will define and enforce uniform rules and procedures for all and that will permit individuals, within the limits of these parameters, to operate as they see fit. In other words, it is a limited order, centered on matters of process, which preserves as much individual liberty as is consistent with maintaining order.

Politics is necessary for the sake of order. But even this necessity is valid only if it leads to an order that cherishes and gives maximum protection to the fundamental political value — individual liberty. It is in the self-interest of individuals to limit their natural liberty, but only if this limitation directly contributes to the protection and enhancement of the liberty that has been retained. Individuals will choose to commit themselves to a common authority. But the common authority must function to make those individuals' self-expressing and self-defining activities more significant. Again, this will not result from creating common authority if the authority is not limited and directed by its commitment to an order that supports the self-assertive activities of its individual members.

The community-centered reading of nature creates a very different pattern of political consequences. Initially, there is no proper role for politics. There is no natural deficiency or inconvenience requiring the compensatory efforts of political authority. Here, nature is not saved by artifice. Rather, this state of nature is somewhat like the biblical Garden of Eden; both are prefatory to redemptive histories and, consequently, both require a "fall." Politics is not required by the pure conditions of nature but by the corruption of natural conditions in history. It is the fall of nature that necessitates a redemptive political response.

Redemption in the communal paradigm requires reorientation to former conditions of natural goodness. In fact, politics becomes necessary precisely because there is no possibility of a simple or pure return to nature. The innocence of Eden has been lost: we know we are naked, and even choosing to be nudists does not restore that innocence. Although politics is the only way around this metaphysical impasse, it was the development of certain political forms that directly contributed to this fall. Jean-Jacques Rousseau, for example, describes the evidence of this process: "Man was born free, but is everywhere in chains."[2] By nature there is no grant of authority to one person over another, but over time, political conventions have developed that permit the domination of many by the few. This artifice of power has not only destroyed the natural freedom of equals, it has destroyed the basis for community by creating a hierarchical structure of conflicting interests that no longer can attract or express common purposes.

Therefore, political artifice must be reoriented to natural principles. Just as political authority initially challenged and subverted the natural community of equals, so now authority must be formulated to reconstitute society, mimicking, as much as possible, the natural principles of vitality. Politics must move from an instrument of power that creates dominance for some interests and subordination for others to an instrument of cooperation for a community of common purposes. The vitality of nature in the communal view is not realized through artificial political remedies. Rather, the conventions of politics must be used to permit and encourage the reinvigoration of nature's intrinsic goodness.

One political value is supremely important to this task — equality. Without equality there is no genuine community, there is no basis for the common good, and there is no prospect for cooperation. Social hierarchy destroys the natural basis for community. It creates conflicting interests. In this view, to "cooperate" is simply an invitation to be dominated and the "common good" becomes nothing more than the product of fantasy, compromise, or coercion. As equals, however, turning to each other, giving to each other, and trusting each other are acts of positive personal affirmation and strength rather than blindly sacrificial acts of self-denial that only contribute to greater vulnerability and eventual death.

Equality creates a social landscape that reflects nature's primal order. It expresses the natural basis for community. At the most basic level, persons living within a community of equals are no less self-interested than persons living in a competitive market society. They have not adopted the life of masochists. But they do understand the nature of the selves about which they are interested quite differently. If, in principle, persons are equal in all essential, intrinsic respects, and if they live in a social order that honors that equality, then their self-interest is, as well, a common interest. Expressed as a common interest, it does not compromise or change their personal interests; instead, it strengthens them as a shared purpose directly relevant to both personal and communal well-being. Because a community of equals is seen as capturing the harmony of particular and universal, personal and collective, interests, it revives the cooperative example of nature. No principle contributes more to the battle against the abuses of history and for the revitalization of nature than does equality.

These two political traditions grew out of the different assumptions embedded in their respective portrayals of nature and resulted in unique agendas for legitimate political authority. In addition, they generated different perspectives, principles, and techniques for the practical definition and implementation of democratic life. At the practical level the implications of political theories touch specific characteristics of governmental structures, political processes, and public policies. The following discussion sketches some of the more telling ways these two democratic voices, the one individualistic and the other communal, differentiate themselves in these political forms.

Nature validates particular rights and interests in the individualistic tradition. Politics, therefore, must honor and protect those validations. A politics is required that is as free as possible from domination by specific persons. The willingness to create a common authority was never a willingness to submit to the tyranny of personal authority; personal rule is always tyrannical. Therefore, the common authority that has been contracted for must be as impersonal as possible. Contract must not be a vehicle of surrender to the authority of another person. It must be the creation of an apparatus that will permit competing persons to continue their competitions under substantially improved conditions of reliability and security.

How is power to be impersonalized? Making power an expression of law is one important step. Law is to be rules, not personal will. Properly formulated, law is impersonal because it is abstract. It is abstract because it is not concrete; it is not an expression of a specific will or of specific circumstances. It is the negotiated result of conflicting wills formulating general rules and standards applicable to all without regard to specific persons or particular circumstances. A science of political technologies is especially important to the depersonalization and abstracting of the law. Techniques for checking and processing personal interests are needed both to construct impersonal standards and to prevent the corruption of the law's abstract standards of justice.

Law's impersonal and abstract qualities are further enhanced by centering the purpose of law in process rather than in substance. Law is not to designate winners and losers, because such choices are always personally interested choices. Law is to provide fair and uniform standards for competition — rules of the game. Fair and uniform standards of process provide the practical basis for order and freedom. They are the only rational limitations competitors can be expected to choose and respect, and they are the only acceptable common grounds for the predictability and security necessary to make playing the game a rational choice.

Although the practicability of law is important for the law's proper functioning as an ordering device in a market society, practicability also affects concerns about freedom. The state is not designed to be a moral agent. The individual is the agent of moral choice and responsibility. Therefore, the impulse to use the state as the agent of moral sanctions must be checked. The state must be committed to the limits of practicability to ensure a secure and predictable process of autonomous, competitive interactions. The highest expression of human liberty — moral agency — cannot be preempted by the political creation free persons have built precisely to protect their free choices.

Traditional language has described this kind of authority as "negative government." Many connotations of this label are misleading, but the essential point is that directions, priorities, values, choices, and interests are not to be determined for individuals by government. They must be the direct expression of individuals or the outcome of interactions among individuals. Government is negative, then, through the absence of its own independent, positive decisions. Its role is to fashion a practical legal process whereby individuals can more successfully define and pursue their own positive agendas. And even in its rule-setting and enforcing role, government should not assert itself beyond the practical needs of public order. If process is too rigidly and comprehensively defined, it will inadvertently prescribe results. This, too, is inconsistent with the requirements of negative governance.

To preseve a proper balance between government and individual authority, a secular realm is created for politics. The resulting spirit of tolerance is not a reflection of indifference or hostility to basic political, religious, or moral choices and values. Rather, it reflects the judgment that the differences among persons on these questions are so deep and persistent that to establish government on any of these principles is to guarantee the sacrifice of order and individual liberty. The only effective way to provide a public order in which free individuals can express and pursue their own political, religious, and moral commitments is to create a secular authority that does not presume to judge these matters because they are not within that authority's range or competence. Precisely because morality must be private and personal, politics must be limited to matters of secular practicality.

Conceptions of the public and the private have always been tools for shaping the extent and nature of politics. Because the individual only needs and wants political authority for limited, instrumental purposes, the public, in the individualistic tradition, is understood in narrow terms. Legitimate public life is limited in its scope and functions. In fact, the more limited it is the more likely it will focus on practical rules of process, leaving positive choices to free individuals, who can center their lives in an expanded and enriched private sector of individual autonomy and market competition.

Democracy in the individualistic view must create a politics that speaks to and for the individual. The people rule when individuals are free and when the government that they have authorized provides an orderly protection for that freedom. Within a democracy, the greatest threat to the rule of free individuals comes most directly from the majority's will. When majorities rule, their constituent members perceive themselves as acting in harmony with their freedom as individuals. But majority decisions are always based on a collective principle — the authority of numbers — not on individual preference, not on reason, not on truth, not on justice, and not on the will of gods in heaven or in nature. A majority's ruling rules simply because of the number of people who support it, regardless of the wisdom or folly of their decision and even if there is no shared rationale for the decision backed by those numbers.

Majorities, therefore, must be checked. Two techniques have been important to the individualistic tradition's checking efforts. The first of these is a strong advocacy for an antimajoritarian principle to counter or balance the majoritarian impulses of any democracy. That antimajoritarian principle is minority rights and protections. The essential difference between majoritarianism and minoritarianism is not the size of the group each represents. Rather, majoritarianism is always a collective principle, whereas minoritarianism is ultimately a principle of individualism. Minority protections are not needed to strengthen society's smaller groups but to protect autonomous individuals. This tradition argues that the democratic process must include a specific form of an antidemocratic bias. Its minoritarianism, however, is not to privilege an elite, presumptuous, and cunning class or social group. It is to protect the political order from the excessive influence of any collectivity — large or small — that could destroy individual liberty.

The second technique is to engineer representational schemes and governance processes that encourage an indirect and negotiated expression of majority preferences. When the majority does speak and rule, as it eventually will in some form in any democracy, its voice must be "compromised." If it is more manufactured than expressive, it will not automatically define responses to other issues or, perhaps, even to similar issues at different times, and it will not necessarily maintain its cohesion and internal sense of rectitude. It will be more limited in scope, less durable, and more psychologically unsettled internally. In short, it will be less likely to abuse individual liberty. It will be able to construct the requisite social order but with a reduced risk of tyranny.

The communal vision offers a different direction for the political implementation of its understandings. Nature has given a special validation to humanity's shared life in community. The images and perspectives that develop the implications of this communal view are often implicitly or explicitly religious. For example, covenant language replaces or supplements contract language. Both contracts and covenants bring people together, by choice, into some kind of association or society. Contracts, however, assume a heterogeneity of interests among the associates, whereas covenants assume a homogeneity of interests among the associates. The act of contracting makes certain kinds of relationships possible that would be impossible without the contractual guarantees and protections. The act of covenanting affirms and deepens intrinsic natural as well as accomplished historical relationships of common purpose and commitment. A covenanted community is one cemented by trust through its shared sense of meaning. If human life is authenticated and fulfilled in a community, then a covenant, or contract of homogeneous interests, strengthens the bonds of a community so that it can accomplish these shared purposes.

Communities tell stories. They tell stories because stories are powerfully moving forms through which communities express the uniqueness of their identities and purposes. Israel, for example, was a covenanted community that sustained and nourished its covenant by telling its story. That story is always about the whole and the particular members of the whole who have best embodied the community's nature and destiny. Israel is the chosen people of God, it is the children of Abraham, Issac, and Jacob, and it is the Jewish people led by Moses. A community is united by its story and the persons in that story who most embody its unique struggles and accomplishments. Common purposes and efforts can only be understood and maintained through knowledge of the community's distinctiveness.

A community of purpose is never content with mere orderliness and process. It must be concerned with the outcomes that result from the structures of governance and the rules of the game. Rules are not legitimated just because they are indifferent to any particular interests and are applied uniformly. They must be evaluated in terms of their social results as those results relate to the community's historic commitments. Only if this attention to outcomes is maintained will the community and the equality of its members be achieved and preserved. If results are matters of indifference, the community's shared meanings will soon fragment into competing particularistic interests, and the vestiges of corruption will soon flourish, creating hierarchies of power and advantage.

Law, in this communal view, in not merely an artifice of procedural order. It is the will of a properly constituted community bringing to political life the wisdom and vitality of nature's truths. It is not manufactured through contrivances but discovered and expressed in the natural vitality of a people. Thus, its purpose and role in society is not merely one of practicality. Its purpose and role is moral. Laws, governments, and public life must contribute to the strengthening of substantive justice over injustice and mere process. The health of a community and its citizens requires a particular kind of order, not mere order. It requires an order as consistent with the natural order as is possible in history, which can only be achieved if the moral responsibility of politics is recognized and attentively pursued. The community cannot be an association of purpose if it is indifferent to the very purposes that constitute its collective life. Thus, morality is not a matter of individual choices but of shared commitments in harmony with nature, and political life must meet a moral standard: a standard of meaning consistent with community resolve and a standard of consequences that support and strengthen that resolve.

This political orientation casts government in a positive role. It deems it appropriate and necessary for government to identify the intended outcomes for the political expression of authority and for government to exercise its authority to achieve the fullest possible realization of these desired results. If political authority manifests a community of meaning and purpose, it has the duty, not just the right, to disclose itself as a positive instrument of that community's values and truths. Politics must function beyond secular standards of practicability and orderliness. In certain respects, political authority must defy mere practicality and order because ultimately it is responsible for the redemption of corrupted humanity. To wage that battle, it must give positive leadership so that the community's proper essence will prevail. Such an effort inevitably will disturb and destroy orders at odds with "natural" communal values and will be animated by a passion contrary to the pursuit of self-interest among persons who have accommodated themselves to the practical necessities of the established social order.

It is not surprising that a communal tradition would press for an enlargement of the public sector. As a result, government, law, and the general life of the community have an expanded public role, which substantially reduces both the form and significance of the private realm. This orientation has deep implications for personal life as well as for political life. Personal meaning and fulfillment are not matters of isolated experiments at self-discovery and self-expression; humans are not natural voids scurrying around trying to authenticate their lives in an environment that makes authenticity nothing more than self-assertion. Instead, nature has given human life a richness that has been challenged by historical conventions but which can be reconstituted through the public purposes of a covenanted community. Personal and social well-being are not antithetical either in their pursuit or in their ends. In fact, a properly constituted community is essential to personal freedom, that is, to personal authenticity. The just order of personal and public life is achieved in concert.

According to the communal view, democracy must create a politics that expresses the shared aspirations of its people as a people. The people rule when the common goals of the community are sanctioned and enforced. The greatest challenge to the popular will of a well-ordered community is the pressure to rule in behalf of particularistic interests, especially when they contradict or seek exemptions from the collective wisdom of the majority. If people live in a well-ordered community, it should be expected that agreement among the largest number of them will represent more than just a quantitative judgment. The majority will is qualitative, as well, because it expresses the dominant understandings of citizens in environments properly organized for democratic choices. It is the voice of a community.

For communalists majority choice must be the directing principle of democratic life. Political authority should be moral and positive, reflecting a strong public-spiritedness. Thus, it must be an authority that expresses the community's majoritarian preferences. Any government that is not fully majoritarian must be severely restrained in its authority. The majoritarian spirit is best served when participatory involvement is encouraged within the spontaneous life of the community. Government, typically, should be simple and direct, unencumbered with elaborations of technique and strategy. And the efficacy of persuasion through benevolence and trust in a well-ordered community substantially diminishes the need for coercive power or cunning.

These two visions of democracy — individualistic and communal — have been presented as purified abstractions. At no point have they been limited to any particular political theorist or tradition of political ideas. This is not because there are no such sources for these views but because these visions are meant to express more of a cultural product than a purposeful and disciplined representation of, for example, Locke or Rousseau, liberalism or radical democracy. In this discussion, the important assertion is not about the Lockean or Scottish Enlightenment sources of these views but about the general coherence of views that were used as raw materials in the evolution of a compound tradition of democracy in America.

This presentation of these two democratic perspectives is overdrawn in two important respects. First, the purity and narrow consistency of each view is artificial. When they are placed within the context of their relevant sources, they become considerably more intricate and subtle. Second, their radical disjunction from one another is artificial. These two visions share some important congruences of sources and consequences that are not adequately reflected in the preceeding discussion.

However, it is precisely because the American political consensus is based on such a complex and multidimensional tradition that it was necessary to identify and separate artificially purified representations of the major elements that form its tense mixture. In one sense, these models are helpful precisely because they are not representations of what we most typically find. We more commonly find a sense of democracy that has a powerful psychological coherence for most Americans but which is filled with tensions, conflicts, and contradictions when scrutinized historically and analytically. The political ideas Americans experience and live as if they formed a unity are really the conditions for conceptual schizophrenia. To unravel the riddle of a tradition that is both profoundly coherent and contradictory requires an analytical method that can chart and inform discussions of both its continuities and discontinuities. And this required a reading that clearly, even if artificially, differentiated these two interacting democratic visions.

The Reagan administration illustrated this strange interplay of consensus and contradiction when the president communicated no sense of disjunction or tension in his advocacy of both the free individual and the good people of this God-fearing nation. In such a view government is both limited and expanded. It is given both procedural and positive roles. Impersonal standards of merit are asserted with a vigor equal to that given to the personal standards of loyalty. The magic of the marketplace stirs the same soul that insists on public determinations of issues of religion, morality, and education. Ronald Reagan is the individualist who is, nevertheless, unable to embrace a classical formulation of individualism — "equal opportunity under the law" — for female individuals. He is the individualist who, at times, can only trust the impulses of communal majoritarianism. However, these are not the unique traits of one man or of one administration. And their deeper significance is not as a basis for judging one man or one administration. This president was "heard" by large numbers of Americans because he spoke for them and thought as they think. He revealed not only the inconsistencies of his own position but also the inherent tensions of American political ideas.

The umbrella of American democratic consensus covers a considerable diversity of views, and Americans are skilled at manufacturing ingenious combinations of this diversity's pieces. When particular combinations are supported by some Americans, they respond to the mix of ideas as they are parts of the democratic consensus, not as these ideas relate to each other analytically. Similarly, when particular combinations are rejected by some Americans, they challenge the combination of ideas, not the relevance of the elements to America's political values. Furthermore, rejected compounds usually are challenged not with conceptually whole responses but with alternative combinations of disjointed ideas. In this way, Americans are unified, even in their political quarrels; and they are quarrelsome, even in their political unity.

The most familiar interpretations of America's political ideas have insisted on a choice between the consensus and conflict — between the integrative and disintegrative characteristics — evident in American democracy. Robert Brown, Richard Hofstadter, and Louis Hartz, for example, emphasize the unity of America's political tradition. For them the Constitution of 1787 is the fulfillment of the events and understandings of 1776. This view sees only a need to explain a profoundly consensual society. Thus, it articulates an unalloyed political tradition, most commonly Lockean in nature. There is much that is valid and significant in this understanding of American political life.

Two chief limitations of this view must be noted, however. First, it neglects or sublimates the original and continuing political conflicts among Americans. For consensualists America is born whole somewhere around 1776 or 1787. The doubts, the disagreements, and the divergences of nearly two centuries of political experiences on either side of these watersheds are ignored. Second, this view implies a teleological role of the Constitution, which results in a reading of all American history in terms of that source, whether the events of 1776 or of 1802 are being discussed. This Constitutional teleology provides the convenience of a single source for a consensual polity, in a form easily identified and understood, and hence an overt structure of institutional authority. It is not that a deeply

consensual character cannot be found in American politics. But recogniz-
ing this trait should not require amnesia about the serious, persistent, and
principled political struggles and conflicts Americans have experienced
throughout their history. Nor should the power of structural continuity
under the Constitution encourage neglect of the vital complexity and
conflict that informal cultural attitudes and processes have added to that
consensus.

Still other interpreters of America have captured the struggles and
conflicts of American politics but have ignored the solidarity and harmony that underlies many American disputes. After identifying and
discussing conflicting American impulses, it is common for these interpreters either to project the "victory" of one of the conflicting traditions
or to assert the evolution of a new, unified synthesis. Either way, consensus
is claimed to be formed and expressed in a purified tradition. In this
respect, interpretations that capture America's political disputes often lead
to perspectives quite similar to those developed through consensus assumptions — visions of a deep unification of political ideals and aspirations expressed by a coherent set of interests and ideas. Vernon L.
Parrington, D. H. Lawrence, John P. Diggins, J.G.A. Pocock, and Gordon
G. Wood give rich and valuable readings of America's conflicting impulses
and, then, propose paths of integration beyond these conflicts. They
conclude that one of the contesting views or a new, higher tradition will
establish the basis for a stable political future.

D. H. Lawrence's exaggerated language is illustrative precisely because
his metaphorical images vividly present an America marred by antagonis-
tic forces. He says that Americans possess a "mind consciousness" dominated by self-regarding calculations designed to achieve orderly control
and security, which is assumed to constitute freedom. It is the technician's
aspiration to be saved from the vitality of unpredictable forces. And
Americans possess a "blood consciousness," a spirit of spontaneous living
and sharing with others, experiencing "the incarnate mystery of the open
road."[3] According to Lawrence, the former is America's white-skinned,
blue-eyed soul as shaped by the artifacts of European, Judeo-Christian
history; the latter is America's dark-skinned, brown-eyed soul as shaped
by the natural vitality of the inherent paganism of an unspoiled new
world. For Lawrence, this continuing conflict must be resolved, and the

resolution will lead either to America's doom or redemption. The fanatical efforts to order life and to save oneself that are inspired by the white mental consciousness will lead to a suicidal doom. The heroic message of the American future comes, instead, through the victory of its darker blood consciousness.

> The soul is not to pile up defenses round herself. She is not to withdraw and seek her heavens inwardly, in mystical ecstasies. She is not to cry to some God beyond, for salvation. She is to go down the open road, as the road opens, into the unknown, keeping company with those whose soul draws them near to her, accomplishing nothing save the journey, and the works incident to the journey, in the long life-travel into the unknown, the soul in her subtle sympathies accomplishing herself by the way.[4]

Lawrence presents a fundamental conflict in American life and, equally, insists that it must be resolved.

The interpretative perspective of this study is different from those offered by either the consensus or conflict traditions. This view finds both deep consensus and significant conflict in American politics, and it finds them in the same sources.[5] The content of American political agreements invites unavoidable controversies. Further, specific resolutions of disputes do not cleanse the larger scope of American politics from further controversies because the various elements that feed these conflicts are rooted in a larger, more fundamental consensus. Thus, "defeated" impulses are never vanquished. At other levels they retain their validity and, most importantly, saliency. For example, Americans have resolved specific conflicts that inevitably arise between freedom and equality. These resolutions sometimes have been balanced toward the primacy of freedom and other times toward the primacy of equality. But none of these controversies nor their various terminations have eliminated the meaningful, continuing presence of both values — freedom and equality — in the national consensus. Both continue to be fully available to fuel tomorrow's quarrels and reconciliations. If America actually transcended the grounds for its political conflicts, it would lose the framework of its consensus as well.

Whether or not the fundamental meanings of the Declaration of Independence and the Constitution of 1787 are more similar to or more different from each other, there is no doubt that the outer forms of these two documents are considerably different. It is also true that Americans continue to respond positively to both of those outer forms. Americans are not divided between those who respond to the Declaration's political images and those who respond to the Constitution's images, even if those two forms are, themselves, differentiated and contradictory. Americans embrace both portrayals of democracy and can be stirred to supportive responses through both images even when they are offered up almost simultaneously. In fact, many Americans read the Declaration into the Constitution and vice versa. They affirm both natural vitality and remedial artifice; they see governance as both implicit legitimacy and formal authority; they characterize interpersonal relations as matters of both trust and suspicion; and they present a politics to the world that asserts they are both a good people with virtuous intentions and competitive individuals protecting their material self-interests. Americans are not troubled by or, more precisely, conscious of the various theoretical incongruities and conflicts inherent in their allegiance to both the Constitution and the Declaration. Yet because American politics finds both deep consensus and significant conflict in the same sources, agreements are a primary generator of disagreements and, simultaneously, the basis for "resolving" those disagreements.

There is a certain dialectical quality to the American political consensus, but it is a dialectic that is neither self-transcending nor teleological. It is a playfully stable dialectic because the negations are always also affirmations. Thus, when Americans resolve conflict, the resolutions are quite clear in their specific implications and determinations. Nevertheless, these resolutions are never really transcending or redefining at the most fundamental level because the American political consensus generates its own controversies and then "manages" those conflicts in terms of the very consensus that gave them birth. In this sense, American political consensus is more of a monolectical process than a dialectical one.

The synthetic vision that binds Americans politically and defines the terrain of their public debates is the constituting tradition of American political assumptions, values, and understandings. It forms a "constitutional" base that, in its own way, is as real and significant as the written document that states the formal structures and principles of national government and authority. Although Americans have always shaped their politics and their constitutional interpretations beyond the limits of the Constitution of 1787 and, sometimes, in ways contrary to that document's most obvious specifications, whenever they speak with self-consciousness of their constitutional tradition they habitually think of the written document alone. However, America has been constituted and continues its constituting process through a framework that, although profoundly influenced by the Constitution of 1787, nevertheless moves beyond the forms and values of 1787 federalism. "Constitution," in this larger sense, not only refers to the overt and formal structures of politics but to the covert and informal processes of political life as well; the term is meant to express fully the nature of all fundamental political values. The narrower sense of constitutionalism in America, which claims to be limited to the intentions and specific meanings of the 1787 document, continues to be fed, affected, and shaped by this larger constitutional form, whether or not it is welcomed or recognized.

Not only does this view require a distinction between the more organic and the more contrived ways Americans have given form to their political life, it requires an appreciation of the constructive interpretations necessary to form and understand this larger constitutional tradition. Actual political practices must be interpreted through analyses of the intentions of the community that houses these practices. The constitution is never reducible to a formal document, because it is a construction within the actual political life of a people. It is the best articulation of the political values and purposes that animate American political practices as a whole. This larger constitution must capture the distinctive constraints and inducements of the nation's politics and identify the diverse dimensions of its political values, joining them together into an interpretation of the whole. The synthetic form of America's constituting vision requires a continuing process of interpretation. Through interpretation of this synthetic tradition, Americans generate conflict out of consensus and discover consensus even within their conflicts.

As Ronald Dworkin has shown, constitutional interpretation is not a matter of conventionalism or pragmatism.[6] There is no frozen formalization of America's political essence that is self-evident and constant. The mechanistic approach to law and principle expressed in the literalism of the conventional view is more a deception than an insight. It hides the constructive interpretations that necessarily give life and direction to the fundamental principles of national life. Yet there are continuing traditions of value and meaning, which constitute the basis for national purpose. The cynicism of legal realism that severs all axiomatic anchors for politics finally abandons visions of justice and satisfies itself with mere change and situationally defined experimentations. American politics is not the story of rudderless experimentations. Its experiments, although considerable in number, have always been conducted within the limits of a stable, even if disjointed, set of assumptions and purposes.

The notion of a constitutional tradition articulated through processes of constructive interpretation combines the backward-looking bias of conventionalism with the forward-looking bias of pragmatism. The constitutional tradition at its most fundamental level interprets the meaning of persistent political practices and ideals through an unfolding narrative. Dworkin's own jurisprudence reflects this idea well.

> [Law] begins in the present and pursues the past only so far as and in the way its contemporary focus dictates. It does not aim to recapture even for present law, the ideals or practical purposes of the politicians who first created it. It aims rather to justify what they did (sometimes including, as we shall see, what they said) in an overall story worth telling now, a story with a complex claim: that present practice can be organized by and justified in principles sufficiently attractive to provide an honorable future.[7]

The initial difficulty, however, is not a matter of textual interpretation or hermeneutics. It is, instead, a matter of sources. In what sources do we find the elements that constitute the fundamental principles of American politics? It is not an easy question to answer, but the start of an answer lies with what is most clear, even if negative. The fundamental nature of American politics, its constituting tradition, is not exhausted by the apparatus and values of the 1787 Constitution. Although American politics is profoundly affected by that source, it has also experienced the significant and sustained influences of principles contrary to or different from those of that document. Americans are often blind to this reality because they simply project alternative principles onto the Constitution.

The complexity of America's constitutional tradition is tacitly understood but, unfortunately, has been attached to a single constitutional document. The problem with this imprecision is practical as well as philosophical and historical. The practical problem is that Americans experience a complex constituting tradition but interpret the meaning of that complexity through a source that does not fully reflect or nourish it. The relative coherence of principles and values underlying the Constitution of 1787 does not sufficiently account for the diversity of ideas that continues to feed American political choices and debates.

There is an ongoing tradition of commitment and controversy centering on a number of fundamental issues. For example, Americans are torn by the conflicts created because of their commitments to both localism and nationalism. They constantly wrestle with simultaneous characterizations of themselves as competitive individualists and as members of a people with shared and virtuous purposes. They want to merge with nature's harmonies and benign mysteries at the same time as they want to tame and control nature's wildness to ensure their own security. The tense coexistence of competitive and cooperative principles, minoritarianism and majoritarianism, and process and substance principles underscores the need to identify the full range of sources for a constituting tradition in which these disagreements grow out of broadly agreed-upon ideals. A single, pure source is not a sufficient parent to the tensions of this hybrid tradition. The diversity and tension of the consensual constitutional tradition in America come from sources that themselves are diverse and in conflict.

No one can doubt the essential role of the Constitution of 1787 in any reading of the constituting tradition of American politics. Americans hold a deep and pervasive commitment to its language, values, and structural order. It defines much of the political language of American politics even when the meanings attached to that language are anomalous and bewildering. And it has shaped most of America's basic structures and processes of overt governance and formal authority. But even if it represents the predominant tradition of American politics, it has never been America's exclusive tradition. American politics cannot be explained exclusively on the basis of its principles. Further, there are many things done within the authority of the Constitution and in the name of the

Constitution that make no sense in terms of Constitutional principles. For example, why do some find a legal pledge to the "equal protection of the law" to be endangering of constitutional values when applied to gender, and why do some find a legal requirement for participation in forms of worship to be consistent with Constitutional thinking? Are these realities best understood as direct expressions of the values and principles of the 1787 document or as expressions of alternative democratic values, which also have had a significant role in constituting the foundations of America's political identity? The latter alternative is the view of this study.

The issue of obscenity is another interesting illustration of American democratic antagonisms. The courts have steadfastly regarded obscenity as unprotected speech. In itself, this poses no constitutional dilemma *if* those same courts can define obscenity and agree on the definition. Because no one doubts that obscene depictions of human behaviors can be forms of speech, they can only be unprotected speech because of their obscene characteristics. But this requires that the nature of their obscene character be specified in the law and shown to be of such a form as to require negation of a fundamental individual right and an absolute constitutional principle. In short, something considerably more than "I know it when I see it" is required. Nevertheless, the current standard is quite similar to Justice Stewart's nonstandard. In *Miller v. California* (1973) the Supreme Court declares that it is willing to regard as obscene anything "the average person, applying contemporary community standards," would find, taken as a whole, to be appealing to prurient interests. In terms of the political principles attributed to the core of the Constitution of 1787 this is a nonstandard. Yet in terms of the American political tradition it can easily be viewed by many as a sensible and appropriate "constitutional" standard.

The Constitution of 1787 exhibits great self-consciousness in pressing for majoritarian restraint. It emphasizes the necessity of a public authority expressed through the abstract and impersonal standards of law. The philosophy of government that created the Constitution of 1787 and which best sustains its essence requires a procedural, not substantive, justification and role for law, especially if that law has the potential to limit or deny an individual's fundamental right. The Miller ruling, however, taps into other dimensions of America's political values. It authorizes particularistic responses, which empower local majorities to impose substantive standards on dissenting individuals.

The most important aspect of the Miller ruling is not that it is in conflict with the Constitution of 1787. Rather, it is that this ruling is accepted by many Americans as an appropriate "constitutional" standard. This acceptance is not a consequence of the ruling's coherence with the theory of Madisonian democracy but a consequence of its place within a tradition of American democracy that has always incorporated challenges to Madison as well as affirmations of his views. Thus, Americans face the challenge of unraveling a great national riddle: why are some things declared constitutional in the name of the Constitution of 1787 when, by that standard, they could be better understood to be unconstitutional?

A source must be identified that directly and positively represents the tacit standards capable of eclipsing those of the Constitution of 1787. It must be a source that has had a significant role in the story of America's political self-expression. That source, which reflects the assumptions and values of America's other democratic vision, is the Articles of Confederation and Perpetual Union. By understanding its political theory, the theorizing of its supportive traditions and then, joining those insights with the political theory of the Constitution of 1787, a much richer and more precise reading of the intricacies, limitations, and possibilities of American politics can be achieved.

The purpose of investigating the political theory of the Articles is not to recreate old conflicts or to invigorate a dualistic reading of America. Rather, it is to develop a better understanding of the uniquely complex form of American political consensus — a consensus that has fostered both stability and change because of its hybridized theory of democratic politics. The Constitution of 1787's tradition represents an essential but incomplete part of this compound theory. Adding the tradition of the Articles of Confederation to the mixture of American political theory raises the tacit dimensions of American democratic thinking to the level of explicit consideration that is warranted by the true nature of American political life.

To speak of the political theory of the Constitution of 1787 is to address the larger tradition it embodies. Just as the Constitution of 1787 represents a tradition of political theorizings that is broader and deeper than the limits of its physical form, so, too, the Articles of Confederation must be read in a comparable manner. Its forms and specifications emerge out of a larger tradition of political assumptions, aspirations, and analyses. Thus, to discuss the political theory of the Articles of Confederation is to engage the elements of the tradition of which it is representative. In both cases the quest begins, it does not end, with the form of their governmental recommendations. What are the values and purposes that underlie these forms? What are the patterns of thinking that lead to the shaping and defending of these forms? Why are alternative forms seen not only as differences of strategy but also as distinctions of purpose?

America's political consensus is no more adequately represented by the theory of the Articles of Confederation than by the theory of the Constitution of 1787. America's consensus is a tense, at times seemingly schizophrenic, compound of both democratic visions. Nevertheless, this study gives focused attention to the articulation of only one part of this hybridized tradition — the part reflected in the theory of the Articles of Confederation. The theory of the Articles requires special attention not because it is either the exclusive or the more essential tradition of American democracy. It can claim neither of these roles. It merits special attention for the simple reason that it continues to have a vital but unrecognized role in America's political foundations. Its vitality has come from Americans' tacit commitment to its principles, which have been subsumed into American constitutionalism. A fuller and more satisfactory understanding of the perplexities of America's formative political principles requires that the implicit be made explicit. Americans must understand the conflicting principles of their "constitution." In part, this means that they must better understand the principles of their constitution that are not those of the Constitution.

A Perpetual Union of Sovereign States

In spite of a bicentennial mania that gripped the United States for more than a decade, there was a virtual amnesia about the Articles of Confederation. This is symptomatic of American knowledge about the Articles in general. The Articles is a document little remembered and even less understood. Although it reflects a political tradition still honored and pursued by many Americans, its political principles are seldom, if ever, connected with this document and its tradition. Few pause long enough to consider the Articles' own positive tradition and its importance to America's past and present political choices. Those who remember anything are generally satisfied with a simple and distortive formula: the Articles fashioned an unrealistic plan of governance that failed, and out of the chaos of its failure America was blessed with the political wisdom of the Constitution of 1787.

Thus, there is little knowledge of either the Articles' content or theory that can be assumed or relied upon. Because of this, it is necessary to start with the document itself. What does it specify? What values, assumptions, and purposes does it imply? What does a careful reading of the document suggest about its view of American politics?

Both the Constitution of 1787 and the Articles of Confederation are dominated by discussions of two broad categories — governmental structures and governmental powers. Neither document is theoretically explicit; that is, neither specifies the assumptions and values that inform its organizations of governmental structures and powers. Thus, one important route to understanding the theoretical tradition of either document is to investigate a simple hypothetical question: what political assumptions and aspirations are necessary to convince someone that the practical political recommendations of the document will result in effective and desirable governance? What is a theory of politics that would lead a supporter of the provisions of the Articles of Confederation to conclude that its specifications will lead to an effective and just political order for the people who had just formed themselves through the Declaration of Independence? Before this question can be addressed, it is necessary to review exactly what the Articles specify as the new government of this new people.

The Articles set up a federal system or confederacy described as a league of friendship among sovereign states forming a "perpetual union." At the heart of this form and intent is a paradoxical interplay between Article 2 and Article 13. On the one hand, "Each State retains its sovereignty, freedom and independence," and on the other hand, "Every State shall abide by the determinations of the United States, in Congress assembled, on all questions which, by this confederation, are submitted to them. And the articles of confederation shall be inviolably observed by every State, and the union shall be perpetual." This interplay of differentiation and integration is reflected by the document's full title — The Articles of Confederation and Perpetual Union.

The governmental form of this perpetual union is rather limited. It explicitly authorizes legislative and administrative structures and implies certain judicial-like forms. The primary legislative body is a unicameral Congress. Representatives to this Congress are selected annually by each state. Each state may determine the number of delegates it wishes to send to Congress within a specified range — a minimum of two and a maximum of seven delegates. No representative may serve for more than three years in any period of six consecutive years. Each state has the authority to recall any of its representatives during their year of appointment and make replacements if necessary. No state representative may hold an office in the U.S. government or receive compensation from the United States. All representatives enjoy the protections of free speech and debate in Congress and protections from arrests and imprisonments while going to and from sessions of Congress except for reasons of treason, felony, or breach of the peace. Finally, whenever the United States "in Congress assembled" acts to decide a question, each state has one vote.

The Articles also specifies the creation of a secondary legislative body, "a Committee of the States." This committee may be appointed by the Congress to sit during congressional recesses and consists of one delegate from each state. The committee shall execute any of Congress' simple-majority powers, which Congress invests in it by explicit action of at least nine states. One member of the committee shall be appointed to preside as president, but no one shall serve in the office of president for more than one year during any period of three consecutive years.

Although the Congress shall be able to adjourn any time within a year and may convene at any place within the United States, no period of adjournment may be longer than six months. Conversely, no period of authorization for a Committee of the States will last longer than six months. The Congress must also publish a monthly journal of its proceedings and must include roll call votes on any question if requested by any delegate.

The Articles creates a quasi-judicial structure to accommodate the responsibilities of Congress in disputes between two or more states. In all such disputes concerning "boundary, jurisdiction or any other cause whatever," Congress is the last resort on appeal. The manner in which Congress' authority shall be exercised in such cases is specified. A state or states shall petition Congress, identifying the issue(s) and requesting a hearing. Congress will notify the affected parties, who will be instructed to appoint, by joint consent, judges to constitute a court to hear and decide the issue. If the affected parties are unable to agree on judges, Congress will name three persons from each state. From this list, each party will alternately strike out one name until the number is reduced to thirteen. Then Congress shall determine the number of judges to be chosen, although that number shall not be less than seven nor more than nine. The specified number of judges shall be drawn by lot from the thirteen remaining candidates. The persons drawn, or any five of them, will hear the case and determine a settlement of the controversy.

Finally, the Articles contains several other features important to its general form and operation. Canada shall be admitted to full advantages of the union if it ever wishes to join. All other colonies shall be admitted only after the agreement of nine states. All bills of credit, borrowed monies, and debts contracted by the Continental Congress will be considered to be charges against the union, and a solemn public pledge will be given that they will be fully paid and satisfied. Finally, an amendment procedure is specified that requires the agreement of Congress and confirmation by the legislature of each state.

Although Article 2 asserts the sovereignty of each state, saying that each state will retain "every power, jurisdiction, and right, which is not by this confederation expressly delegated to the United States, in Congress assembled," the Articles expresses some general standards of conduct that are restraints upon the states even though they are not delegated powers to Congress. These restraining, nondelegated standards of conduct are designated probably because the Articles is also committed to a perpetual union of friends. For example, Article 4 introduces their specification with a statement of rationale: "The better to secure and perpetuate mutual friendship and intercourse among the people of the different states in this union."

These specified standards of mutual friendship have several dimensions. There are "privileges and immunities" to protect all free inhabitants of each state; in short, the rights of citizenship are honored from state to state. The people of each state shall have free ingress and regress to any other state, and shall have the same privileges of trade and commerce as the inhabitants of any particular state. All states must honor extradition requests for persons guilty of or charged with "treason, felony, or other high misdemeanors" in any other state. And "Full faith and credit shall be given in each of these states to the records, acts, and judicial proceedings of the courts and magistrates of every other State." Whenever states are authorized to raise land forces, the state legislatures must appoint all officers under the rank of colonel. Finally, all states are charged with maintaining a well-regulated and disciplined militia.

In addition to the delineation of things each state must do, the Articles lists things each state is prohibited from doing. Some of the prohibitions are absolute and others are conditional. The absolute prohibitions include the following: no state may lay imports or duties that interfere with or violate any operative U.S. treaty. The other two absolute prohibitions apply equally to state governments and to the United States in Congress assembled: no title of nobility may be granted, and no governmental officer may accept any compensation or entitlements from any foreign nation.

The conditional prohibitions limiting the powers and actions of the states can be modified by explicit actions of the U.S. Congress. No individual state may send foreign delegates or enter into treaties, nor may any group of two or more states do the same without the consent of the United States in Congress assembled. All states are prohibited from maintaining vessels of war and a body of armed forces during peace except as the United States in Congress assembled permits for defense of each state and its trade. States may not engage in war without the authorization of the United States in Congress assembled. But there are two circumstances that provide the grounds for exceptions to this prohibition. States may engage in warfare on their own if they are actually invaded by an enemy or if there is reliable knowledge of an Indian attack that is timed to preclude normal consultations with Congress. No state may grant commissions for vessels of war unless there has been a formal declaration of war by the United States in Congress assembled. However, even the commissionings permitted by this criterion can only be used against specifically declared enemies.

The powers actually delegated to the United States in Congress assembled are of two types — those consisting of sole and exclusive rights and powers and those of last resorts on appeals. The latter type is more limited. The United States in Congress assembled is designated as the last resort on appeals regarding all present and future disputes between two or more states. And all disputes concerning private rights of soil claimed under the different governments of two or more states will be settled on last resort appeal by either party to the Congress of the United States.

The United States in Congress assembled is granted sole and exclusive rights and powers to determine the conditions for peace, to declare war, to send and receive ambassadors, to enter into treaties and alliances, to establish rules for legal confiscations and their appropriation, to grant letters of marque and reprisal in peace, to appoint courts to try piracy and high seas felonies, and to determine appeals in all cases of captures. Congress also has a sole and exclusive authorization in a number of regulatory areas: setting the alloy and value of coins struck through its own action or those of the states, fixing standards of weights and measures, managing trade and other affairs with Indians not in any state, establishing a post office and postage system, appointing all officers of land forces excepting regimental officers and all naval officers, and managing the regulation and direction of all land and naval forces.

The most significant and general power granted to the Congress is the authority to determine all charges of war, all expenses for common defense, and all expenses for the general welfare. All of these authorizations are to be defrayed from a common treasury supplied by the states. The states, in turn, are to be charged in proportion to the value of each state's land. Congress shall specify both the manner by which the value of land shall be estimated and the time period within which states shall raise the tax revenues necessary to establish the common treasury of the United States.

All decisions of the Congress, except adjournment from day to day, are to be determined by majority votes. However, there are some areas of authorization and responsibility where the necessary congressional majority is nine votes rather than the mathematical minimum majority of seven. The following decisions require this larger majority vote: all fiscal decisions, designating the commander-in-chief and the number of forces, regulating the alloy and value of coins, granting letters of marque and reprisal during peace time, ratifying of treaties and alliances, and declaring war. Not only must Congress pass actions in these areas with a minimum of nine supporting state delegations' votes, but the Committee of the States, which may be invested with powers by Congress to act in its behalf during recess, may not be authorized to act in any of the areas reserved for action by a nine-vote majority in Congress.

The Articles of Confederation created a rather truncated set of governmental structures, a somewhat more amplified picture of authorizations and processes, and a singular, explicit purpose — to form a perpetual union of sovereign states whereby those states may protect and defend their mutual friendship, liberties, and general welfare. The Articles does not offer any overt articulation of the theoretical basis for the governmental form it creates, and the best accounts of the Articles' formation have emphasized the practical political disputes and choices of the era. Therefore, to make theoretical sense of the governmental form proposed by the Articles, a process of induction must be followed because the Articles provides no explicit basis for deducing its own theoretical principles. The challenge is to decipher the theoretical perspectives that would encourage the creation, adoption, and commitment to the political organization offered by the Articles — an organization that its authors and supporters expected to provide a viable governmental foundation for America, both practically and normatively.

The most intriguing dimension of the Articles of Confederation is its simultaneous commitment to the pursuit of sovereign statehood and to a perpetual union of states. Neither value is ingenuous nor expendable. Therefore, the location of sovereignty in the states, which is the exclusive emphasis in most representations of the Articles, is a real but incomplete principle of the political theory that shaped it. The challenge is to identify the theoretical basis for sovereign states *and* for a form of perpetual friendship — for free and independent states that are, nevertheless, obligated to obey the actions of Congress under the charter provisions of this perpetual union of states.

I propose that the key to this riddle is a particular set of understandings about community. The Articles of Confederation implicitly expresses its political concerns in terms of groups of people or communities. It reflects life in communities, not the anxious press of individualists. Thus, the Articles resonates more with the assumptions of covenanted communities than with those of self-interested competitors driven to contract for protection and stability.

The Articles' sense of community is reflected in different forms. Primary or foundational communities are represented by the states. A state is portrayed as the maximal level of meaningful, direct self-definition, and it must be protected as a primary communal form. Thus, it is the unit of formal sovereignty. Its freedom and independence must be protected not as a political telos but as an essential political foundation. It is the depository of all powers, jurisdictions, and rights not expressly delegated to Congress by the Articles. States are the primary political communities and the nature of their primacy is expressed, finally, in their formal authority — their sovereignty. It is in this context that the people formally constitute themselves, so this is where formal constituting authority is centered as well.

However, the Articles implies that states are not the fullest expression of the people's political unity. A national community is possible and desirable. It is not, however, the purpose of the national community to displace the primary communities of the states. Rather, the national community is to extend the parochial limits of these primary units. The national community is not to deny or replace primary communities but to organically extend them into broader spheres of public life.

The evidence in the Articles of a difference between a state as a community and the nation as a community is keyed to formal authority at these two levels: states are the centers of formal authority and coercive powers; the national community, on the other hand, has delegated responsibilities and must act largely through informal moral power and persuasion.

The differentiation and integration of state and national communities suggest that the Articles sought more complex and positive political objectives than those based solely on suspicion of power and fear of its abuse. Although states provide a basis for primary associations that must be protected, these communities also must be transcended to secure and protect the general welfare of the enlarged or national community in a just society.

On the other hand, there are practical limitations of space and interest that must be recognized and given their due in any design of formal authority. There must be a setting or space for communal life that makes it possible for a people to interact freely and meaningfully with one another. Such a space provides an environment within which shared perspectives and interests will develop. It is not that all citizens must or will simply echo each other's views. It is that there must be a shared source for the choices a free people will and must make. States represent the perceived limit for such a common setting. They extend as far as possible the limits of practical and meaningful communications through which a people can come to know itself as citizens and formally express their citizenship. And they are the limits for coherent patterns of social and economic activities that give any people a concrete basis for determining a common identity with shared purposes. In other words, states represent not the fullest expression of the theoretically desirable community but the fullest expression of community attainable through the formal self-definition of a people.

Expressed differently, states represent the practical limits of coercive authority and formal structures. They are invested with coercive authority not because they are the most extensive community but because building a democratic community requires limits of coercion. States are the most extensive political units within which a free people can define itself without creating a public order indifferent to virtue and liberty. In the lexicon of the Articles of Confederation, the most unambiguous expression of formal, coercive authority is "sovereignty." And it is the states that are sovereign. They are the units of formal, coercive authority within this perpetual union.

But the Articles of Confederation also expresses the vision of and commitment to a national community that will be more integrative than the community offered by any single sovereign state. In this it expresses the assumption that this national community will not be and, by implication, should not be the product of formal, coercive authority. Instead, this national community is to be fashioned indirectly through the persuasiveness of moral authority. It is a community of allies "to secure and perpetuate mutual friendship and intercourse among the people of the different states in this union." Although all sovereign states are obligated to abide by the actions of Congress taken within the Articles' grants of power, there is no coercive recourse specified for Congress if they do not. Despite traditional understanding, the Articles does not lack a vision of a more comprehensive political community than that offered by individual states. Nor is there a lack of commitment to that national vision, unless a person arbitrarily assumes that this commitment can only be assessed as genuine if it is expressed in terms of formal grants of coercive authority. The Articles expects that this will be a community given by people in state communities, not a community taken from them or imposed on them.

This willingness to allow the most comprehensive political goal to evolve within an environment of friendship and trust beyond coercive control reflects basic assumptions about the nature of politics and the nature of humanity. It suggests that an organic order is assumed to underlie the orders of history, civilization, and human contrivance. It also implies that if access to this order is not blocked or hidden because of the closures insisted upon by formal authority acting beyond its proper span, this organic order will move a free people to emulate its harmonies. Thus, the fundamental political task is to establish a basis upon which political principles will reflect the vitality of that natural order. Building a democratic, national community is based on the strengthening of persuasive power through trust, common purpose, and friendship in the spontaneous life of a virtuous people. The nation is not the basis for its people's virtue and freedom; rather the people's virtue and freedom are the basis for nationhood.

The rationale for the Articles is not to establish the public basis for the stable and secure expectations necessary in a society based on egoistic competition. Stability and security of expectations are not built into the provisions of this political association. In fact, these provisions, taken on their own terms, introduce insecurities and new possibilities for instabilities. The Articles also is not designed to define a maximum scope of individual discretion. Individuals, even free individuals, are always citizens — equal participants in community. The preoccupation of the Articles is community building — not as an act of willful imposition but as a consequence of shared adventures in mutual self-discovery. The Articles fashions a framework within which this adventure can be launched and pursued.

Even when Article 8 charges Congress with a responsibility to authorize expenditures in behalf of the general welfare, this does not occasion an abandonment of the Articles' designated mode of congressional action. The Congress is to pursue this positive and comprehensive charge just as it pursues its more negative and limited charges. It must base all of its actions on patterns of cooperation and commonality that it develops through the deliberative interactions among the thirteen state delegations and that they establish with their respective state legislatures. Congress does not define the common good and thereby establish the terrain for cooperation. Cooperation in the congressional process gives expression to specific forms of the common good.

The Articles of Confederation creates a political environment dominated by an important form of egalitarianism. It is not an equality of individuals that is directly expressed but an equality of primary communities. This is another reason why coercive authority at the national level is not endorsed. There is neither a substantive basis nor a procedural one by which prior judgments can establish a hierarchy among states. When each state is valued similarly and when authority is persuasive, the principle of equality is significantly supported. Although this creates a majoritarian thrust, it is more a majoritarianism of consensus rather than of a sufficiently large number. For example: actions on lesser issues require a mere majority, actions on more fundamental issues require an unusual majority of nine states, and actions on provisions of the constitutional order itself require unanimous consent.

In addition to endorsing the value credited to each community constituting the nation, egalitarianism and communalism also underlie the Articles' provisions for annual elections, limited terms, and recalls. To be sure, these features reflect a suspicion, if not distrust, of persons with formal grants of political power. They heighten accountability and break up potentially arbitrary or abusive consolidations of power. But they also reflect more positive attitudes and possibilities. They imply that the defense against the political abuses of power by individual representatives is an attentive, remedial community. The model of representation encouraged by these short reins is a representation closely tied to, strongly reflective of, and immediately responsive to the life and perspectives of the constituent community.

Again, these provisions imply a kind of egalitarianism. Society's proper governance does not require the special skills of any particular subgroup of society. Neither a class of hereditary rulers nor a "natural aristocracy" is needed or wanted to supply invested political leaders. Instead, the Articles assumes that a vital community will provide a continuing supply of able citizen/delegates who have been nurtured by this parenting source. The exceptional contributions of individuals uncommitted to the community are feared and discouraged. Trust is in the large and self-replenishing stock of persons rooted in and nurtured by a wholesome and purposeful community.

It is important to know what the Articles of Confederation is not as well as what it is. Such an awareness helps to clarify the differences of balance and orientation between it and the Constitution of 1787. The

Articles does not center its attention on autonomous individuals. This is not to suggest that it does not care about liberty. On the contrary, the Articles specifically mentions the securing of liberties as one of the primary purposes of the confederated league. The liberty it wishes to secure, however, is that of the states — or, more precisely, that of the primary communities, which are the states. To express this in personal terms, the Articles pursues traditions of liberty that are available to persons as a consequence of their membership in a larger, particular community. The Articles does not reflect a tradition that conceives of liberty as belonging to individuals qua individuals without regard to their social affiliations.

The Articles of Confederation does not provide a system of governance well suited to the dominance of competitive self-interests. This is not to say that competitive self-interests do not dominate, but to argue that if they dominate the Articles is not designed to govern effectively. The language of friendship, mutuality, and communality sets the document's tone. And the expectation of cooperative accommodation is assumed to be the basis for operations within the structures and authorizations it provides.

Unlike Madison's metaphor describing the Constitution of 1787, the Articles of Confederation is not designed to be an order-producing machine. Order, especially a humanly achieved and designed order, is not at the center of its approach to politics. Article 2's provision for state sovereignty is order-centered. But characterizations of the Articles informed by the perspectives and priorities of the 1787 Constitution seize this element of order and make it the essence of the whole, implying that the Articles offers a simple system of decentralized state control.

For better or worse, however, the Articles of Confederation is not a project dependent on humanity's political inventions. It is better read as an attempt to establish an environment within which the authentic order of nature can be reestablished and expressed. It offers a political framework that puts its citizens in touch with one another rather than contriving an endless array of isolating and fragmenting contexts for both social and personal life. It is more hopeful than fearful. It anticipates the revitalization of a natural order; it does not manufacture an order that will either stabilize naturally destabilizing factors or compensate for natural deficiencies or inconveniences. The Articles' underlying orientation en-courages confidence in the ordering possibilities of the intrinsic and spontaneous structures and processes of human life in community.

Finally, the Articles of Confederation is not hostile to a positive and vital nationhood. If it is assumed that the only criterion that can identify a genuine national commitment is a grant of centralized, coercive author-ity, then of course it is impossible to claim a strong national orientation for the Articles. But this is an arbitrarily narrow criterion. It may be that the Articles' national orientation is not fully practical on its own terms, but that does not make it any less real in principle as an expression of national commitment. You do not insist on perpetual union and inviolable observation of Congress' acts by sovereign states if you do not invest the national association with substantial value. There is little doubt that supporters of the Articles took perpetual union as seriously as state sovereignty.

This examination of the Articles of Confederation has been narrowly cast. It is an effort to specify the theoretical perspectives that best express the positive orientation of the Articles. Assuming that the organization of governance that it presents was written and supported by persons who believed it would result in a proper and workable polity, what are the coherent values, assumptions, and principles that supported this political approach? What were the theoretical perspectives that encouraged those people to frame the Articles, to defend the Articles, and to assume that the Articles offered the United States the appropriate basis for its political institutions and procedures? The attempt to answer these hypothetical questions resulted in the outline of a democratic theory that emphasizes community and community building, the egalitarianism of people in community, and the value and validity of intrinsic and spontaneous principles in the pursuit of justice and the common good. This is a democratic theory focused and balanced quite differently than the one offered by the Constitution of 1787. However, it does represent a practical, governmental extension of the community-focused ideals in America's original social contract, the Declaration of Independence, and in America's complex, self-conscious process of choosing and defining independence.

Colonial Ideologies: Republican and Democratic

America's political experiences during the last decade of colonial life not only led to political independence, they were also the immediate parent of America's first constitutional order in the Articles of Confederation. The Articles incorporated the theoretical perspectives that shaped the dominant justifications of America's movement to political independence.

The works of four men have made uniquely valuable contributions to contemporary understandings of the theoretical grounds for the American revolution. Bernard Bailyn identifies the role of country ideology in colonial America. J.G.A. Pocock explores country ideology's relationship to classical republicanism. Gordon G. Wood traces the development of republicanism in revolutionary America. And Merrill Jensen ties these trends to the ideological and social debates between the democratic/radical federalists and the aristocratic/conservative nationalists that informed the creation of both the Articles of Confederation and the Constitution of 1787.

Although Bailyn claims that his study of the pamphlets of revolutionary America "confirmed [his] rather old-fashioned view that the American Revolution was above all else an ideological, constitutional, political struggle and not primarily a controversy between social groups undertaken to force changes in the organization of the society or the economy,"[1] his work points to the unique impact of a particular social group, "the unsophisticated ... independent, uncorrupted, landowning yeoman farmers."[2] His claim that they did not seek social or economic interests as a primary goal is not easily sustained by his own findings. Bailyn asserts that the entire ideology of independence was rooted in the intention of saving the moral basis of a healthy, liberty-loving society that was still uncorrupted by the avarice of commerce and power; the ideology of a new constitutional order was needed precisely to protect and nurture the social possibilities of a purified, or relatively pure, agrarian America.

The dominant sources that served this American ideology were those of opposition theorists and country politicians in England. John Milton, James Harrington, Henry Neville, and Algernon Sidney were important, but Americans especially looked to the eighteenth-century writers who modified traditional opposition thought to accommodate contemporary applications: John Trenchard, Thomas Gordon, Benjamin Hoadly, Robert Molesworth, Francis Hutcheson, Philip Doddridge, Isaac Watts, Francis Bacon, Thomas Hollis, Andrew Eliot, Richard Price, Joseph Priestley, John Cartwright, James Burgh, and others. On the one hand, these writers voiced the conceptual commonplaces of their age. Their key concepts — natural rights, contract, liberty, and mixed constitution — were the popular elements of mainstream liberal thought. On the other hand, they did not imagine that the current state of government or society constituted a sufficient realization of these principles. The values that many took for granted as already fulfilled, they feared were being corrupted or lost.

The revolutionary theory of politics identified by Bailyn illustrates the central importance of questions of power. What are the grounds for the dominion of some persons over other persons? What are the social consequences of this dominion? What are the techniques by which dominion can be limited and reviewed? Bailyn notes that power is never static. It is aggressive and expansive. Bailyn describes "its endlessly propulsive tendency to expand itself beyond legitimate boundaries."[3] The natural prey of power is liberty. Thus, liberty is also a natural antidote to the corrupting and consolidating patterns of power. A constitutional order of mixed governance will limit the exercise of power and support the realization of natural rights, which are at the heart of liberty. This English model was respected, but the colonists expressed some deep anxieties about their ability to limit power within the practical setting of everyday English politics.

More and more, Americans saw themselves as freer and purer than their English counterparts. They emphasized the simplicity of their social life, the rectitude of their personal lives, and the noncoercive character of their political life. The perception of their own virtue was their primary hope against the deepening corruptions of the home country. Consequently, the practical basis for protecting their indigenous virtue became increasingly clear — rebellion. As Andrew Eliot wrote in 1765 when faced with the advances of corruption, "submission is a crime."[4]

Whether they spoke of a conspiracy against their liberty or of a conspiracy of power between crown and parliament, argues Bailyn, they were looking at similar corruptions that directly threatened their freedom and virtue. It was not difficult for the colonists to corroborate their worst fears. Evidence of malevolence was easily discovered: standing armies, plural office holding, attacks on the independence of the judiciary, executive patronage, and a badgering — if not unconstitutional — colonial tax policy. Soon these pieces of perceived ill will were ample enough to be woven together into a theory of deliberate conspiracy to reduce the colonists to a state of servility. These Americans were convinced that it was not only their freedom and virtue that were threatened but that their freedom and virtue were their best tools in any effort of self-preservation. Thus, the qualities of freedom and virtue were both ends and means — colonists' aspirations and colonists' weapons.

This position was more than a rhetorical ointment designed to calm the symptoms of the colonists' distress. It expressed a transformation of their political understandings that went to the heart of the entire issue of political power. What had been seen as their weakness or powerlessness — American isolation, simplicity, natural primitiveness, and formally weak states — was now seen as their virtue and strength. To many colonists, their perceived virtue was not just a point of contrast with conventional notions of political power in a corrupted home country but an alternate model for organizing and expressing the nature and form of political power itself. Political power had to be based upon and reflect the characteristics of a whole, healthy people. Previously, these characteristics had been associated with weakness. Now they were empowering.

The full empowerment of this new political form required that it be based on its proper foundation. In the first place, this meant that social and political arrangements must be in tune with the order of nature. The corruption of England, Bailyn shows, was increasingly associated with its dissociation from nature and its surrender to the mere conventions of history. Historical artifices were seen as coercive and violent in structure, establishing patterns of unwarranted domination. Instead, they believed, an uncorrupted people must live within a totally different plane of experience. Power should be the consequence of harmonious associations not of coercive control against the spontaneous life of the whole. In its proper form, power is the closest approximation of natural vitality that human contractual choices can achieve. This reconceptualization of power, with its switch from the standards of history to those of nature, is an important aspect of the colonists' radical change in the expression of their grievances. Colonists thought of themselves as English. Their claim against England was that, as colonists, they were being denied the chartered rights of that people's history. But as the conflict deepened, the nature of their complaints substantially changed. Their status was now natural, not historical — human, not English. This change not only offered the colonists an effective strategy for pursuing political independence; it drew Americans into new ways of thinking about forms of government and the nature of political power more generally.

Bailyn ties this evolving sense of power to issues of representation. The crucial issue at the core of any legitimate grant of power is the nature of representation. Coercive power is taken more than given. Persuasive power is given more than taken. Taking control is a top-down process. The taker is the source of initiative and authentication. Giving authorizations is a process of building upon a common, well-ordered base. Persons who are given public authorizations have power but only because of the actions of those to whom they are accountable.

Bailyn refers to representation as the first serious theoretical problem to come between England and the colonies. Essentially, the colonists abandoned the English norm of virtual representation, which had shifted initiative and power from the represented to the representative. They returned to a view of representation that was like the medieval notion of representation ("local men, locally minded, whose business began and ended with the interests of the constituency"[5]) and yet one that simultaneously expressed the preferences of a more broadly participatory and nature-oriented democracy. That democracy's basis for virtue and vitality is a well-ordered community. Therefore, it would be self-defeating to provide for the practical matters of everyday governance by disconnecting those charged with such governance from the guidance of a democratic community grounded in nature.

Locke's metaphors of popular contractual consent are never attached to continuing, specific actions in real time, but in this view of representation, consent of the governed was no longer occasional or metaphorical; it was substantial and literal. This new view of representation made consent a continuous everyday affair whereby the actions of government through its representatives accurately mirror the will of a well-constituted, public-spirited people. This is a more participatory notion of democracy, because in it the people are not just a check on government — they are the government.

While the people are to govern actively, they also are to be checked. Americans were quite conscientious in their efforts to disengage political principles and basic institutional forms from the positive actions of government. The latter were to be the expressions of popular will guided and limited by the former, a fixed set of written rules and forms based on the universal structures of nature. Thus, the legitimacy of specific expressions of political authority rested on a two-step process of authentication. First, particular actions of the government were to be consistent with the will of the people. Second, the expressions of popular choices were to be based on and be consistent with the requirements of nature.

The momentum of these changed perceptions of power placed the colonists on a collision course with their home country. As the colonists evolved a political understanding built more on local community autonomy and direct associations with nature, the contradictions of their colonial status became increasingly clear and untenable. The tensions between decentralized, persuasive authority norms and a centralized, formally coercive system of authority could not be sustained indefinitely.

Bailyn amplifies our sense of these transforming perspectives among the colonists.

> To conceive of legislative assemblies as mirrors of society and their voices as mechanically exact expressions of the people; to assume, and act upon the assumption, that human rights exist above the law and stand as the measure of the law's validity; to understand constitutions to be

ideal designs of government, and fixed, limiting definitions of its permissible sphere of action; and to consider the possibility that absolute sovereignty in government need not be the monopoly of a single all-engrossing agency but the shared possession of several agencies each limited by the boundaries of the others but all-powerful within its own — to think in these ways, as Americans were doing before Independence, was to reconceive the fundamentals of government and of society's relation to government.[6]

The concerns of those colonists who withheld their support for this transforming set of understandings illustrate the nature of the changes. Not just in the 1780s, but in the late 1760s and early 1770s, some Americans feared that ideas had come to prominence that were incompatible with the practical needs of a stable and secure public order. They saw this new vision of society as one based on a spontaneous communalism of consent and equality. The opposition feared more than the possibility of a new social order in which one set of rulers overthrows another set. They feared the establishment of a set of political principles incompatible with society itself. They feared that the refusal to defer to traditional understandings of authority could only lead to anarchy or tyranny. The depth of this opposition underscored the novelty of the newly ascendant ideas and the centrality they had in the political thinking of many colonists. For those enchanted by these ideas, they expressed a vision of a new day and an aspiration to transform all political orders into conditions that would allow a freer life for all. However their success is measured or judged, it was the energy of their political theory that generated American independence, formed America's first governmental structures, and expressed a unique sense of American identity and mission. These political ideals are still capable of capturing the energy of Americans, especially when Americans compare themselves to other peoples and their national life and when Americans seek renewal and redirection.

The split in colonial views, which intensified during the decades immediately prior to independence, has been described in terms of the court and country alliances in England. Bailyn's account describes the increasing dominance of the views associated with the country party. Court apologists in America wanted a strong and vigorous national government, an aggressive foreign policy, a standing army with revenues sufficient to wage war, and ample administrative structures. The country forces wanted a limited government dependent on voluntary cooperation, restrained taxation, a militia, and frequently elected representatives.[7] The country ideology, which dominated the movement to independence, has been interpreted by Pocock as the revival of the republican ideal of civic humanists. The republicanism Pocock describes captures the sense of dynamic virtue, threat of corruption, and affirmation of moral personalities in civic action that marked the American "country." In building this connection to civic humanism, he is concerned that the complex relationship between the American revolution and English and renaissance cultural histories not be lost or overlooked. This is a valid, significant concern.

Nevertheless, Pocock's representation of civic humanism does not reflect key aspects of American republicanism in a fully satisfying way. I believe that Pocock exaggerates the historicism of the American movement and at the same time deprecates its naturalism. His own apparent passion for a secular, nonabsolutistic commitment to res publica is admirable, but it is not a sufficient expression of eighteenth-century American views. There is much about American experiences and perspectives that does reflect and contribute to the republican orientation he explores. But the American revolutionary ideology was not dominated by a historical orientation. Increasingly, it separated itself from the traditions of English constitutionalism, not to affirm the contingencies of another people's history but to avoid the arbitrariness of the accidental, circumstantial, and corrupt factors it attributed to identities based solely on history. Its ally in this process was particular forms of naturalism.

Nature, they claimed, represents a dimension of universals, neither independent of time and space nor historically contingent and subrational. The abstract principles of nature are simultaneously concrete. They penetrate the particular manifestations of things. Although factors of time and space are historically particularistic and fortuitous, as expressions of nature they reveal universal purpose. Americans thus projected a morally and politically stable republic in the midst of corrupt and irrational events without a metaphysical principle that superceded their own attempts to express civic virtue. Yet for them nature functioned like a metaphysical principle. Its constructs were immanent rather than transcendent, but they were also a source of fixed meanings and guidance. The American ideology that most actively fed the movement to independence did not make the historical act of rebellion subordinate to eschatology, or to transcendent mystery, or to ultimate redemption; but neither did it ever suggest that "they were placing their virtue at Fortune's mercy."[8] The explicit and implicit Deism of revolutionary America was built on a firm naturalistic foundation that was a primary source of American confidence and naivete — "with a firm reliance on the protection of Divine Providence." Also, this naturalistic cast of American republicanism encouraged a less elitist and more egalitarian expression of civic humanism in the new world.

Because nature is a principle of immanence many characteristics of civic humanism can be seen in the American setting. There was a keen sense of the interplay of virtue and corruption. Americans sensed that virtue was not the essence of some realm of escape but that it must be the form of their actual historical community. However, because the community takes its form in time it will be threatened with the corruptions of time as well. In this sense, Pocock's emphasis on a Machiavellian moment over Lockean eternity is most appropriate. American ideology was not an unalloyed return to nature and to the Lockeanism that has been associated with that return in the conventional wisdom. Rather, the American experiment was launched by a complex reading of the interactions of nature and history, related to what Pocock calls "an ambivalent and contradictory dialogue between virtue and corruption."[9]

My limited quarrel with Pocock concerns only the extent to which the American view of virtue is denaturalized in his account. Perhaps because of their naturalistic beliefs, the colonists were not particularly melancholy about the struggle they accepted and pursued. There was a complex and continuous battle to be fought between virtue and corruption, but the alternatives were not perceived as being two forms of secular preferences. Nature provided both immanent principles that defined virtue and specific conditions of being that provided means for effectively pursuing virtue. Nature created a foundation for considerably greater hopefulness than could be established by mere will and intentionality.

Thus, the Declaration appeals to the god of nature to verify "the rectitude of our intentions." Perhaps this is why the quarrel with modernity is not as directly reflected in American thought and practice as Pocock asserts.

Gordon Wood, in *The Creation of the American Republic, 1776–1787,* captures this interplay of corruption and virtue, history and nature, and conservatism and radicalism at the birth of American independence. Because the American model for civil society was organic and developmental — not abstract and mechanistic — a sense of interaction and process was encouraged. Also, the immanence of nature drew Americans to history but not necessarily to particularism. Thus, they could justify a break from England without abandoning the "free and ancient principles" of the English constitution.[10] Those historical principles were worthy of their continuing allegiance not because they were the mere artifacts of English history but because they were historical forms true to basic principles of nature. The break was because of the principles' corruption in England not because of the principles per se. To the end, an uncorrupted English constitution was one of the primary ways Americans expressed what a constitution should be. But they found the uncorrupted English constitution more securely represented by nature than by current English practices.

Nevertheless, the political theory in the American view that dominated the movement to independence was not focused on forms of government. Its attention was centered on the character of American society. This is reflected in its concept of republicanism. It is quite common today to define republicanism in terms of formal structures of government such as representative institutions. It was common for them, however, to define republicanism as being based on the spirit of association it endorsed and fostered. The struggle between virtue and vice was understood in both existential and political terms as a battle that is intrinsic as well as environmental. Attentiveness to nature guides both personal and political success in this struggle. For example, rural life was celebrated not because it permits wild excesses but because of its rigor and simplicity. It restores access to humanity's intrinsic independence and dignity, fostering fortitude, temperance, and restraint. These personality traits result in lives of devotion and duty to country not because of fear and coercion but because of trust and commitment.

The key to both health and sickness was the character of the people. The path to social strength and health was through the unique traits of the yeomanry — frugality, industry, temperance, and simplicity. Charles Lee's utopian plan for an American republic was representative of this view. He wanted a simple agrarian society free of a competitive commercial life, which would only "emasculate the body, narrow the mind, and in fact corrupt every true republican and manly principle."[11]

The simple independence of an egalitarian yeomanry, however, was not understood as the basis for isolation or social estrangement. To the contrary, that independence nourished a spontaneous sense of common feelings that were proper social bonds for consent. The great failure of existing governments was twofold. Either they coercively extracted compliance to a common good or they sacrificed the public good to the private interests of a small group of rulers. America's republican sense of the public or community required that the shared take precedence over the discrete and that consent be honored above coercion. Colonists recognized clashing interests within their communities but did not make them an integral basis for their political theory except in the conflict between the rulers and the ruled. Otherwise, they represented the community as a moral unity animated by the good of the whole. An anonymous colonist wrote in 1776, "No man is a true republican that will not give up his single voice to that of the public."[12] Factions are disease. They express malfunctionings of the parts, and they jeopardize the whole. A healthy society, on the other hand, is the harmonious integration of all parts of the community. Americans pursued an integration of the universal and the particular with an innocence that was unimaginable to Jean-Jacques Rousseau.

Colonial Americans emphasized the importance of building republicanism within an environment of commonality. Specifically, they sought shared time and space as the basis for common interests. Therefore, the primary unit of formal authority necessarily had to be small in territory to be unified in purpose. Common interests were neither coerced nor suicidal. They expressed the satisfactions that come through the assertion of consent. Shared experiences within coherent space could produce a broadly shared sense of common identity and purpose that would result in the fulfillment of both selves and the community. The community would be healthy because it would be able to organize itself around genuinely common interests. And individuals would be healthy because this pursuit of common goods would serve their proper particular needs as well.

This pattern of joining the common with the particular is also evidenced in their handling of liberty. As Wood shows, American republicanism in 1776 saw liberty as fully compatible with a public realm harmoniously integrated in all of its essential parts. It expressed a public or communal sense of liberty rather than a distinctly private or individualized one. It was the liberty of their communities they feared losing and that they sought to protect or, as necessary, establish. At the onset of American independence the dominant view of liberty was the public right of the people against the particular and privileged interests of arbitrary political rulers or economic elites. This view did not encourage an awareness of or concern about majoritarianism because the people were not seen as a self-serving faction. Instead, the people were presented as a harmonious unity. Tyranny by the people was virtually inconceivable. The power held by the people was their liberty and the abuse of that power was seen only as anarchy or licentiousness. Individual liberties played little role in their political theory, especially if such liberties contributed to opposing the people's majority will.

For the individual, their notion of political liberty or freedom of the community was not so much a protection for dissent as it was the basis for proper obedience. They felt no need to hide or deny this reality but did believe that the obedience of community members' behavior was an expression of their commitments, not their fears. In this respect they expected a radical transformation of the nature of authority. Their recommendations for governmental powers were not based on the constant need for coercive control but on a largely uncompromised assumption that the people would willingly obey governments worthy of their obedience. They expected this public virtue from the citizenry and saw it as the unique characteristic of their republicanism. Governments, specifically republics, are sustained by the virtue of their people not by the terror of their powers.

Preserving these republics and the virtue they assumed required a society of equals built on the possibilities of commonality in small and coherent states. As Wood demonstrates, much of the egalitarianism of these Americans was ambiguous and strategic even if it was conceptually valid. The ambiguity was not that they did not possess strong egalitarian sentiments. Americans then, as now, were uniquely sensitive to any claims of status superiority. This sensitivity is reflected by the long American tradition of wealthy politicians who present themselves through the imagery of log cabins and tales of former drudgery and want. The ambiguity was that these Americans also coveted and pursued the symbols of status. This tension of values created a serious challenge to their republican theory. Their egalitarianism was also strategic. It could be used to dramatize a disjuncture with the authority of the crown. Their conflict with the crown, in turn, avoided conflicts among themselves. Further, their egalitarian resentments were a tool with which radical leaders could counter the traditional deferential habits of the common people not only to the crown but to any formally or traditionally established leaders. Egalitarianism not only provided a theory that positively joined personal and community interests, but that helped convince the people that they rightfully had a share in their own governance.

The years immediately surrounding the war for independence express America's initial political objectives. Americans have continued to affirm these objectives even if with an increasing sense of melancholy and nostalgia. It was a time of self-restraint and cohesion when communities seemed to be purposefully united. Even to a critic such as the Reverend John Witherspoon, who took strong exception to the republican ideology of his fellow colonists, the "degree of public spirit ... [which] has prevailed among all ranks of men" strained credulity.[13] But for many Americans, perhaps most, this homespun version of republicanism was more than credible. It expressed their self-respect, their sense of urgency, and their acceptance of the challenges at hand. They knew that their virtue was not complete or inevitable. Their hope for what was possible and their fear of what could be lost intensified their republicanism and drove them into revolt. Reflecting back on the time of independence, David Ramsey in 1778 observed, "In vain we sought to check the growth of luxury, by sumptuary laws; every wholesome restraint of this kind was sure to meet with the royal negative." Therefore, if Americans had not revolted, "our frugality, industry, and simplicity of manners, would have been lost in an imitation of British extravagance, idleness, and false refinements."[14]

Republicanism became the American version of the alternative life both politically and morally. Wood carefully traces this blending of republicanism, revolution, and regeneration in the American mind. Republicanism, together with Deism and Christianity, encouraged honesty, benevolence, and self-denial in a democratic society. It expressed a vision of transformation and a basis for achieving those changes. It projected a positive role not only for public life but for government too. Properly ordered, government was part of the elevation of ordinary people. The regenerative effects of republicanism were the basis of John Adams' confidence in the revolution. He did not trust in a spontaneous natural virtue and he did not accept assertions of realized historical virtue. But he did have confidence in the transformational capabilities of republican values and institutions on human behavior. The American revolution promised a new kind of politics, not just a new set of politicians.

The concrete setting for working out these new political forms was the states. In fact, the business of the Continental Congress was severely complicated because of the number of delegates who returned to their home states to participate in the creation of new governments there. For many of the most revolutionary-minded colonists, the erection of new state governments was thought to be the most expeditious means of severing political ties with England. Nothing, argues Wood, engaged the interests of the Americans more in the period around 1776 than the framing of these governments. In fact, he reads the Continental Congress' May 15, 1776, resolution calling on the states to form new governments as the real act of revolutionary independence.

An evaluation of the states' responses to this call reveals several patterns. The states had an inordinate anxiety about magistracy. But it mattered little to most colonists whether that magistracy was elected or hereditary. In the executive they sought little more than service to unavoidable administrative functions. In all states, through a variety of devices — redefined Executive Council powers, separation of the executive from the legislative process, impeachment provisions, short terms of office, rotations in office, and elimination or severe control of appointment powers — the substance, if not the form, of an independent magistracy was destroyed.[15] This reduction of the magistracy to specified executive functions, and those mostly administrative, had an inevitable impact on the nature of government overall. Designs that sought political vitality from governmental structures were avoided. Instead, the colonists preferred nonstructural and informal grounds for public vitality and wholeness. This principle of unity and direction was the people; specifically, the majority.

Although colonists were fond of rhetoric praising Baron Montesquieu's precepts on the separation of powers, the actual practices of state governments were widely divergent from that norm. There was an intensification of legislative domination over other governmental functions. Formally and informally, colonial legislatures had become heavily involved in judicial and executive activities, and these developments were readily understood and accepted as appropriate and necessary for the protection of the people's welfare. The Articles is an unambiguous statement of this legislative domination not only because of the formal exclusivity and primacy of the Congress but also because of the channeling of all interactions with the states through state legislatures. Wood summarizes this blurring of magistracy with distinctly legislative responsibilities.

> The state constitutions of 1776 explicitly granted the legislatures not only tasks that they had claimed with varying degrees of success in the course of the 18th century but also functions that in the English constitutional tradition could in no way be justified as anything but executive, such as the proroguing and adjourning of the assembly, the declaring of war and peace, the conduct of foreign relations, and in several cases the exclusive right of pardon.[16]

Initially, separation of powers was a means to protect the people and their directly representative bodies from executive manipulation. The prohibition against plural office holding illustrates this point. Previously, magistracy could manipulate and dominate the people by offering their representatives appointments to other executive or judicial posts. Now magistrates' powers did not allow this possibility. Also, one of the major reasons why judicial independence did not develop in revolutionary America was that legislative intervention was seen as a necessary antidote to executive manipulation of the courts. This problem was so severe in most colonists' minds that they had great difficulty fitting the judiciary into their scheme of government. Separation of powers had a unique thrust in revolutionary America; in practice it was the legislative separation of powers from the magistracy in the name of the people.

State legislatures were more than lawmaking bodies. Now they held most of the prerogative powers of colonial governors. Centering power in the body most directly attached to the people gave a distinctly democratic quality to the changes of 1776. As was noted earlier, the theory and practice of representation was the crucial dimension in identifying and serving the will of the people. Nearly everyone agreed to the practical impossibility of convening the whole people directly, even in state contexts. These Americans had theoretical direction, but they did not trap themselves in theoretical straitjackets. Yet precisely because they accepted representative linkages, they were extraordinarily attentive to the precise nature of representation plans and their implementation. The new state representative bodies did not universalize representation, but they consistently expanded the number of representatives and eased access to suffrage rights relevant to the selection of those representatives. The new state assemblies were larger than the colonial ones. All of them retained some kind of property or taxing provisions for voting eligibility, but the amount and value of property or tax required for voting was typically reduced. These qualifications were not viewed as a priori denials of democracy and popular rule. Instead, the real challenge to democracy, especially in the south, was any denial of the equal representation of the citizenry.

Wood characterizes colonists' theories of representation as being complex, unstable, and somewhat self-defeating. When the issue of representation was formulated in terms of their experiences with England, they insisted on the more protective advocacy of actual representation. However, when representation was tied to their domestic republican aspirations, they sought the more integrative voice of virtual representation. Support for actual representation was needed psychologically to cope with their political fears and strategically to exempt themselves from parliamentary authority. Yet this pressure for actual representation and the implicit heterogeneity of interests it serves formed an unintended challenge to their republican ideology and its assumption of an organic society with a fundamentally common interest. Americans blended these notions of actual and virtual representation, picking and choosing more in accord with a standard of expediency than with one of theoretical unity. The one consistent pattern that can be charted is their tendency to insist on the protections afforded by actual representation when dealing with formal political structures and authority, especially the more comprehensive and remote those institutions were in relation to popular supervision. In this sense formal domestic institutions were seen as analogies of English institutions. The other part of this pattern was their willingness to endorse virtual representation's greater ability to act decisively when dealing with their own communities and when the informal processes that mark the shared life of a people were considered.

Their language patterns illustrate both the confusion in their theories of representation and the informal differentiation they evolved regarding virtual and actual representation. They spoke of both petitioning and instructing their representatives. When the representational interchange was perceived as being within the basic harmony of the community, they used the term "petitioning" — language more applicable to virtual representation. When the issues were transcommunal or intercommunal, they more often spoke of "instructing," using the language of actual representation. The immediate result was not a discrediting or death of the republican ideal but a driving of that ideal into more and more localized manifestations. It also suggests that these colonists were not as naive as many have accused them of being. In actual political practice, they did not take the homogeneity of the people's interests for granted; that was a possible achievement, not a realized achievement. To fulfill the possibility they had to build from a proper base and they had to maintain important distinctions of structure and method.

The colonists revered the principle of mixed governance in the English constitution. Their history, ideology, and democratized society, however, offered them no clear way to implement this principle in America. The focus of the efforts they did make was within the legislative element and is best seen in the development of bicameralism. Revolutionary Americans did not oppose the leadership of their more cultivated fellow citizens, but they did oppose hereditary and arbitrary privileges.

Upper houses were acceptable in most states because they gave the impression of mixing governance and diversifying the voices of the people while at the same time resembling unicameralism. The cosmetic change preserved their abstract concern about checks without introducing a genuinely heterodox principle of representation or of society. Wood finds that these state upper houses pressed no social interests distinct from the lower houses. The result was two homogeneous branches that closely mirrored each other. Even when states specified different qualifications and different bases of representation for the two houses, the people elected similar kinds of people to both.

American bicameralism and unicameralism seldom opposed each other, especially in local settings susceptible to the operation of a moral majority where dominant values, perspectives, and styles shaped formal structures and transcended apparent distinctions. When distinctions are without a difference, pose no impediments to majority will, and provide a way to presume the presence of an honored ideal, they are likely to be attractive to a democratic society. The real battle about bicameralism and unicameralism arose as the idea moved beyond local and state contexts. Persons who comfortably lived with and endorsed bicameralism in Massachusetts, for example, were likely to insist on unicameralism in the Articles. This was more than a form of blind bias. It was a form of political judgment about the different ways informal processes express themselves in local and in national settings. What can be ameliorated in one setting may be exacerbated in another simply by following the same organizational scheme.

Initially, combining bicameralism and mixed governance offered a convenient union. But the more these two principles were seriously studied in relationship to each other, the clearer were the incongruities between them. The colonists discovered that, in fact, you could have an acceptably democratized republic with two houses, but then the essential point of a mixed government — the empowering of distinct social interests — was lost. Most states adopted bicameralism and dropped mixed government rationales. The end result was a tradition of republican bicameralism. Only in Pennsylvania was there a substantially different pattern. There an aggressive and deliberate rejection of bicameralism and the mixed polity ideas most frequently used to explain and defend it stimulated a significant and effective opposition. This opposition directly argued the merits of mixed governance and of bicameralism as an important means to mixed governance's implementation.

It was easier for the more radical Americans of 1776 to abandon or transvalue an honored principle such as mixed government because of new directions in their concepts of law and constitution. Already they had evolved a unique understanding of constitution. A constitution was a superior law, preferably written, with authority that stood above the forms and processes of governance and against which those and all other expressions of law were to be evaluated and interpreted. As this view established itself, it became harder for Americans to accept the so-called English constitution as constitutional at all. The English constitution was in no way distinguished from English government and governance. It was, instead, the collecting and integrating of institutions, laws, and customs that describe the system of relationships between authority and the people. Americans, instead, wanted to identify fundamentals of politics and assumed that these fundamentals would not be synonymous with patterns of historical usage. For example, their colonial history fed a deep desire for political rights and convinced them that the basis for those rights had to be superior to the actions of presently constituted authority. This constitutional perspective applied fully to legislative bodies representing the people. The constitution had to be beyond mere legislative enactment, even if those legislative responses were shaped by the instructions of the people.

The idea at the heart of this view of constitutionalism, argues Wood, involved some kind of compact among the people. The most fundamental aspect of a constitution was not its descriptions of the forms and procedures of the state but its specification of those jurisdictions invested in government and those retained by the people. In essence it expressed the form in which society constitutes itself more than the organization of governance. Such a formation of the political community was fundamental in another respect. It could only be achieved by the people themselves — not their representatives. The work of representatives presumes that the more fundamental work of the people has already been accomplished. A Massachusetts colonist illustrated this view and its divorce from English constitutional standards. When someone suggested that representatives in the legislature could define for society whatever constitution they pleased, he attacked the suggestion, describing it as "the rankest kind of Toryism, the self-same monster we are now fighting against."[17]

Revolutionary Americans had a strong preference for codification of the constitutional principles, but they were never willing to limit their rights or political principles to what was codified at any particular point in time. The writing did not create these rights and principles, it only affirmed their natural existence. It was not the actual source of those principles. Americans took legislative enactments quite seriously but never reduced obligation to mere positive law. They obeyed the enactment because it was perceived to be in the spirit of fundamental principles of justice and law. In this way Americans gave themselves a dynamic, interpretive framework more than a formula. The result was a pattern of responses that were often difficult to interpret. For example, as Eldon J. Eisenach has shown, the use of English common law tradition is marked with both attentiveness and carelessness in America.[18]

Eventually this emphasis on higher principle could not be maintained without developing judicial independence and discretion. At the time of the revolution, however, Americans were trying to find legislative solutions, and therefore rejected an independent judiciary as the source of constitutional interpretation. The linkage of the legislature to the people and of the people to the constitutional order made this the obvious focus of their search. Before Americans developed a judicial remedy, they adopted a unique pattern of extralegislative action by the people. Their conventions and committees were constitution-making bodies considered to be superior, for this purpose, to ordinary legislatures. Shortly after independence, they expanded their activities to a wide range of political and economic issues and became increasingly associated with the behaviors of mobs and, even, mob violence. They are important theoretically because they reflect the deep distrust of all authority set above or beyond the effective control of the people. The deeper challenge was whether the people could ever be embodied in any representative institution. Certainly this atmosphere invited a constant stream of schemes to define and redefine the will of the people and to play those schemes off against almost any institutionalized authority.

This strategy was effective largely because of the deep-seated commitment to the primacy of the people's will. The sovereignty of the people was a settled matter, but what it meant for the people's instruments of political power or government was muddled. The essence of sovereignty was the making of obligatory law. The power to do so was theoretically held by the people anterior to government. Actually, this was a power of specified representational bodies. By designating governmental sovereignty, Americans feared they might lose the representational basis of government and reduce politics to the power of command. Americans on the eve of independence responded by adopting a sovereignty that rested on the political base — the states — rather than on the political center — the nation. Regardless of this political arrangement's practicality, placing sovereignty in the states was not the expression of a theoretical denial of or hostility to the national union. In this sense the normative issue was not localism or nationalism but the nature of and basis for their proper relationship. National virtue required the vitality of a representational system in which power was as much a matter of consent as of command. In this judgment, building the union out from state communities in which representation could be more fully achieved and monitored was the preferred way to accomplish America's nation-building objectives.

Although Merrill Jensen resists versions of American history based on a monopoly of "federalist" ideas and honors the Articles' expansion of political possibilities, he illustrates the exaggeration of American political agreement just prior to and at independence. The initial phase of the revolutionary process did not fully reveal the conflicts between the economic upper-class interests and the interests of the masses in the towns and on the frontier. The ascendency of the democratic radicals at the time of the revolution hid important internal political struggles. Conservatives frequently united with radicals because of external issues — such as the conflict with England — not because of a principled consensus. In fact, the radicals' assumptions of internal revolution often encouraged conservatives to restrain the movement toward independence even though they commonly aspired to a political separation of the colonies from England. Therefore, the radicals were able to dominate the ideology of the revolution not because they had engineered an overwhelming ideological agreement and not merely by the volume of their own numbers, which were considerable, but because they were able to exploit the external issue of British authority for internal advantages. The perspectives, values, and assumptions that were most effective against the claims of British rule were simultaneously most beneficial to their immediate domestic interests and values.

The sense of a national bond uniting each of the former colonies was real and grew stronger as the revolution neared. It was a bond that also came voluntarily. It came freely because of a sense of common problems and threats, not because of coercive authority. In fact, the principle of a single coercive authority as proposed in 1787 would have been suicidal between 1774–1776. Even the colonial establishment, which would have favored a more unified and rigorous national authority in theory, was deterred from implementing such a design because it might place the government in the hands of the more radical masses. Also, forcing the formalization of the national union at this juncture could have resulted in more fragmentation than unity. The divisions among the colonies cut in many different ways and were not simply contained within the borders of states or groups of states (New England, middle states, southern states). There were differences between states with small and large populations; between states with small and large geographic areas; between states with many and few slaves; between states with western land claims and states with no credible western land claims; between states with different religious traditions and traditions of religious tolerance; between states with different population mixes and patterns of rural and urban development; and between individuals of strong and mixed minds. It was neither naive nor a failure to insist that common bonds be given voluntarily. To force the union beyond the processes of consent could have jeopardized the entire project of nation building. America's initial national unification was accomplished under circumstances marked with deep and pervasive divisions and yet without coercive authority. Therefore, the choices of 1776 cannot simply be dismissed as mistakes corrected in 1787. It is quite likely that the possibilities of 1787 arose only because of the colonists' patience, restraint, and goodwill in dealing with the circumstances of 1776.

Radicals' domination of the revolutionary ideology is also reflected in the actions of the Continental Congresses. The First Continental

Congress launched its sessions on September 5, 1774. One of its first debates indicated the direction its proceedings would take. The more socially and economically conservative colonists wanted a political analysis of the colonists' plight based on the principles of the British constitution, even if exemptions were necessary for current parliamentary authority within that constitution. The more radical voices insisted on a law of nature argument and the more extensive basis for political experimentations it made possible. Although the final statement was in the form of a compromise, its real effect was to authorize, not limit, the claims of the radicals. This statement based the rights of the colonists on "the immutable laws of nature, the principles of the English constitution, and the several charters or compacts."[19] Nature trumped history. The restraints of British precedence, the limitations of articulated rights, and the prohibitions against rebellion could readily be transcended.

The delegates most committed to independence were able to beat back every attempt to restore the union with Britain and to create the domestic equivalent of Parliament — a strong central government. The first congress had given them a strong basis for future effectiveness: the inclusion of natural law claims; the denial of parliamentary authority except in the regulation of trade and even then only with the consent of the colonies; and the tacit authority to meet force with force in dealing with the home country.

The Second Continental Congress met in the late spring of 1775. By this time it was clear that British strategy had forced the cooptation of the conservative colonists. Their participation in the revolutionary ideology was not a matter of choice or commitment but the unavoidable consequence of preempted choices. Because the British pursued forced subjection, their call for reconciliation translated too easily into surrender. In the choice between surrender and independence, the conservatives chose political independence, if not the underlying theory that supported it.

Also, the advocates of independence were quite cunning in their own efforts. They did not directly press for independence but rather for the de facto conditions that constituted independence: creation of a common military capability, formation of an association, and opening up of ports to the world. Jensen observes, "Congress was maneuvered into a position in which it was practically fighting for independence though the word was not mentioned."[20] Such maneuvering was another means of effectiveness, building of informal, voluntary processes to achieve political goals without recourse to the traditional exercise of formal, coercive power.

The issue of the form and powers of a central government was not just a matter of fundamental values and theoretically derived conclusions. The more immediate and concrete form of the issue related to British authority itself. Did the colonists want to create a new, Americanized form of the British government or not? One group wanted to create something like the prior order minus the British role. The other group wanted an informal association that could work together to achieve common goals such as pressing the war against England, forming alliances and international support, and raising funds. The radicals had no intention of setting up an alternate authority that could easily do what they were trying to shed from British rule.

In the end the formal independence of the states was most important. Radicals saw this arrangement as essential to achieving the kind of government they desired. They valued democratized communities. They could foresee a national union built upon the base provided by these communities, but they did not believe that these communities could be built from the top down or on the basis of threatening coercive power. There should be a contagion of virtue and common interest to the whole. But formal political integration alone neither fostered nor required virtue or shared commitments.

The theoretical orientations that gave life and form to the American revolution are directly relevant to America's first constitutional order, formally expressed in the Articles of Confederation, which was built on assumptions, values, and orderings that still inspire and shape American political dialogue and policy. If there is a key to revolutionary America and to the Articles perhaps it is the assumption that the people, in some fundamental sense, have primacy — not formal authority or government. This is the most significant sense in which the Articles is democratic. It proposes a polity that will only be practical if it works from the base up. It depends on the building of power, not the imposition of power.

Government is sustained by the virtue and activity of its people, not by the terror of its authority. This is the conviction many Americans used to contest British authority, to design indigenous authority, and to inspire themselves even as they moved into their third century of nationhood.

The transformation of conventional images of powerlessness into authentic power animates the search for a perpetual union without coercive power at the center or the top. The power of a simple, whole, and healthy people is to lead the way to this high goal. These Americans assumed that it was their character as a people, not their institutional forms, that ultimately would determine the success of their public aspirations. Even their republicanism was not a theory of structural forms and procedures. Rather, it communicated the moral basis of a good people. Ultimately, government had a higher role than mere order. The proper life of government would be the expression of an elevated people, not just coercive control.

The coercive power that was established was localized where, it was presumed, it could be watched and checked more effectively. Further, it could be more easily transformed there because it was tied to a communal unity of purpose based on consent and equality. Consent then became a continuous aspect of governance, and justice was tied to natural principles. Universal moral principles, they believed, have concrete manifestations that tie politics to nature. The constitutional model that launched autonomous American politics was an organic/developmental one. Even though American politics subsequently embraced an abstract and mechanistic constitutional model, it never totally discarded the organic patterns of the dominant political vision's founding.

The Second Continental Congress, which convened from May to July 1776, took several actions important to the future structure of American political life. In May it called upon each colony to form its own government. In July it issued the formal declaration of America's political autonomy. And by mid-July it had received John Dickinson's draft for a confederation and perpetual union among the thirteen former colonies. It is the second of these events that has been the most remembered and celebrated. The Declaration of Independence, unlike the Articles of Confederation and the Constitution of 1787, is a statement of principle, rather than a practical plan of governance, which builds a theoretical justification for the revolutionary actions of the Americans.

The Declaration of Independence continues to have a great rhetorical appeal to Americans more than two hundred years after its writing. This appeal is not exhausted by its powerful statement of what America was and why Americans did what they did in founding their nation. It moves Americans today because in some fundamental ways it expresses what America still is. In a unique sense, it was in 1776 and remains more than two hundred years later a "constitutional" document. Obviously, it is not constitutional in any specifically governmental, technically legal, or directly practical sense. Its constitutional character derives from its principles of nationhood and the continuing credibility they have had for the American people whenever they interpret their past, whenever they organize their present, and whenever they project their future. In fact, the Declaration's lack of legal standing and absence of institutional forms makes its moral and conceptual hold on American political ideas all the more unexpected but significant. And the importance of this state of affairs is further enhanced because the formal, legal, and structural order that has been established since the ratification of the U.S. Constitution in 1789 is primarily based on an alternate tradition of political values and assumptions.

The Declaration is constitutional in a more specific sense too. Its interpreters have attributed a more passive role to it than may be warranted. For example, Arthur E. Sutherland describes the Declaration as a manifesto of the new nation that merely announces a fait accompli.[1] This is a common interpretation in which the Declaration expresses the values that government should serve and the grounds from which government must come but leaves the specifics of these constituting issues to be defined in state codes and other fundamental documents. Although in many ways this is an accurate description of the Declaration, it misses further implications. The Declaration of Independence is constitutional vis-à-vis the American nation — it expresses the constituting of the American people. This is especially important for revolutionary America, even if it did not constitute any formal government or "state." The state was to be established within a well-formed community. Political society had to be constituted before proper political authority in government could be established. The Declaration of Independence represents the formation of a people. It gives composition to the American nation. In this sense it is more than an eloquent rationale for specific political actions. It ties those actions to the positive need for a people to properly constitute themselves as a political community.

The habit of reading American politics forward and backward from 1789 has detracted from a sharper understanding both of the foundational role of the Declaration in defining American nationhood and of the discontinuities between the Declaration of 1776 and the Constitution of 1787. John P. Diggins points to both the continuities and discontinuities of these two documents. He does not focus his attention on the Declaration per se, centering his argument more generally on Thomas Jefferson and the nature of America's political society. Overtly, he offers a Hartzean portrait of American politics — America as the place of unrelieved liberalism. However, the revolution brought America two forms of liberalism — liberal individualism and liberal pluralism — Diggins tells us. Presumably, the former is most relevant to the Declaration because Diggins describes its essence through the political ideas of Jefferson and Thomas Paine. Liberal pluralism is best represented by Alexander Hamilton and James Madison and the 1787 Constitution.

Thus, America is interpreted as being formed through the interactions between individualistic and statist forms of Lockeanism. In his words, "One expression of liberalism valued freedom, autonomy, and the sufficiency of the individual, the other power, stability, and the efficacy of the state." Together they robbed America of a tradition of political virtue and of any meaningful elevation of its political vision. Liberal individualism blocked a moral community just as liberal pluralism barred national purpose. "Both identified happiness with property and material pleasure; neither committed America to political ideals that appealed to man's higher nature. Individualism provided the means by which Americans could pursue their interests, pluralism the means by which they could protect them."[2] Diggins' lament is that American political thought and culture is best characterized not by the presence of civic virtues but by the absence of uniquely Christian values.

It is not clear why distinctly Christian values must determine virtue for the American people. It is clear that virtue at the time of the American revolution was not shaped in an exclusively or traditionally Christian way. In the first place, it is debatable whether or not there even is an active, positive form of political virtue available within biblical Christianity, which is the primary foundation for Christian views uniquely powerful in America. Biblical Christianity, at least on its New Testament foundations, offers no possibility of redemption or self-authentication. It only affirms our worthlessness and need for salvation. If salvation is the story, humanity's best is necessarily tainted or, in some essential respect, not virtuous. In the second place, American revolutionary thinking about public virtue was disproportionately influenced by deistic ideas, which held that in this setting, the world does not need a savior. It does not need to be protected from the consequences of its own nature. Rather, the world is potentially self-fulfilling and self-authenticating whenever it is true to its own being. Virtue in this view is not paralyzed by sin and futility but animated by wholesomeness and possibility.

   Diggins correctly understands the non-Christian character of Jefferson's worldview. But his representation of Jefferson does not do full justice to Jefferson's and revolutionary America's political ideas. Diggins's image of the self-sufficient individual, for example, does not adequately summarize the essential form of Jefferson's political thinking. Jefferson celebrates the virtuous independence of the yeomanry, yes, but this neither comes from nor does it lead to the celebration or recommendation of isolated, self-sustaining, egoistic, amoral individualists. Cultivators of the earth are not, for him, the most important class of humans qua humans. They are, specifically, the most valuable type of citizens. Their contribution is not to self but to the community. Their vigorous independence and virtue ties them to their nation and weds them to its liberty and common interests by the most reliable and lasting bonds of affection and commitment.[3] Jefferson strongly supports lives that are attentive to their own business and that do not meddle in the affairs of neighbors, but the primary benefit of this lifestyle is never expressed in individualistic terms. Instead, its value is a nation whose life is tranquil, where laws are mild and well obeyed, where strangers are received with sacred respect, and where the virtuous disposition of all members is encouraged.[4] "The small landholders are the most precious part of a state" because of the virtues their lives foster and because of the vices their lives avoid.[5] What is Jefferson's reason for antipathy to the yeomanry's social alternatives — artisans and merchants? Such persons are "the panders of vice, and the instruments by which the liberties of a country are generally overturned."[6] They pander vice because they are self-centered. Their independence does not contribute to the health of the whole but only to particular advantages obtained at the potential expense of the whole.

   For Jefferson, therefore, the yeomanry represent a social order more than a type of individual. Both collective and individual perfections depend on the form of society for whatever virtues might be obtained. Society is the great educator of humanity. It is the concrete setting through which persons learn the laws of their own being as ordained by nature. Yet in order to be so educated, nature and its universal principles must be directly accessible to society. Jefferson understood the impact that customs and traditions have on particular cultures. They can lead to estrangement or to a unity of purpose. They can create bewilderment and dependency in the name of self-sufficiency, or they can be legible to every reader and be pursued with little dependency or distortion. In this sense Jefferson projects a kind of individualism, but it does not imply an antithesis of civic morality and virtue. Jefferson's individualism is the result of a politics centered in a virtuous community's harmony with nature. For the individual this setting leads to trust and affection, not suspicion and hostility. In his First Inaugural Address, Jefferson formulates this point explicitly. The challenge faced by America was not one of principle but of affection. "We have called by different names brethren of the same principle. . . . Let us, then, fellow citizens, unite with one heart and one mind. Let us restore to social intercourse that harmony and affection without which liberty and even life itself are but dreary things."[7]

The Declaration of Independence asserts the political liberty of the American people. It is the freedom of this people, not of its individual members, that the Declaration explains. Frequently, Americans have transposed the proclamation of American national independence into an assertion of their individual status as independent Americans, but this is not the message of the Delaration itself. The document offers the unanimous declaration of a united people in thirteen United States of America. The unanimous ratification and amendment requirements of the Articles directly extend this spirit and letter of nationhood.

The document itself is eloquent in its directness and conceptual simplicity. It presents its argument in three parts — assumptions, evidence, and conclusions. The first two paragraphs state the presuppositions of the American position. The first paragraph implies that rebellion involves more than a formal right to rebel. A mere right of rebellion could be exercised whenever any offenses or violations occurred. But the Declaration limits itself to those specific circumstances that force a people to take the drastic step of political dissociation: "When in the course of human events it becomes necessary for one people to dissolve the political bonds which have connected them with another." We are first asked to consider what one people has done to another in history that has left the victims with only the protections of their natural status, "the separate and equal station to which the Laws of Nature and Nature's God entitle them."

There is a right to rebel, but it must be fully warranted by historical conditions and its exercise should be readily explainable to all humanity — it should show "a decent respect to the opinions of mankind."

The second paragraph summarizes the specific natural presuppositions of the Americans' position. Even before all men are explicitly declared equal, the Declaration assumes self-evident truths. This seemingly simple idea has important theoretical implications. It projects a natural order or, more precisely, an accessible natural order. And when a people holds to the principles of this order as if they were self-evident, we should expect that they will be committed to making those principles effective in the life of their political community.[8]

The holding of self-evident truths by a people also implies an equality that is subsequently directly asserted. If truths are asserted to be self-evident, they are knowable because of the potential harmony that exists among nature, human nature, and the nature of all particular humans. The highest truths are characterized not as the discoveries of esoteric reasonings but as the sense — equally available to all — of our own being. As Garry Wills has argued, Jefferson was probably attracted to the Scottish Enlightenment's philosophy of moral sense, in part, because egalitarianism was an essential ingredient of its vision too.[9] Francis Hutcheson, for example, believed in universal access to virtue embedded in human nature and based on internal senses of affection, benevolence, and fellow feeling.

The initial self-evident truth asserted by the Declaration is an explicit insistence on equality — all men are created equal. This is not an equality of particular characteristics but one of essence or worth. Regarding those things that make us human and constitute the essence of humanity — human nature — we are the same. This means that there is no natural authority of some persons over other persons. In positive historical terms such equality leads to democratic authority — the equal empowerment of all members of a political community. Further, the form of the asserted equality is substantive rather than procedural. It describes something essential about what all human beings actually are. It does not describe the environmental or procedural conditions within which they live. That we "are equal," for example, is a totally different political value with different implications than an assertion of "equal opportunity." Politically, equal opportunity is not about persons but about the circumstances within which persons operate. The fundamental political value protected by equal opportunity is freedom, not equality. "The equal station" of all persons, however, asserts a different reality, gives primacy to a different political value, and encourages a different set of practical political implications.

The second self-evident truth is that nature has imbued our beings with unalienable rights. The difference between an unalienable and an alienable right is the difference between a natural right and a civil right. The former is a consequence of our humanity; the latter is a consequence of our political association and citizenship. The former can be violated, but it can never legitimately be taken away. There is no legitimate alienation of a natural right from any human because it is an intrinsic, common part of human nature. The latter can be violated too, but it legitimately can be taken away as well. It can be taken away in exactly the way it is given in the first place. It is given as an act of the political association and the political association can take it away.

Building on this natural rights assumption, the Declaration does more than grant all persons an equal claim to the protection offered by basic human rights. It establishes a context in which government and politics are to be limited by and answerable to principles beyond their own authority and control. And it gives vitality and validity to the natural order in shaping human associations. Natural rights define much more than a basis for individual choices. They clarify some of the fundamental characteristics of the way things are and should be within a contractual association guided by nature. They express a framework for order more than for choice. They define, more than give, options. They orient the political order to the criteria of an asserted natural order and away from the whimsy of rootless, immediate, personal volitions. Politics is not to be the mere story of order or authority. It must be based on a just order corresponding to the authentic principles of nature.

The specific unalienable rights cited by the Declaration are life, liberty, and the pursuit of happiness. Wills traces the direct relationship between Jefferson's triad and the moral sense school's view of rights.[10] David Hume and Francis Hutcheson did not begin (as did Thomas Hobbes, John Locke, and Jean-Jacques Rousseau) with the idea of rights as the basis for self-rule. Jefferson agrees: "To ourselves, in strict language, we can owe no duties, obligation requiring also two parties. Self-love, therefore, is no part of morality."[11] Moral principles are principles of sociability directed by benevolence to others, not principles of self-love directed by selfishness. Thus, a right for Hume and Hutcheson was a moral expression that affected others for a common good. In Hutcheson's full articulation of a right, the test is the public good. "Whenever it appears to us that a faculty of doing, demanding, or possessing anything, universally allowed in certain circumstances, would in the whole tend to the general good, we say that any person in such circumstances has a right to do, possess, or demand that thing. And according as this tendency to the public good is greater or less, the right in question is greater or less."[12]

Hutcheson divides rights into two categories — perfect and imperfect. Perfect rights pass the public good test and, consequently, can be defended by private force. Imperfect rights, because they less clearly or consistently pass the public good test, cannot be authorized as fully. Hutcheson identifies the two primary perfect rights as the right to life and the right of liberty and identifies benevolence as the basic social bond. No being can love another without life and respect for life itself. In short, life is not the grounds for self-love but the precondition for loving others. Hutcheson defends the right of liberty similarly.

> As nature has implanted in each man a desire of his own happiness and many tender affections toward others in some nearer relations of life, and granted to each one some understanding and active powers, with a natural right to exercise them for the purpose of these natural affections, it is plain each one has a natural right to exert his powers, according to his own judgment and inclination, for these purposes, in all such industry, labor, or amusements as are not hurtful to others in their persons or goods, which no more public interests necessarily require his labors or require that his actions should be under the direction of others. This right we call natural liberty.[13]

These rights express duties. They are not authorizations for individual discretion. They reflect the structure of human nature and identify responsibilities in society that correspond with that nature. Humans have a duty to stay alive and to stay free in word and deed. The obligation or duty is the basis for the right and for the right's high standing.

The great curiosity, of course, is why Jefferson dropped the specific language of "property" if his political thinking is as specifically Lockean as conventional interpreters of him and of the Declaration have insisted. The issue is not whether Jefferson saw property as a right or not. Certainly he did. He maintained notions of property rights but not as unalienable rights. Here too his orientation parallels Hutcheson's. Hutcheson called property an "adventitious right" not a natural right. Rights of productivity are more fundamental than rights of possession for both men. Property's real purpose is not as an end to be appropriated but as a means of goods and services transactions to stimulate the productivity of all humans. Hutcheson's view has a clear Jeffersonian resonance: "Lands must be dispersed among great multitudes, and preserved (thus dispersed) by agrarian laws, to make a stable democracy."[14]

This idea is at one with Jefferson's desire for the constant transfer of property. He believed that such a process was necessary for the healthy development of society. This is one of the primary reasons he insisted on limited contract periods. Jefferson deeply mourns the concentration of property in France and observes more generally: "Whenever there are in any country uncultivated lands and unemployed poor, it is clear that the laws of property have been so far extended as to violate natural right."[15] If laws that protect the possession of property can violate natural right, it is obvious that property rights are not themselves natural rights and that "pursuit of happiness" as a natural right is not just a euphemism for conventional property claims. Jefferson grants primacy to the right to labor and to be productive over rights of possession. He summarizes this view in a 1785 letter to Bishop James Madison, cousin of the Constitution of 1787's draftsman.

> The earth is given as a common stock for man to labor and live on. If for the encouragement of industry we allow it to be appropriated, we must take care that other employment be provided to those excluded from the appropriation. If we do not, the fundamental right to labor the earth returns to the unemployed. It is too soon yet in our country to say that every man who cannot find employment, but who can find uncultivated land, shall be at liberty to cultivate it, paying a moderate rent. But it is not too soon to provide by every possible means that as few as possible shall be without a little portion of land. The small landholders are the most precious part of a state.[16]

This issue of rights and how they are expressed reflects an important difference between Jefferson and Locke about the nature of society itself. Locke's system makes society instrumental — it is for individuals considered separate from society. Jefferson's view starts with social drives and interdependence and builds on principles that nourish the well-being of this social base. This view relates directly to the primary right that Jefferson offers as the replacement for Lockean property — the pursuit of happiness. The right to pursue happiness is the duty to follow human nature: to honor "the magnetic response of . . . nature."[17] Jefferson does not imagine that the natural right to pursue our happiness is ever an absurd claim to be and do whatever we want. The pursuit of happiness is neither undefined nor self-defined. Jefferson has presented natural law in the form of natural right. This is not a trivial or self-evident assertion. When the laws of human nature are seen as rights, then human beings can act freely, knowing that their deeds are in concert with the natural order. In discovering what humans should pursue, they learn that they had a right to pursue it.[18] The pursuit of happiness, therefore, is not a vague or idealistic concept, and it was not rooted in assumptions of individualism or privacy. The pursuit of happiness is about the public scale of political actions sanctioned by nature.

> [Humans] are really cheated of their happiness in being made to believe that any occupation or pastime is better fitted to amuse themselves than that which at the same time produces some real good to their fellow creatures. . . . If the public good be the principal object with individuals, it is likewise true that the happiness of individuals is the great end of civil society. . . . If the individual owes every degree of consideration to the public, he receives, in paying that very consideration, the greatest happiness of which his nature is capable.[19]

The highest human achievement is to perceive the natural impulses to happiness and to build life through them. The benefits are both personal and communal.

Governments, we are told, are empowered by the consent of the governed to protect these natural rights, which — given the meaning of these unalienable rights — is also to say that governments have the duty to serve the common good. Correspondingly, whenever governments act against the will of the people or against the laws of nature, the people must act to alter or abolish them and to institute a new government that will secure their safety and happiness — in other words, one that will protect their rights to life, liberty, and the pursuit of happiness.

Jefferson moves from the variations in historical conditions to the identification of laws and patterns in nature. His interpretation of history, and especially of history's interplay with the natural order, is rooted not in the meaning or authorizations of particularistic incidents but in patterns of events, which reveal more than accidental meanings. He does not encourage outrage at accidental, fortuitous, or incidental acts — only at intentional and essential ones. However, when a people is confronted with "a long train of abuses and usurpations pursuing invariably the same object, evinces a design to reduce them under absolute despotism," direct rebellion is required, not just permitted. "It is their right, it is their duty, to throw off such government, and to provide new guards for their future security."[20] This formulation emphasizes the role of patterns, not that of mere incidents. And it underscores the intimate relationship between rights and duties in the Declaration of Independence's formulation. Natural rights identify fundamental responsibilities, making them dutiful as well. And as duties they authorize rights. In either form, they express the primary principles, dictated by nature, necessary for personal and communal well-being.

The presuppositions have been stated. Now Jefferson presents and considers the relevant evidence. Have the colonies been subject to patterns of abuse clearly indicating malevolent intentions against them? Have the colonists suffered patiently? Does the history of their patience and suffering now warrant rebellion? The Declaration says "yes" and supports its case with a checklist of offenses against the colonists for the consideration of "a candid world." This case is not based on any particular offense or the sum of particular offenses but on the design evidenced through these specifics and the intentionality suggested by this pattern.

The offenses charged against the crown probably reveal more about revolutionary American thinking than they do about specific British behaviors and intentions. This is not to take the British off the hook but to focus attention on the precise nature of American sensitivities. Whether or not this list of offenses constitutes the full and actual explanation for

American actions, it does express American sensitivities and reveals the rationale Americans saw as their best case before the court of world opinion.

Interestingly, the first offenses of the crown are for things not done: he did not support laws necessary for the public good, he did not permit laws of immediate and pressing importance, and he did not permit the representation of larger districts of people. The representations of the people and service to their good were also violated by what he did. He manipulated the meeting of representative bodies, dissolved representative bodies for their support of the people's interest, and refused to reconstitute representative bodies once they were dissolved. He not only subverted the representation of people, he obstructed the populating of the colonial lands. He hindered the administration of justice. He corrupted politics by using appointments to public office to control government and the representation of the people. His use of the military was directly abusive of a free people: he kept standing armies in peace without popular consent, he allowed military power to be independent of and superior to civil power, he forced the quartering of armed troops by private citizens, and he protected his troops from punishment for their offenses against the people. There were offenses of commerce: he cut off American trade, taxed without consent, and plundered American seas and towns. A proper system of justice was denied the Americans: trials by juries were often denied, foreign jurisdictions were illegitimately imposed on the colonies, and colonial charter provisions were abolished. Finally, the crown initiated acts of violence against the Americans: he introduced foreign mercenaries, forced captured colonists to bear arms against their confederates, and instigated domestic insurrections.

These offenses were frequent and diverse enough to demonstrate a patterned intention to tyrannize the American people. In terms of general principles, despotic purpose was seen in the violation of four essential precepts: (1) the crown acted against any reasonable understanding of the public good; (2) the crown took no guidance and accepted no restraint from representatives of the people; (3) the crown assumed authority without consent; and (4) the crown pursued a strategy of political corruption that denied the colonists the benefits of their own virtuous community. It is a simple and familiar formula. It was the principle ideology

Americans used both to divest British power and to shape indigenous authority.

The colonists did not suffer these offenses in silence. They claimed repeated humble requests for redress. But they only received renewed injury — as one would expect from a tyrant. The penultimate paragraph of the Declaration, however, asserts the most radical dimension of colonial rebellion. It says, in effect, that the colonists have a much more fundamental quarrel than the one generated by the crown's governmental abuses. If the abuses of the crown constituted the full dispute, colonial rebellion would have been that of Englishmen or Britishers attempting to reconstitute British governmental authority. This was not, however, the colonists' project. They took exception to the British government and the British nation. They denied the authority of the crown and declared themselves to be a new people — Americans. The Declaration insists that every kind of appeal was made to their "British brethren." Details of their plight were specifically presented and appeals to "their native justice and magnanimity" were offered. All of this was to no effect. Neither justice nor natural affinity was able to move their brethren in Britain to challenge these governmental abuses. Therefore, it was necessary for the colonists to separate themselves from the British people, hold them as enemies in war, and declare the formation of a new and independent nation — the people of the United States of America.

Even in the form presented by the Second Continental Congress, the Declaration clearly extends colonial rebellion beyond Crown and Parliament to the British people. That is, it makes clear that this is a national, not just a governmental, act of separation and rebellion. In the earliest draft of the Declaration, Jefferson draws this point out in a more specific and extended discussion.

> These facts have given the last stab to agonizing affection, and manly spirit bids us to renounce for ever these unfeeling brethren. We must endeavor to forget our former love for them and to hold them as we hold the rest of mankind enemies in war, in peace friends. We might have been a free and a great people together, but a communication of grandeur and of freedom it seems is below their dignity. Be it so, since they will have it.[21]

The last stab hurt so much, largely because the pain of the British people's former stabs was so great. Even after Congress sanitized the pointedness of Jefferson's language, the meaning expressed by Jefferson was not lost.

The tone of Jefferson's language is equally significant. These are certainly not the words of a hard-nosed Lockean individualist. Personal and material interests have no play. The language is that of affection: "agony," "unfeeling," "brethren," "love," and "dignity." As Wills quips, "What kind of revolution begins with the recollections of a jilted lover?"[22] But this is not just romantic drivel offered up for mere effect. It is language that must be taken seriously because it was offered seriously at the climax of Jefferson's most significant public utterance. It is the language of the theoretical tradition that shaped his perspectives — the language of benevolent affections and their role in shaping the form and substance of justice and virtue in a people's life.

The Declaration's conclusion is a moving statement of the dominant political ideas and images of revolutionary America. In asserting American independence, Jefferson affirms proper representation, popular consent, and public virtue. The appeal to the Supreme Judge of the world is to certify the rectitude of their intentions. Both the representatives of the American people and the American people themselves take this step on a proper moral footing. It is not an expression of narrow self-interest. It is not an action disharmonious with the principles of nature. It is a course of action designed for the common good through the consent of a virtuous people. These Americans could assume a firm reliance on the protections of Divine Providence precisely because providence was intelligible. It was, for them, the rule of nature's order. They were acting in concert with the fundamental principles of that order and thus could know that they were to be providentially blessed.

Already in the Declaration of Independence, American politics is introduced to the riddle at the center of the Articles of Confederation. That riddle is to understand a perpetually united people who fragment their formal instruments of public authority. That condition, evident in the Articles, is the circumstance charted initially by the Declaration. Governmentally, the colonies are declared free and independent states with all the powers properly assigned to sovereign states. However, the agent that establishes the autonomy of these diverse governmental units is one people — the good people of these colonies. Not only are these independent states created by a united people, they bind themselves to a perpetuation of that unity on the grounds of the most fundamental natural principles — their lives, their fortunes, and their sacred honor.

Again, the language is telling beyond its denotative meanings. It is the language of virtue, fidelity, and honor. In the spirit of the Declaration the American revolution is not presented as an action merely narrowly or technically permissible. Nature requires it. And there is no higher expression of virtue than life in harmony with nature. Honor, in fidelity to nature, is the highest human accomplishment. "For the greatest happiness a moral-sense theorist can bestow on others is the sight of virtue inciting to virtue, the intercourse that alone makes all parties truly happy."[23]

The Declaration of Independence stands as a clear expression of the dominant political ideas at the time of American independence and of the political theory that informed the shaping of America's first formal constitutional order under the Articles of Confederation. It constituted the American people on principles they could use when it was time for them to constitute American government. These were principles of virtue tied to human nature through the universal efficacy of benevolent affections; principles of sociability directed by benevolence, whose test was the public good; principles of rights as responsibilities in society ordered by nature, which protect persons in community; principles of popular consent; principles of proper representation; and principles of public virtue. These principles were essential to a social contract based on the uncoerced unity of a free people.

The thirteen-year period from 1776 to 1789 encompasses the writing, ratification, and formal implementation of the Articles of Confederation. These phases of development and expression also reveal a theoretical pattern of assumptions, ideals, and analyses consistent with the dominant political theory of the revolutionary era and with the implicit political theory of the two primary documents of America's first decade of independence — the Declaration of Independence and the Articles of Confederation. The discussions of this chapter summarize the theoretical issues central to the writing of the Articles (1776), to the ratification process (1776–1781), and to the period of the Articles' formal authority (1781–1789).

WRITING THE ARTICLES OF CONFEDERATION

Even before the Second Continental Congress appointed a committee to draft articles of confederation, Benjamin Franklin had drafted a charter of union for the colonies, which he submitted to Congress in July 1775. Franklin's draft, which proposed a government based on centralized sovereign power, shows that the governmental form of 1787 was preferred by some Americans even before the Articles was drafted. The failure of Franklin's proposal also suggests the strength of a theoretical perspective that saw centralized, coercive authority as contrary to the proper foundation of the American revolution.

In 1776 thirteen men were appointed to an official drafting committee responsible for proposing a governmental design for the new nation.

They presented their document to Congress on July 12, 1776. The greater numbers and personal influence among the committee members were with those who were spokesmen for more socially and economically conservative interests and with those who preferred more formalized and centralized organizations of political authority. There were two fence sitters, Roger Sherman and Josiah Bartlett, and only two committee members who represented the more dominant political perspectives of American society in mid-1776 — Stephen Hopkins and Sam Adams. The rest of the committee members were oriented to still other political views — less local, less participatory, less majoritarian, and less consensually based than those that eventually dominated this process. These representatives were John Dickinson, Edward Rutledge, Robert R. Livingston, Thomas McKean, Francis Hopkinson, Thomas Stone, Joseph Hewes, Button Gwinnett, and Thomas Nelson.

Dickinson, as chair, was able to dominate the committee's proceedings. He is the primary author of the draft proposal, and this draft document provides a picture of his political vision. It made the organization of the central government the basis for defining the rights, powers, and duties of the states. Yet he did include a general clause that granted each state "as much of its present Laws, Rights and Customs, as it may think fit, and reserves to itself the sole and exclusive Regulation and Government of its internal police, in all matters that shall not interfere into the Articles of Confederation."[1] States were to maintain militia and appoint commissioned officers for troops serving the common defense, and they could lay imposts if they did not violate any treaty provisions. No other powers were reserved for the states. Further, the language of Article 3 limits these powers to those matters that will not interfere with operation of the Articles. State powers were limited in number, based on grants from the center, and restricted in their potential range. There was no doubt where sovereign or coercive power was centered — with Congress and the central government.

If the draft is examined from the opposite point of view, there was only one significant restraint on Congress: it could not directly tax citizens. There also were restrictions that required three-fourths majorities for certain specified actions, such as declaring war, and there were prohibitions against congressional interference in a state's internal policing when it was unrelated to the functioning of the Articles' provisions. In spite of these limitations, Congress and the central authority held the stronger grant of powers and the theoretical balance of power in the Dickinson draft.

The quarrels among the Congress' political minority of 1776 were closely related to the larger controversies in American society across all parts of the political spectrum: How should powers and duties be apportioned between the states and the Congress? Dickinson's draft is significant because it offered a model balanced much like that of the Constitution of 1787, even if less polished and less explicitly developed. Thus, together with the effort of Franklin a year earlier, the general political sentiment of the Constitution of 1787 was very much present as an active alternative in 1776, but it was knowingly turned aside.

In the reworking of the Dickinson draft, however, the states hold fundamental authority and Congress acts by specific grants of powers. The Continental Congress changed eighteen subject matter areas of the Dickinson draft. Many of these changes strengthened the role of the central government, but most of them were designed to strengthen accountability (for example, a delegate's appointment) or to make adjustments to accommodate the diminishment of central authority overall (for example, treaty and military powers). The most significant changes, however, all weakened the authority and role of the central government and correspondingly strengthened that of the states. This pattern of weakened central government is most obvious in the changes to Article 3, on the nature of the union; to Article 4, on interstate comity; to Article 9 on maritime jurisdictions, Indian affairs, and western lands; and to Article 10, on the military powers granted to the Council of States.

By August 20, 1776, Congress agreed to proceed with a second draft version of the Articles of Confederation. As Merrill Jensen has pointed out, this brought the constitutional process to the point where four issues remained for settlement: the equal representation of all states in Congress, the basis for the apportionment of common expenses, the grant of powers to the central government over western lands, and the distribution of power between the states and Congress to define the precise location of sovereignty. This last issue was resolved quickly but pointedly. Formal coercive authority was to be located in each individual state. Yet the final draft was completed only after protracted and difficult debates on the other three issues.

The issue of state representation in Congress was much more complicated than just the immediate, practical problem of balancing larger and smaller states. It directly related to first principles — exactly what kind of union was this to be. If it was to be a single national state, more compromise and experimentation was appropriate in arranging state representation in Congress. However, if the union was an alliance of independent states, each state had to be equally represented, regardless of differentiations in land holdings or populations or else the very essence of that kind of union would be violated. Another way of looking at the issue was to ask: Was this to be a perpetual union of government or of people? Larger states, especially Virginia, used "national" arguments but were no less animated by their local interests than were the smaller states. In the end, it was the natural interests of the smaller states and the principles of a group of men committed to keeping coercive power on a short tether that controlled determination of this issue. They wanted and got a federal union of sovereign states, not a national government.

Another issue, one of great material interest but with fewer direct theoretical stakes, was the criterion to determine each state's fiscal obligation to the common treasury. The position offered by Dickinson was that the states should pay in proportion to their total populations, excluding Indians, who do not pay taxes. Some states, predictably, objected. They proposed an apportionment system based on land values. The document from Congress in August left this issue much as it was in the original formulation offered by Dickinson. The New England states, on the assumption that their lands were much more valuable than the lands of other states, objected to any land-based value system. In the end, a land value criterion was adopted and it posed no unique stumbling block to ratification in New England. This issue demonstrates that these events involved men who were well aware of practical, material implications, but who also distinguished between questions of mere interest and questions central to basic principles.

The most acrimonious disagreements were over control of western lands. The states without western lands or land claims wanted authority over these lands to rest with Congress. In fact, they wanted to establish the principle that all public lands lying outside the jurisdiction of any state should belong to the union through Congress. The states holding western lands wanted to continue their control. To them, giving Congress control over these lands was paramount to creating a domestic equivalent of British rule. They knew the depth of their displeasure with the British on this question and had no intention of duplicating this frustration in the governmental system they designed for themselves. Dickinson's first draft gave support to the position of the states lacking western lands. But by October 1777, the states with western lands had achieved its reversal. They had secured, in the final draft of the Articles, constitutional guarantees against the claims of the other states and of land speculators working through land companies.

It would be foolish to describe the debates over this issue as those of high principle, but principle, inadvertently, may have had a greater impact than imagined. The western lands issue was obviously an issue of interest — landed states fearing the piracy of landless states, and landless states fearing the opportunism of the landed states. As a question of self-interest there were no clear grounds for settlement of the issue. Neither side had any distinct moral leverage, and there was a near balance of practical power between them. Both sides used common interest arguments to bolster their claims, and in both cases this rhetoric lacked broadly persuasive credibility. Nevertheless, in one respect the landed states had an argument of theoretical significance to the revolution's political norms. Their position coincided with the strong bias to limit the formal powers of government beyond the authority of the states.

The most basic issue addressed during the writing of the Articles was that of sovereignty. Would it be plural — centered in each state — or singular — centered in Congress? Within the framework of Jensen's classifications, the "conservatives" favored a single sovereign with "superintending" power over states and citizens. They saw this form encouraging the more active development of the union, especially its economic development. "Radicals" saw their political battle as a struggle against coercive, centralized power, especially in their conflicts with the British and with the colonial governing class and economic elites. Viewed positively, their political goal was a union given through consent and trust, not seized and then coercively applied. To radicals governmental decentralization was a noble and inspiring experiment that permitted a large-scale union achieved through persuasion and friendship. To conservatives state sovereignty was a dangerous misconstruction that subverted all positive purposes of the union.

It is virtually impossible to separate matters of interest from matters of principle in this debate over a federal association of states versus national centralism. Practical ambitions and ideals were tightly woven together for both parties. High principles were directly connected to immediate, practical stakes. And pragmatic issues were consciously developed and expressed within comprehensive theoretical frameworks. The radicals at this juncture had the theoretical edge. They could build within the theoretical home provided by the Declaration of Independence, and they could more clearly and persuasively distance themselves from the British and their domestic equivalents.

Centralized, coercive authority had been the essence of economic and political life in the colonies. And it had moved Americans to rebellion. The most radical expression of this rebel opposition was the doctrine of the sovereignty of the people. During the 1770s this principle symbolically meant the empowerment of the base, not the top or center. Structurally, it meant the people organized as independent states. Challenges to this arrangement were ineffectively developed in 1776, but since independence, the issue of the relationship between state governments and a common central government has been and remains at the center of American political choices and perspectives.

John Adams argued correctly that the principle of popular sovereignty did not settle the choice between creating a single sovereign state or a number of confederated sovereign states. And continuing debate moved the issue away from abstract claims about the sovereign people. The basic division became one between those who called for a federal government within a confederacy and those who supported a national government. The issue of popular sovereignty was milked by both parties to their best advantage, but the real choice was how that sovereignty was to be organized — federally or nationally. Thomas Burke of North Carolina, in the course of his extended debate with James Wilson, moved the issue to this more concrete, but still theoretically interesting, form. He saw that

Dickinson's third article not only jeopardized the political independence of the states but threatened to consolidate effective governance in one centralized form — the national government. To counter this national government solution, he proposed an amendment to the draft of the Articles, which gave it the federal character that appealed to its eventual supporters. His amendment stated that "all sovereign power was in the states separately, and that particular acts of it, which should be expressly ennumerated, would be exercised in conjunction, and not otherwise; but that in all things else each State would exercise all rights and power of sovereignty, uncontrolled."[2] This amendment was expressed as Article 2 of the final document. Its approach authorized two levels of government: original authority vested in the base and delegated authority in the center. This arrangement was more readily understood as consistent with the popular sovereignty tenet than one that organized governmental authority further from the life and direct scrutiny of the people.

Once the specific issue of locating sovereignty was settled, there remained for the Congress only a few housekeeping chores. These mostly consisted of further limitations on the powers given to Congress in the Dickinson draft. For example, Congress had no formal recourse against states that violated treaty-based regulation of trade, and the Committee of the States was changed from a permanent body to a temporary one, making it a less substantial introduction of quasi-executive organization. The final form of the Articles of Confederation was achieved by November 15, 1777.

A letter to the states was prepared to accompany the printed document. This letter highlights the riddle of the Articles — strong hopes for unity based on wholesome intent, not coercive control. The purpose of the Articles was to form the basis for a "perpetual union." Achieving this end among states with so many different habits required not authority and coercion but time, reflection, and a disposition of conciliation. Pleading for ratification, the letter insists that ratification is "essential to our very existence as a free people, and without it we may soon be constrained to bid adieu to independence, to liberty and safety."[3] Although the letter does not explicitly make this assertion, it is easy to imagine that for many revolutionary Americans the threats to independence and liberty were internal as well as external. Despotic power did not have to be British or

European. It could come as easily from American equivalents of British rule.

The Articles of Confederation and the Constitution of 1787 had single individuals who were the primary authors of their initial articulation — John Dickinson and James Madison, respectively. And both of these authors moved within a set of political predispositions that were related and similarly oriented. The essential cast of government offered by each man's draft proposal was remarkably similar. Nevertheless, the differences were probably more significant than these impressive similarities.

Their general orientations may have been similar, but Madison possessed a theoretical self-consciousness and purposefulness, to say nothing of practical effectiveness, unevidenced by Dickinson. And thus, the fate of their constitution crafting was quite different as well. Madison's model was sound even if compromised; in fact, compromise contributed to the strength of the Constitution of 1787 partly because there was such a clear and strong sense of the primary theoretical nature of the basic political model. Under these circumstances compromises on secondary matters served to make the core proposal more broadly acceptable. Compromise was more difficult to accommodate in Dickinson's model largely because its basic design was not as crisply worked out in either theory or practice. Neither man presented his proposals to a collective review process. Both could have carried the day and both could have lost. Dickinson failed and Madison prevailed, in large part, because theoretical awareness and normative purpose was more developed and effective among Dickinson's adversaries and among Madison's allies. The end result was not only the positive act of selecting principles of political association in 1777 contrary to Dickinson's and Madison's, but in doing so, rejecting the crypto-Constitution of 1787 offered by Dickinson. This underscored the active, two-sided debate about constitutional issues that originated in American colonial experiences and came to a mature expression in 1776. The recommendations of 1787 were already present and active in 1776, but in 1776 they did not prevail both for reasons of interest and principle.

RATIFYING THE ARTICLES OF CONFEDERATION

The ratification process, even though not nearly as smooth as projected by the language of the transmittal letter, reflects the social domination of the political principles inherent in the Articles' organization of governance. For example, within the state legislatures' ratification debates, the more common concern was not the weakness of the Congress but the enfeeblement of the states. This issue was pointedly expressed in South Carolina where it was broadly felt that most of the important powers had been granted to Congress, not to the states. William Henry Drayton charged that once the powers granted to Congress and the restrictions placed on the states are accounted for, "scarce the shadow of sovereignty remains to any state."[4] The South Carolina legislature empowered its delegates to ratify the Articles as presented but offered up numerous amendments, whose purpose was to clarify areas of possible ambiguity so that Congress' role would be more limited and state authority would be strengthened and freed of potentially limiting ambiguities. In the end, ratification was supported and the most vigorously pursued reservations were those supporting even more decentralization, not more centrally controlled, coercive authority.

Most states acted expeditiously in ratifying the Articles, which also suggests that there was a strong base of support for the theoretical direction of its proposals. Within about eight months, ten of the states had instructed delegates to support ratification. Maryland, Delaware, and New Jersey were the holdouts united by a concern about the western lands question. The latter two states reluctantly acceded to ratification by January 1779. Both took exception to the Articles' provisions leaving western lands questions to the jurisdiction of individual states. They opposed this specific dimension of state sovereignty, not the principle of state sovereignty itself. Yet in the end they voluntarily consented and, in the process, affirmed the most fundamental principle of the Articles' union — confidence in the goodwill and integrity of independent states to reach voluntary agreements.

Maryland's protracted ratification process expressed a genuine disagreement but not a conflict or stalemate over any fundamental principle of government. In Maryland's eyes, its reluctance represented the prudent concern of a landless state about the unguided intentions and actions of states with extensive western lands, especially its southern neighbor Virginia. Western lands represented a significant invitation for corrupting temptations. That possibility had to be limited.

Ironically, even Maryland's inaction did not prevent de facto implementation of the Articles' constitutional order. Between 1776 and 1781
the Continental Congress and the thirteen states conducted American
military, economic, and political affairs by the standards and in the forms
specified by the Articles. The final ratification of the Articles, therefore,
unlike the ratification of the Constitution of 1787, did not initiate new
political processes on the basis of political analyses guided by new
assumptions and purposes. Instead, it gave de jure status to the de facto
political forms and processes already in effect. The fact that it represented
the formalization of accepted and acceptable functioning patterns only
strengthened the practical credibility of its noncoercive political solution.
It did represent a high ideal, but not one without known, concrete form
and practical, everyday successes.

Also, Maryland's refusal, in effect, to join the union created a response
from the other twelve states that underscores the two-dimensionality of
their political purposes. The process of affirming individual state sovereignty was to be part of the process of creating a national union. The
obvious choice posed by these dual purposes was expressed well by the
Connecticut delegates to their governor: "shall we send to all the States
for their consent to a Confederation of twelve, or wait for Maryland to
consider better of it and accede?"[5] Maryland was not only left alone to
fight the issue of western land control but was itself viewed critically.
William Whipple expressed this when he charged that Maryland "has
seldom done anything with a good Grace. She has always been a froward
hussey."[6] Nevertheless, the commitment to form a complete national
union prevailed even in the face of Maryland's seemingly perverse
opposition.

Even the states that had accepted the Articles' arrangements for state
control of western lands recognized and openly discussed the potential
problems that could arise within this format. Maryland's concerns, as well
as those of Pennsylvania and New Jersey, were reenforced when Virginia
took repeated actions to cancel the land claims of individuals from those
states. Thomas Jefferson, Richard Henry Lee, and George Mason all took
active roles in opposing what they characterized as the land schemes of
the middle states. They voided all land purchases from Indians within
Virginia's charter claims as well as the claims of the Transylvania Company,

the Indiana Company, and two lesser companies — all with memberships mainly centered in Maryland and Pennsylvania. Further, Virginia offered to use its lands as a bounty to soldiers both to support the war effort against the British and to encourage Maryland to ratify the Articles. Maryland, however, only saw this gesture as clearer evidence of Virginia's unwillingness to accommodate claims other than its own and its willingness to use its claims in a narrowly self-interested manner — for the vile motives of power and/or money. Maryland insisted that these lands should be regarded as common property because they were being seized from the British by the shared blood and treasure of thirteen states.

By the spring of 1779 the Virginia legislature decided to invite land companies to present their claims. They considered the claims of the Indiana, the Illinois and Wabash, and the Ohio companies as well as those of George Croghan. After considering these claims, the legislature declared all of them to be null and void. Virginia insisted on its own monopoly right to purchase land from Indians and interpreted all British purchases as, now, rights of the state. For the land companies the only hope was the one insisted upon by Maryland — jurisdiction and action by the Congress. Maryland appeared to be well on the way to building a collection of allies beyond its isolated and eccentric stance, but the underlying reality was not this straightforward.

Because of the close association of the land companies and the middle states' political establishment, their demands for congressional control of the west reflected an agenda different from and more specifically self-interested than that of Maryland's. Maryland was not using this issue to subvert or challenge the revolutionary ideology rooted in land. Its concern was more with the ability of its community to pursue western land claims and interests within an association that gave exclusive jurisdiction of those lands to only one of the rival claimants. The political establishment of the middle states had more comprehensive fears. The more the west opened up the harder it would be for them to control the trade of the west. Eventually, a developed west would outnumber them. This would quickly result in more votes and the political displacement of the current establishment. Further, this possible political and economic displacement represented more than just changes of particular individuals in power. In addition, there was a quite different set of assumptions, values, and goals in the middle states' establishment and in western agrarianism. The land companies joined with the forces of the establishment because that was their only route to short-term legality and long-term realization of their land-based interests.

The strategies of the middle states' establishment relative to Spain illustrate its attitudes toward the west. Many Americans thought it would be advantageous to bring Spain into its war with Great Britain. But from Spain's perspective there was little difference between an alliance with Great Britain and one with the United States. Thus, the American proposal was to give Spain a special enticement for its support — assurances that there would be no American empire in the west. At the same time as these politicians were insisting that Virginia's charter claims should become the common property of the confederation they were trying to persuade Congress to concede to Spain the empire west of the Alleghenies and, especially, full navigation rights on the Mississippi River.

Virginia tried to calm the fears of the landless states in the fall of 1779 by announcing that it would limit its western border to the Ohio River. But it was New York that actually took the step of ceding western claims to congressional jurisdiction. New initiatives were made to get the confederation ratified and into formal operation. Virginia, influenced by British control in the south, was willing to move but wanted some guarantees regarding any lands ceded to congressional jurisdiction. In January of 1781 Virginia made its conditional land cession. Most notable among these conditions was the voiding of individual purchases of land from Indians — the lifeline of land company claims. That same month, the Maryland legislature passed a resolution of ratification. Unanimous consent had been obtained even when a serious block to ratification had to be resolved. The Articles of Confederation and Perpetual Union went into formal effect on March 1, 1781.

The ratification process suggests that the basic principles of the Articles were not deeply contentious for sizable majorities in almost every state and every state legislature. The delay was caused by a particularistic objection a minority tried to exploit for larger purposes. Although Maryland's immediate concern was not the national interest, it was not dominion either. It wanted what all confederates always want — their just share of the pie and prudent discouragements to corruption when virtue is essential. The final difficulties in the ratification process were not a particularly pretty spectacle, but this episode must be read in terms of its full significance. First, defenders of the confederacy expected that there would be serious controversies among the member units. It is only latter-day detractors of the confederacy who ridicule assumptions of an uncontentious harmony of interests as unrealistic. The positive vision that stood behind the arrangements of the Articles did not imagine a natural harmony of interests as the ontological base of historical politics. It did believe that such a balancing and integrating of interests could be the teleology of a well-constituted historical politics. Maryland's exception, by itself, did not disprove their political understanding. It provided an unavoidable and necessary testing of their political project.

Second, it is not clear whether or not this two and one-half year extension of the ratification process illustrated the success or the failure of the Articles of Confederation's political assumptions and structures. On the one hand, it created substantial delays and frustrations for American efforts in the war and in getting on with the larger business of independent national life. And it warned of the disproportionate power any one state possesses because of its ability to hold the rest hostage. Clearly it was in the British interest to keep the colonists divided or not fully integrated. This would remain just as much a concern after 1781 as it was between 1776 and 1781. On the other hand, the controversy was resolved without political breakdown, chaos, or the exercise of formally coercive authority. In fact, the very processes proposed by the Articles were the ones that operated in this case and with ultimate success. Also, the collective effort of the majority of states in Congress was able to evolve a settlement that probably could not have been asserted or claimed directly without being considerably more disruptive. Not only did this approach overcome Maryland's resistance, it may have been more effective in dealing with the probable resistance of landed states if the proposed resolution had been formally to divest them of their western land claims.

The advent of the Articles' era was not the dawning of political ignorance or inexperience. It was the natural outcome of the dominant revolutionary orientation in the colonies and of the practical tests of drafting and ratifying a constitutional order. There was, however, a real division in the political thinking Americans used to interpret these experiences. The experiences of establishing political independence, of drafting constitutional principles, and of overcoming the impediments to ratifying that order were interpreted through a set of principles that convinced some Americans of the dangers to political order from this voluntaristic and pluralistic approach. Others, in fact most Americans in 1781, saw a more promising outcome largely because they perceived a fit between their practical experiences and their general principles and aspirations.

Merely stating the facts of their colonial and early independence experiences did not and could not settle the differences between these two groups of Americans. These differences were not simply based on the lack of experiences or on the lack of critical reflections about the practical meaning of these experiences. These differences were and continue to be based on the different theoretical constructions that have been used to interpret these experiences. The hierarchy among these theories changed considerably over time, but as a function of persuasive consent, not formal authority. Decentralization, noncoercion, and locally formed authority may be associated with what is called "conservative" rhetoric today. But in revolutionary America these norms offered a particular brand of radicalized, agrarian democracy. In either form at either time they indicate political issues and political interpretations of continuing significance to the history of America's fundamental political order. The theory of 1787 was present in 1776 just as the theory of 1776 was not extinguished by the choices of 1787. More than thirty years after the drafting of the Articles, more than twenty years after the drafting of the Constitution, and less than ten years after Thomas Jefferson became president, John Adams summarized the unique character of American constitutionalism with this suggestive image: "I have always called our Constitution a game at leapfrog."[7]

The ratification of the Articles did not stop the struggle for more formal authority in a national government that would support the engines of commerce and industry. Immediate attempts to amend and reinterpret the Articles were made by the nationalists. Their proposals were not merely common sense responses to the pragmatic realities of the situation. In fact, their full arsenal of criticisms and failures was stockpiled — and long before 1781. For them, criticism of the Articles was not a simple matter of performance assessment. The Articles formed the wrong kind of government and political order. It reflected errant assumptions, undesirable objectives, and empowered the wrong interests and the wrong people. Within the national setting they saw the Articles as inept; within the states it fostered, in their view, a politics that would dismember their positions of power and advantage. At this juncture, however, they simply were unable to fabricate their political objective — an American political equivalent of British colonial rule: centralized authority with legitimate control of state laws; power to enact general and uniform legislation; power to use the military to control rebellions within states; and power to stoke the engines of commerce.

GOVERNING BY THE ARTICLES OF CONFEDERATION

Conventional wisdom, as well as many voices of intellectual expertise, have emphasized the failure of the Articles of Confederation. The Articles is presented, if it is not totally ignored, as a mere organization of government without any informing tradition of values or theory of politics. It is described on the basis of post-1787 assumptions that take for granted the vigor and relative dominance of the national government. "The Constitutional Convention was called because of a general recognition that the national government formed under the Articles of Confederation was weak and ineffective."[8] This familiar interpretation implies that the movement to the Constitution of 1787 was based on an atheoretical consensus about "what works." In fact, the movement to the Constitution of 1787 was neither a consensual movement nor one simply driven by pragmatic evaluations of practical performances.

It is frequently assumed that the states under the Articles lived too independently to achieve nationhood, especially in terms of the foreign, military, and economic dimensions of national life. Yet the system of governance formulated by the Articles operated from 1776 to 1789, during the time that America declared and achieved political independence and nationhood. Even before 1781, in spite of the dearth of formally coercive authority, the Continental Congress was both vigorous and successful. It contracted offensive and defensive alliances with France, it established independence, it financed the War of Independence, it established and administered an army and a navy, and it successfully prosecuted its claims against England. Even after ratification, when the Articles' system was formalized as the institutional basis for American politics, failure and ineffectiveness are far from adequate representations of the confederacy's record. Gordon Wood, who articulates a strong malconstruction interpretation of the Articles, nevertheless acknowledges its surprising achievements.

> What is truly remarkable about the Confederation is the degree of union that was achieved. The equality of the citizens of all states in privileges and immunities, the reciprocity of extradition and judicial proceedings among the states, the elimination of travel and discriminatory trade restrictions between states, and the substantial grant of powers to the Congress in Article 9 made the league of states as cohesive and strong as any similar sort of republican confederation in history — stronger in fact than some Americans had expected.[9]

Even after the War of Independence, the record of the confederacy was not simply one of failure and paralysis. American commerce revived relatively quickly after the war. Navigation acts of the states contributed more to this revival than did any similar legislation by the national government after 1789. In fact, the evidence is of steadily expanding commerce after 1783, not of stagnant or declining commerce with idle ships and bankrupt merchants. By the end of the decade American shipping was handling larger and more diverse cargoes, and trading activities were more broadly distributed throughout the colonies than before the revolution.[10] Part of the merchants' intense criticism against the Articles, it turns out, was evoked not because inactivity or stagnancy resulted from this system of public order. Rather, they were frequently displeased with the form and direction of the activism. For example, state governments were often vigorous in fostering domestic manufacturing vitality through the use of protective tariffs. The sharp differences among Americans regarding tariff strategies is important, but the issue is not a simple matter of governmental activity or inactivity.

Jensen's examination of this era's newspapers found that "the insistence on the basic soundness of the American states and their economy are as common . . . as are gloomy predictions of chaos to come."[11] He continues:

Thus, the picture by the end of 1787 is not the conventional one of interstate trade barriers, but a novel one of reciprocity between state and state. American goods were free of duties, and foreign goods arriving in American ships were charged lower duties in most of the states than when brought in in foreign ships, and particularly, in the ships of nontreaty countries. Cooperation between the states extended to other matters than trade. Ancient disputes about boundaries and navigation rights were discussed and settled rapidly. . . . The usual procedure was for the states concerned to appoint commissioners, and, once these had agreed, for the legislatures to adopt the agreement, a process still followed as problems arise among American states.[12]

Assertions about the Articles' negative performance were the rationalizations, not the reasons, for ditching the Articles of Confederation. The same persons and perspectives that opposed them before ratification opposed them after ratification and were already strongly oriented to the political directions of 1787 before 1776. There is little reason to believe that had the Articles experienced an even smoother run between 1776 and 1787 that these persons would have been converted to its support. Probably the only Americans for whom performance evaluation was an intrinsically important part of their political calculus were those who wanted to maintain the basic structure and principles of the Articles but who saw a need for some modifications and refinements, especially in the powers of Congress relative to foreign policy, military activities, and finance. But their willingness to support an amending process only played into the hands of others who wanted a totally different political construct — not just an amended Articles.

The important issue is not assumptions about the intrinsic rectitude of either political orientation. The fundamental premise of this discussion remains the same as it was initially: the nature and character of American politics has been shaped by and has benefited from two distinct traditions of democratic theory, which over time have been fused into a hybrid but logically contradictory tradition of American political values and understandings. One of these traditions is closely related to the values and assumptions that gave positive expression to the Articles of Confederation; the other is related to those that patterned the Constitution of 1787. Also, the important point is not that the formal shift from the Articles to the Constitution was simply, or primarily, based on assessments of the Articles' practical performance record. Its accomplishments were never as shabby as its detractors' rhetorical excesses asserted. And almost no achievable level of performance was likely to have satisfied them.

What must be seen is a vigorous contest between two quite distinct conceptions of democratic politics. In such a battle the successes of one's adversary are often read as failures, and even if they cannot be easily dismissed, they do not typically persuade those who are conceptually opposed to them to abandon their view and convert to the model that is currently enjoying practical success. Instead, they just stimulate new efforts to debunk the "success."

This discussion does not assume a disjunction between political ideas and political interests. The political interests of individuals and of various kinds of socioeconomic groups inevitably develop rationales. The rationales or political theories should provide a sensible and successful instrument for linking interests, means, political results, and basic political values. The more comprehensive, sophisticated, and persuasive the developed theory is, the more effective it is likely to be both in building a base of legitimacy and in realizing the concrete circumstances that are the preconditions and results of its objectives. It may work differently in heaven or in a very different kind of temporal setting, but in a world of epistemological, moral, and ontological finitude, the association of political theory with interests is inevitable. This inevitability is as much a function of the nature of political ideas in human life as it is a consequence of the power of interests. Political theories identify choices and chart directions among choices. In this world it is not only legitimate to debate these choices and to align ourselves differently relative to the options they encourage and oppose; it is necessary to do so.

The depth of humanity's longings for truth and justice, unfortunately, does not ensure the full or reliable realization of either goal in word or in deed. Consequently, every political theory has a certain polemical or partisan character to it, which serves historical interests more directly than pure absolute truths. Although verifying the absolute claims of political theories is beyond demonstration, it is possible to show that political theories actually can support the specific interests of some groups and individuals and limit or threaten the specific interests of other groups and individuals because of the way theories structure historical choices.

This general relationship of theory and interest is very much in evidence during the formative decades of American independence. Charles Beard's interests and Bernard Bailyn's ideas, for example, do not represent two different realities between which we are compelled to choose. Individual and group interests typically operate in concert with an intricate set of principles and values. And abstract principles and values never operate without direct and substantial implications for the interests of different individuals and groups. The ideological alignments identified by Bailyn and Beard's economic interest alignments are not negations of one another. They are two different manifestations of a common whole. Although this particular discussion has noted matters of interest, its language and attention has emphasized ideas. This is not meant to imply an absence or irrelevance of material issues. Rather, political theory has been stressed because it offers a more complex representation of the choices at hand. Theory gives both a particular and a general representation of the issues and choices; it identifies assumptions and objectives; it expresses and interprets abstract and concrete voices; and it organizes with depth and complexity the choices vying for power and legitimacy in the public life of a people.

This close association of theory and interest is even more evident in the American case, where ideas and speculation have always had a conscious and purposeful association with the interests of practical affairs. Americans have spawned practical political traditions considerably more influential than any of their homegrown philosophical traditions. This practical bent of Americans does not mean that they lack an active pursuit of political ideas. It means that Americans have been quite strongly attuned to the practical stakes of their theories and to the theoretical needs of their utilitarianism.

The ironic twists in American political life in the 1780s are also noteworthy. Irony is found in seemingly chance discontinuities between intentions and consequences, which when examined closely can be shown to have unexpected, but real, causes in the intentions.[13] Thus, irony reveals a unique form of morality and accountability. The contradictions between the high moral assumptions and aspirations Americans posit for their political community and the practical results they are left with may not be the mere accidents of fate but, at least in part, the effects intrinsic to the intentions in their own moral crusades. When events are significantly shaped by irony, the story line is not about the victory of fate, alternative power, or higher truth. The ironic story is the story of a certain kind of moral suicide — an unintended, but no less real, act of self-inflicted harm or destruction. If the changes symbolized by the events of 1787 were in important respects ironic, they represent, in large part, the fate of colonial republicanism at its own hands. The decade of the 1780s is partly the story of what revolutionary republicanism did to itself.

The republicanism that shaped the acquisition of independence as well as the initial form of the republic had clearly discernible characteristics. It was a political vision deeply rooted in a sense of community. Independence was sought for a people and for that people's liberty. This notion emphasized the priority of common purposes and the general good over particularistic interests. Virtue was the essence of this common good and the objective of the people in community. The practical manifestations of a virtuous public association were directly related to the principle of popular sovereignty upon which it was based. There was an emphasis on people, not things; for example, rights of the people were the focus, not rights of property. There was a strong commitment to majority rule and the wisdom of a well-ordered people. There was a powerful participatory bias. After all, this was a people armed with both power (they were sovereign) and moral truth (they were virtuous). Their claim for participation, thus, was rooted in both principles of authority and legitimacy. Formal governmental authority was based on local home rule preferences. Keeping the reins of political power short was most consistent with the positive supervision of a community of purpose and virtue.

Finally, the larger setting for this vision of a political community was not shaped by norms attributed to the patterns of history or to the order of well-designed and well-constructed artifices. This was to be a community in history, but echoing nature. Its successes and virtues were assumed to be the consequences of persuasion, consent, trust, and harmonies of interest. The underlying assumption was that coercion and the violence it fosters represent threats to the liberty of the community and disorient the community by pushing it away from the vitality of natural principles, which ultimately are the grounds for the community's proper virtue. Politics in this view is not primarily shaped by formal structures and procedures or by the authority of governmental institutions. Rather, politics is most fundamentally affected by the character of the people who constitute the political community. Their character must reflect the sentiments and the idealism of humanity's natural affections. This leads to noncoercive community standards that properly link the story of a particular people with the order of nature. In this way, the unique national story will simultaneously be universal — a story for other peoples as well. Americans will have a story uniquely their own, which nevertheless is for all.

Those Americans who held this republican ideal for their national life benefited from the dramatic contrasts it presented when compared with the images of British rule. Britain represented to the ordinary American a coercive, centralized, elitist rule organized for the benefit of parts of its jurisdiction at the expense of the whole. American republicanism, even when it was regretted or challenged, was implicit in the entire process of achieving and defining America's political independence because it expressed a clear and positive alternative to the political forms that were being questioned and rejected. The agrarian roots of the American yeomanry were quick to respond to the elevation of their practical and principled standing and to the invalidation of British claims offered by this view. Local home rule, majority rule, decentralization, character, virtue, legitimacy, nature, and persuasive consent spontaneously expressed constituted clear and dramatic repudiations of the political alternatives of imperial sovereignty, aristocracy, centralization, institutionalism, power, authority, history, and coercion.

Once independence was achieved, those who opposed the governmental model of the Articles and preferred an American equivalent of the British mixed government system faced the challenge of displacing a set of political ideas and institutions that had a powerful hold on a sizable American majority. Whenever the opposition's alternatives were brought to mind, they refreshed the American commitment to the contrasting images of republican ideology. It is not difficult to appreciate why the political theory of the Articles was able to dominate the independence process. It is more difficult to see how it could speedily be displaced, especially when the political objectives represented by the supporters of the 1787 alternative challenged home rule with nationalism, majority rule with institutional process and special opportunities for political minorities, decentralization with centralization, character with structure and process, virtue with order, legitimacy with authority, nature with artifice, and persuasion with coercion.

Yet, in fact, the theory of the 1787 document was able to establish itself at the center of American politics. This development was not the atheoretical consequence of the Articles' ineptitude at conducting everyday political affairs. Even after the unifying power of a common external foe (Great Britain) was removed by the Treaty of Paris, the American union and its individual member states were remarkably prosperous, stable, and cohesive. The Congress and the legislatures of the states did much to stabilize finances and the domestic economy. There was no default on payments of the public debt because it was being assumed by the states. And commercial prospects had already began their upswing by mid-decade.

The Constitution of 1787 also did not succeed in establishing itself because it finally gave expression to the American people's previously unstated aspirations. It is not easy to exaggerate the wide and deep popular disfavor with which the new constitution was received among ordinary Americans. Its formulation did not represent a culminating release from their suppressed preferences. If democracy means, broadly, the empowerment of a political community's human base, then the movement to the Constitution diminished democracy. And the masses saw and felt its impact in precisely these terms. Under the Constitution majorities are more effectively controlled by political minorities. Power is transferred to the few from the many. Vernon Parrington succinctly summarizes the social dimension of this transition: "Polite culture and professional learning joined forces to write down the agrarians."[14]

The formal introduction of the Constitution of 1787's political theory was more than a pragmatic response to the limitations and failures of the Articles, but it was not the articulation of previously suppressed or unexpressed perspectives of average American citizens, and it did not represent the successful conversion of large numbers of Americans to a new set of political values or to a new picture of their national identity. For example, localism was still valued, limits on coercion were still insisted upon, the political ideal of virtue remained, and a political community informed by nature continued to be a central part of American political talk. Thus, the establishment of new and, abstractly, opposite principles did not result in abandoning or dissolving the American people's original political theory. The new principles must be seen as being in a continuing relationship with their earlier competitors. The dominance of either theory did not result in the demise of the other. It is in this context that a concept of irony is helpful. The shift from the Articles' theory to the Constitution's theory charts a significant transition that is not directly or consciously intended by any of the parties contributing to the change and which, in itself, does not necessitate denying or debasing the subverted original intention.

The grip of irony can be seen early on in the existential political center various Americans adopted for themselves after ratification of the Articles. Although formal authority was to be locally centered, the claim of the Articles and the sentiment of most Americans was to create a firm league of friendship and perpetual union. Ironically, even though they intended to limit the coercive dimension of politics and to develop the cooperative dimensions of their association, they acted not unlike those with whom they quarreled. They focused their attentive energies on the center of coercive power, their states, and on the local self-governance of their communities. Their organizational effectiveness at the national level degenerated and was soon lost. Although establishment interests and theories made little headway in the states, they were left effectively uncontested at the national level. Further, the very futility of the opposition's efforts in the states only strengthened its resolve to press for the protections of a stronger central government. The political framework of the Articles failed partly because its defenders did not sustain the level and form of organization they had created and exercised to declare independence and to draft and ratify the confederacy. Their commitment to the union had to remain more than an abstract ideal not just so that they could realize a positive national association, but also, ironically, so that they could maintain the local autonomy they cherished under the Articles of Confederation.

Gordon Wood thoroughly traces another ironic twist that strengthened the nationalist principle as a counter to the psychology of localism that dominated American independence prior to the mid-1780s. The advocates of a nationalist perspective were never successful in their attempt to weaken the idea of sovereign states from above. That is, they were not able to strengthen Congress' authority on the basis of arguments that called for weakening the states. In this formulation of the issue localism never lost its punch. However, the nationalists were successful in challenging state authority from below. Repeated, intense charges that state legislatures did not adequately speak for the people did have considerable impact. First, these charges put the advocates of state sovereignty on the defensive. And then they positioned state sovereignty advocates as the defenders of state legislatures against the people. It had been the principle of the sovereign people that provided the original basis for their advocacy of localism. Now their advocacy of a particular form of localism was jeopardized by the very norm of a sovereign people. The essence of this development, Wood says, is this: "In the contest between the states and the Congress the ideological momentum of the Revolution lay with the states; but in the contest between the people and the state governments it decidedly lay with the people."[15]

Wood's scholarly exploration of the charge that state legislatures inadequately represented the people suggests that it was a claim capable of sustaining its political impact regardless of the empirical facts of the matter. In *The Creation of the American Republic* he offers a detailed elaboration of the "disintegration" of representation in state legislatures and the "disembodiment" of government to which this led. His description is of a process whose logic took the people out of governing in the name of putting them in it. "By weakening the representativeness of the people in the legislatures through resort to conventions, instructions, and other out-of-doors action, by expressing as much fear and suspicion of their elected representatives as of their senators and governors, the Americans were fundamentally unsettling the traditional understanding of how the people in a republic were to participate in the government."[16] Accordingly, he argues, the criticisms of state legislative bodies centered more and more on what they were not able to do rather than on what they did. The people, specifically jurisdictional majorities, increasingly were assuming for themselves powers that they previously had delegated to legislative bodies. Wood describes the history of this period in the states as one of mob activities and a profusion of special committees and conventions, which, through specific instructions to their members, became de facto substitutes for state legislative bodies. The people disobeyed, ignored, and fashioned alternative legislative enactments. They also intimidated lawmakers, especially by the norms of instruction developed in local districts. In effect, representation had become increasingly passive for the individual representative, and for the numerical majority — the people — it had become a vacuous concept.

An effective majority transformed representation into direct participation. This denigration of legislative authority and representation, ironically, resulted in a keener sense of nonrepresentation and nonparticipation among individuals or groups that did not agree with the methods or ends of this highly mobilized segment of American society. Thus, a movement keenly sensitive to a meaningful relationship between the people at large and their elected representatives compromised that very relationship by limiting its sense of the people to an effective majority directly empowered. The result was an increasingly trivialized meaning of representation. Under these circumstances it was not the power of the state legislatures that raised questions regarding their adequacy as the keystone of America's governmental system. It was their powerlessness to resist being dominated and circumvented that forced many people to advocate with increasing credibility an alternative arrangement of authority better designed to speak for the people.

However in another essay, "Interests and Disinterestedness in the Making of the Constitution," Wood describes state legislatures as the engines of democratic excesses. The democratic politics of state legislatures is represented by "the scrambling of different interest groups, the narrow self-promoting nature of much of the lawmaking, [and] the incessant catering to popular demands."[17] In this reading of the state legislatures the real issue was not the weakness of the Articles, but their pernicious strength — as argued by James Madison, the "multiplicity," "injustice," and "mutability" of state laws and legislatures. From this perspective, the state legislatures did not speak properly for the people either. They became no more than the means for authorizing private interests. They did not speak for "the people," only for particular people. Therefore, the people must be served by a principle of disinterestedness superior to private advantage and not found in the behaviors of state assemblies. Consequently, whether the state legislatures are described as being powerless to resist organized interests or as being the powerful instruments of organized interests (and Wood offers both views), they embodied a similar problem. Either way, state legislatures were vulnerable to the charge that they did not properly speak for the people and, therefore, needed to be replaced as America's primary governmental institution.

Another ironic dimension of the American situation during this time concerns expectations and self-criticism. Just as the problems in the economy have often been exaggerated, so too, the lapses of American virtue and goodwill may have been overstated. Because the supporters of American independence really did aspire to something more than mere separation from Britain, successful administering of the war and even reasonable economic healing were not sufficient to confirm the full success of their political enterprise. They had embarked on an utopianlike adventure designed to remake the nature of democratic society every bit as much as to sever British authority from the conduct of everyday business. Given these high ideals and aspirations, it was possible to see clear evidence of failure. Revolutionary theory constantly fed doubt and defeat to its proponents and provided ammunition for charges of failure to its opponents even in the face of relative practical success.

The yeomanry behaved in a more narrowly self-interested fashion than had been expected. Elitist critics jumped on the yeomanry's failures, charging that a society driven merely by the power of majoritarian numbers was harming the development of talent and the rewarding of hard work. Commitment to a community of equals was not creating pure harmony. Public-spiritedness was being pushed aside in an increasingly factionalized society. A growing number of Americans feared that they were perverting the promise of their national liberty. Not only were sentiments of trust and fellow feeling seen losing ground to selfishness and greed, but, correspondingly, there was decreasing hope that noncoercive principles could provide sufficient cement for the kind of society most Americans wanted.

Power in the hands of the people did not move America nearer to the prophesied chaos of license, but it did give specific form to the previously neglected problem of majoritarian despotism. The majoritarian expression of the people's will was seen by more and more Americans as capricious and arbitrary. Property was confiscated, paper money schemes were developed, tender laws were enacted, and contrivances were created to suspend normal means for the collection of debts. All of this and more was the work of a majority through its instructed or displaced delegates, not the work of an unaccountable magistracy. The fact that the ills of the old order were manifesting themselves at all, even if to a limited extent, introduced a disturbing sense of vulnerability to America's revolutionary ideals.

Ironically, the republican ideal became normalized precisely as its practical validity became more problematic. The form and focus of American political debate then shifted from whether or not America should be a republic to whether America had the ability to sustain any kind of republic, and, if so, exactly what kind of republic it could sustain. Americans had to find, according to Madison, "a republican remedy for the diseases most incident to republican government."[18] The difficulties and limitations of representation, majoritarianism, virtue, and persuasion, for example, Madison saw as endemic to republics. But this did not lead him to an overt repudiation of republicanism. He pursued, instead, republican corrections for republican errors. However, this project led him to a dramatic revision of both republican theory and the form of the republican state.

Republicanism had been a uniquely modern attempt to honor the classical ideal — benevolence and virtue within a community of common purpose. In this form it functioned as a significant restraint to the individualism of market societies. Republican virtue, it was held, could be achieved by education in a society of happy, frugal yeomen. Moral reforms and the regeneration of sentiment would remedy human viciousness. A republic, in short, was a political community whose collective character could be transformed by the character of its citizens and the nature of their associations with one another.

Many Americans remained committed to the validity of this vision, but doubts and challenges increased in number and in impact. The result was not a direct repudiation of this ideal, but a transformation of its republican meanings. The new defenders of a "republic" sought to ensure political order in the absence of public virtue. Because the human spirit cannot ensure its own redemption, government must assume humanity's sinfulness. This new view required a machine to compensate for organic failures — mechanical devices and institutional contrivances to organize America's political life. The coercive power vested in institutions of governance, carefully arranged and balanced, would make it possible to manage an unvirtuous people and achieve, indirectly, the public good.

Therefore, as the republican ideal became a nearly universal aspiration, it became more problematic and fragmented in its meaning. American republicanism, consequently, became a less distinct political alternative, and became, instead, a general heading for quite diverse political assumptions, strategies, and objectives. Madison's mechanical republic did not replace Jefferson's organic republic. They both had substantial, committed support, but their joint, yet separate, vitalities made it increasingly difficult to understand and use "republic" as a vehicle of any precise political meanings. Nevertheless, rather than discard the concept, Americans have retained the language of republicanism and filled it with the instability and contradictions of divergent meanings. Ironically, the victory of the republican configuration of American politics opened up new republican possibilities and complicated any precise and focused understanding of the nature and direction of American republicanism.

The move to the Constitution of 1787 and to the principles of nationalism, centralization, and institutional coercion that came with it was not achieved directly by converting American opinion to enthusiastic support for these principles. It was achieved, in large measure, indirectly and ironically. The move was a political response to problems in the conduct of state governments and in the activities of popular majorities. It was presented as a republican answer that, nevertheless, was strikingly different from the republic of the Articles of Confederation and the political theory that supported the Articles. The new direction of 1787 was not achieved by vanquishing the dominant theory of 1776. The ratification of the U.S. Constitution in 1789 merely initiated a new phase in the entanglement of these two political visions in American politics.

Unwitting Common Sense: 6
Paine and Jefferson as Theorists
of the Articles' Democracy

The Constitution of 1787 offers a well-studied and familiar theory of politics. It also has equally well-known theorists, both original and contemporary. James Madison's significance as a theorist of the Constitution is unparalleled and substantial. He was the principal architect of this constitutional document. He played a telling role in working his model through the Constitutional Convention's deliberations, provided an effective and memorable theoretical explanation and defense of this instrument of governance in the *Federalist Papers,* and implemented its structures and processes firsthand as president of the United States. Furthermore, Madison has never carried the Constitution theorist's burdens alone. There was and continues to be a rich tradition of Constitution theory beyond the efforts of Madison: John Jay and Alexander Hamilton directly associated themselves with his efforts and were followed by a lineage as varied as, for example, John Marshall, Noah Webster, Abraham Lincoln, John Dewey, Joseph Schumpeter, Robert Dahl, and Theodore Lowi.

The story is rather different for the Articles of Confederation. The political theory that is embedded in its organization of politics is not commonly recognized and is not a subject of broad or intense curiosity. In fact, the typical nontreatment or superficial treatment of the Articles suggests that it is theoretically inert or, even, atheoretical. Identifying a theorist of the Articles seems to be an even more challenging task than articulating the Articles' political theory.

John Dickinson is the person most specifically identified with the Articles because of his primary role in shaping the 1776 draft proposal.

But he was unable to save the underlying principles of his original scheme in the Second Continental Congress's deliberations. The final document sat Dickinson's draft on its theoretical head. A document that has been either neglected or subsumed into other realities, especially the ideological realities of the 1787 Constitution, is unlikely to generate its own clearly defined tradition of dialogue for which it is the primary reference point. Further, advocacy for the political ideas central to the Articles has not dominated the efforts of America's economic, political, and intellectual elites. Although the Articles of Confederation embodies a political vision with a specific theoretical foundation, one important reason why this is seldom realized or considered is that it lacks the voice of a definitive theorist.

Two men who were quite clear in their opposition to the Articles may, nevertheless, serve as its most useful theorists. Certainly neither Thomas Paine nor Thomas Jefferson ever imagined himself as the theoretical defender of the Articles of Confederation's political theory. Yet both Paine and Jefferson provide important understandings and support for key principles essential to the Articles' political vision. They quarreled with the specific architecture of the Articles but they were influential and articulate spokesmen of the theoretical terrain within which the Articles and its political tradition came to life and lived.

Thomas Paine was not a friend of the formally structured government offered by the Articles of Confederation. Especially in his writings to Washington's troops, published as *The American Crisis,* Paine emphasizes his preference for a national union of the states over the political independence of the states. Here he develops his recurring criticism: "The continental belt is too loosely buckled."[1] The primary association must be the union of the states. State affairs are local and parochial. America's proper sovereign base must be the nation as a whole. Thus, America's existence as a nation requires that it move on one center. "Our union, well and wisely regulated and cemented, is the cheapest way of being great — the easiest way of being powerful, and the happiest invention in government which the circumstances of America can admit of. — Because it collects from each state, that which, by being inadequate, can be of no use to it, and forms an aggregate that serves for all. . . . . Our great title is AMERICANS — our inferior one varies with the place."[2] But this opposition to the key structural characteristic of the Articles — state sovereignty — is perhaps not as determinative as it appears to be and hides the extent to which Paine offered important theoretical insights into the larger and deeper political principles supportive of the Articles.

The typical starting place for most discussions of Paine's political theory is his January 1776 pamphlet, *Common Sense*, through which he fired American passions for political independence from Great Britain. Nevertheless, it is two later works, *Age of Reason* (1794) and *Agrarian Justice* (1795–1796), that provide a fuller view of his political perspectives. Overtly, *Age of Reason* is about theology and the dispute between naturalistic (deistic) and nonnaturalistic (Christian) understandings of God. For Paine the resolution of these issues was of critical theoretical and practical importance to any proper understanding of public life. Why?

Paine addresses two forms of religion that are contrary to his own version of creationism. The first of these, historical religions with national churches, he dismisses as quickly as it is introduced. Such religions teach no truths larger than one people's unique appropriation of the incidents of their national life. They are religious voices trapped in particularism. Therefore, they are not religious in any large and meaningful sense. The second form of religion is revealed religion, which for Paine is best represented by Christianity. The most significant and authoritative revelation for Christians is, of course, the composite revelation of the Bible. It offers up a multitude of revelations — to Abraham, Moses, Isaiah, Mary, Jesus, Paul, and many others — which have been combined to form the basis of authoritative truths for persons who have not had these same revelations. Paine contends, "It is a contradiction in terms and ideas, to call anything a revelation that comes to us at second-hand, either verbally or in writing."[3]

If a revelation is not directly experienced, it is not a revelation at all. Instead, it is an instrument of personal authority based on an account that is, at best, second-hand and, typically, quite a bit more remote and dissociated from the supposed truth being communicated than even second-hand claims. Nothing illustrates this transformation of revelation from an instrument of truth to an instrument of power better than the fate of Jesus, who Christians claim is the fullness of revelation. The only accounts available portray Jesus to be "a virtuous and amiable man."[4] Yet

Christianity in its institutional form, the church, has set up a system of religion directly contradictory to the character of the person in whose revelation it claims authority. Although the rhetoric of humility, love, and forgiveness persists, Christianity has pressed its followers into the boldest presumption, self-righteousness, never-ending selfishness, and ingratitude. A Christian, notes Paine, does not even know how to pray in a manner consistent with the revelation claimed in Jesus. A Christian prays dictatorially: "when it is sunshine, he prays for rain, and when it is rain, he prays for sunshine; he follows the same idea in everything that he prays for; for what is the amount of all his prayers but an attempt to make the Almighty change His mind, and act otherwise than He does? It is as if he were to say: Thou knowest not so well as I."[5]

Christianity is the betrayal, abuse, and perversion of God's revelation. There is, fortunately, a proper revelation of God, argues Paine. It is a genuine revelation — a direct communication to every person independent of second-hand accounts. And it is a revelation that affirms God and the Word of God. This Word of God is the creation, and it is through this Word that God speaks universally to every human being, independent of the varieties of human language and speech. Everything in and about this creation suggests that it did not create itself. Creation reveals God as the first cause or creator, but it does not clarify other attributes of God's being. Revelation teaches us that God is and that the world God made, the Word of God, speaks a knowable language of universal principles. These are principles humans did not make but that they can discover. These are principles humans cannot change but that they must obey.

Through its misunderstanding and misuse of revelation, Christianity has become a religious denial of God, it has become a unique but significant form of atheism. It treats the world of God's creation as a conceit. It imposes falsehood on humanity through mystery, miracles, and prophesy. Mystery is "a fog of human invention."[6] The God of nature, says Paine, is not a God of obscurity but of revealed truth, whereas miracles and prophesy play on mystery's deceptions and hidden meanings, denying that the order of creation directly makes known its own truths. Thus, Christians deny God and God's word. They despise the language that shows us God's own existence. Christian parents even use mystery and miracles to hide the real principles and teachings of their religion from

 Mystery is a fog of human invention

their children. Paine suggests, for example, that we tell a child the story of God the Father putting his son to death and, simultaneously, convince the child that this is an act of love designed to make human life better and happier. It is a message that can only survive with the camouflages of mysteries, miracles, and obfuscations. For Paine, the conclusion is clear: "any system of religion that has anything in it that shocks the mind of a child cannot be a true system."[7]

Paine's theological quarrels with Christianity are quite clear. But why does a man of practical affairs, deeply absorbed by the political issues of his day, press such a controversial argument? Why does he risk public support for his political agenda by insulting the public on a religious issue, which — from a secular, pragmatic view — achieves nothing more than a displaying of eccentric theological beliefs? He did this, I believe, because the issue was as fundamental to his view of politics as it was to his view of religion; it was a matter of public order not merely one of personal faith. In Paine's mind this issue had a clear and direct relationship to politics. Politics was a matter of properly ordering human associations. Properly ordered human associations require moral principles. Moral principles must be anchored in truth. And truth must be accessible to all associating humans.

Christianity is, for him, the great enemy of morality and a just public realm. It reduces politics to matters of order and power rather than elevating politics to principles of justice and legitimacy. And it makes truth transcendent and esoteric rather than immanent and practical. Morality is replaced by faith; facts are replaced by notions.

> Of all the systems of religion that every were invented, there is none more derogatory to the Almighty, more unedifying to man, more repugnant to reason, and more contradictory in itself, than this thing called Christianity. Too absurd for belief, too impossible to convince, and too inconsistent for practice, it renders the heart torpid, or produces only atheists and fanatics. As an engine of power, it serves the purpose of despotism; and as a means of wealth, the avarice of priests; but so far as respects the good of man in general, it leads to nothing here or hereafter.[8]

It holds humanity in ignorance of its God, of its world, and of its rights.

For all of his political radicalism, it was Paine's classical commitment to the moral basis of politics that is the recurring element in his argumentation. Politics must be built on the truth — moral truth — not on power. Moral truths must reflect the essences of their universal forms, not merely particular meanings. Particulars uncorroborated by universals are the sources of arbitrary meanings. They establish meaning through imposition, not through the convictions of open inquiry and examination. Paine is not just pointing to the historical association of Christianity with Roman emperors when he charges that Christianity was established by the sword. He is pointing to the particularisms characteristic of Christian revelations from which "the most detestable wickedness, the most horrid cruelties, and the greatest miseries that have afflicted the human race" have originated.[9]

Furthermore, universal moral truths must be knowable. They must have an accessible home in this world. Even though Paine is often dismissed as a mere pamphleteer — not a real political philosopher — he pursued the ontological and epistemological basis of his ideas with great care and at great potential cost to his practical success. He insisted that genuine moral truths must be in and of this world and directly knowable by all human beings. In this sense Christianity denies what Deism offers. This is why he reads Christianity as a corruption of morality and politics. This is why morality, which requires a religious basis, must insure that its foundation not be Christian. Paine had to choose between offending American Christians and inspiring Americans to a new form of public morality. His choice was theoretical integrity, not mere pragmatic prudence. Beyond expediency, there was nothing to be gained theologically or politically by surrendering to the contentment of American Christians.

Paine asks us to consult the bible of creation. It reveals the order of this world, the principles upon which this order is constructed, and it makes knowledge of this order and its principles directly available to every human being. The ignorance and dependency of humanity, which is both the cause and consequence of despotism, should and can be shattered. Houses of worship that call for the repudiation of humans and their world and, thereby, sanction the deformity of both must be replaced with schools of science that teach the true principles of humanity's best possibilities.

Thus, eliminating Christianity is essential to eventually eliminating despotic governments.

Paine's naturalism is the religious alternative to Christianity necessary for the kind of politics he projects. Christianity offers believers protection from the consequences of their corrupt personal lives and unjust governments. Paine offers moral agents the challenge of establishing just communities through virtuous lives. To affect this change, the stranglehold of transcendence must be broken. Deism offers a cosmology of immanence. Thus, moral truth is available as a potential characteristic of human life in community, not just as the perfection of another kind of being in a different order of being. And just as moral truth is now ontologically available, so too, it is epistemologically available to all. Knowledge of truth is no longer the basis for human dependency — whether that dependency be on a totally different world or on the power and authority of a few persons and institutions claiming to express the truths of the other world for those in this world. The moral truths of nature are knowable precisely because they are the principles of the world we live in and of ourselves in this world. Truth is not a principle of alienation but one of egalitarian wholeness.

In *Age of Reason* Paine prepares for a tradition of public virtue based on radically new religious and political principles that, among other things, erase the distinction between sacred and secular life. The cultural hegemony of Christianity posed the greatest theoretical obstacle to his new vision. He met this challenge head on. On the specifically practical side, the acquisition and holding of property was the greatest obstacle to his design. The groundwork for dealing with this challenge was developed in *Agrarian Justice*.

There are three kinds of possessions identified by Paine: those of the intellect, those of liberty, and those of property. Property is held in two modes. Natural property is held in common according to natural principles. Artificial or acquired property is held according to the requirements of human inventions that vary greatly in detail but that uniformly establish inequalities, which create poverty. Contrary to the biblical adage frequently used to justify artificial property systems and the poverty they create, Paine insists that poverty is not a natural condition. It is a condition created by the conventions of human civilization. Human inventions have created patterns of greater affluence for some and greater destitution for others. What does this condition hold for a new politics of morality based on principles of nature? First, the romantic ideal is an unavailable option; that is, there is no return to a natural state from a civilized state no matter how disfigured the civilized state has become or how attractive the natural state remains. However, this does not excuse or justify civilization's deformities. Everything possible must be done within civilized conditions to remedy these ills and to preserve as much of nature's beneficence as possible.

Although humans will never again have direct access to the spontaneously natural life of the species, no one should face worse conditions in a civilized state than were faced in nature. Yet this is precisely the condition of many, perhaps most, persons today. They now find themselves living lives of poverty, destitute of property, whereas in nature they had been born into property claims. Naturally there was a right to occupy land but no right to locate personal property in perpetuity in any particular part of it. Nevertheless, Paine acknowledges benefits from civilization. "Civilization is at least one of the greatest natural improvement ever made by human invention."[10] Cultivators, therefore, do have a right to the improvements they introduce. Unfortunately, this benefit and its corresponding right have also produced the greatest evil faced by humanity — individual land monopolies.

Paine supports a principle of justice that, he believes, gives its due to both the cultivator and the destitute. Cultivators must receive the part that is the improvement their artistry introduced and no more. The destitute must receive the natural part that they have been denied and no less. For Paine the accumulation of personal property, even as it is produced through the work of one's own hands, always is a consequence of living in society. Justice requires, then, that the artificial accumulation of property made possible by the conditions of social life must be limited and directed, with the balance returned to its source — the social whole. Such an adjustment will benefit all without harming any. To achieve this, a harmony of interests must be established wherein the interest of the social whole coincides with the interests of the particular members of the society. Paine's specific proposals, he says, are designed to "consolidate the interest of the republic with that of the individual."[11]

The plan developed by Paine to solve the problem of property's improper distribution in civil society was based on the creation of a national fund to provide all citizens with the means for an equal, minimal property base, one comparable to the property base that they would have had under natural conditions. Under the plan, all citizens shall be paid the sum of fifteen pounds sterling at age twenty-one in partial compensation for the loss of their natural inheritance because of society's landed property system. Also, ten pounds per annum for life will be paid to every person now fifty or more years old and to all others as they reach the age of fifty. Paine's plan for funding this program was rather simple: appropriation of value released when citizens die. In effect, he formed a fund to establish an equal property base for all persons in civil society by, at the same time, eliminating the intergenerational transfer of distributed property and wealth. This eliminated the transfer of property from people whose cultivation of property created a claim by heirs based exclusively on the latter's greed and acquisitiveness. By eliminating the intergenerational transfer of property monopolies, Paine could simultaneously correct the abuse, as he saw it, of natural property claims, and honor the property claims acquired through the initiative and hard work of citizens.

Paine's search for morality in politics led to a direct confrontation with the issue of equality. This is reflected in several ways. Natural standards of truth and value must be uniform. As principles of nature rather than history they must be similarly relevant to all humans as a function of their humanity, not as a consequence of their artificial characteristics and standings as members of civil societies. Paine's emphasis on nature and the laws of nature provided a universal standard within which all persons were to participate directly and equally. Equality required not only a uniform standard for all but also this standard's ability to be known and effectively acted upon by all. And, finally, the standard of equality necessitated removing artificial impediments that prevented or subverted meaningful realizations of humanity's natural commonality. Properly expressing equality and effectively countering artificial barriers to it made it possible to transform the politics of contractual societies into closer approximations of nature's truths, which unify the whole and ennoble each member of the whole. Based on this ideal, Paine developed an elaboration of politics that was quite relevant to the dominant currents of thought in revolutionary America.

In addition to these principles of justice and equality, there is a third principle central to Paine's effort to honor the natural status of humans and the obligation of political associations to order themselves in keeping with nature's requirements. This principle asserts that the nation — the people — must be the source of all public authority. The authority of governments, of all other human institutions, and of any individual is derived solely from a sovereign people. Government is derivative and instrumental; in this sense it is a necessary evil. It is formed by a people to limit defects in humanity's moral virtue. Societies serve human well-being positively by uniting persons through benevolence and affections. Governments serve human well-being negatively by restraining personal vices.

Although governments must be founded on a moral theory, the greater part of virtue will always come from society's and humanity's natural constitution, not from government's coercion. This is because society itself is a direct, positive expression of human nature. Nature has made human wants and needs greater than individual powers can satisfy. Thus, we are naturally drawn to each other, spontaneously expressing "the mutual dependence and reciprocal interest which man has upon man."[12] Nature has drawn us into society for the reciprocal aid of each other, and it has given us a web of social affections essential to our happiness. Whether humans have found themselves in nature or in civilization, they have never found themselves without a need and love for society. Humans' social character begins and ends with human existence in both natural and artificial contexts.

Government, however, is another matter. It is a contrivance often needed but never always needed in the past nor necessarily always needed in the future. Societies have performed for themselves everything that civilization ascribes to government. In *Rights of Man* Paine states this principle directly: "Government is no farther necessary than to supply the few cases to which society and civilization are not conveniently compe-tent; and instances are not wanting to show, that every thing which government can usefully add thereto, has been performed by the common consent of society, without government."[13]

The safety net for human felicity comes not from governments but from the mutually and reciprocally maintained principles of nature in society. The constituting of government does not constitute society, just as the dissolution of government does not dissolve society. In fact, as civilization achieves moral progress, the less need it will have for government because society will recapture its positive abilities to govern itself. The fundamental laws of any just society are the laws of nature. "They are followed and obeyed because it is the interest of the parties so to do, and not on account of any formal laws their governments may impose or interpose."[14] Unfortunately, governments too often destroy or damage this natural order. And the evidence of perdition is easy to spot: excessive and unequal taxes and the poverty of the many.

Properly functioning governments will be nothing more than national associations acting on the principles of society. Not only is their function and authority totally derivative, they have no natural or organic standing. Their structure is merely that of a contrivance. Paine calls this contrivance a "common centre" that connects with all parts of society. It is the center in which every radius meets. These assertions about government, as we will see, create ambiguities of interpretation. For example, is the structural requirement of a "common centre" primary or is its status reflective of government's derivative status?

Unfortunately, this is not how most governments view themselves, or how most citizens view their governments, or how most governments actually have been constituted. Governments, according to Paine, should be based on a charter from the people and not on a deal among the governors. The people are to constitute governments; governments are not to be self-constituting. But most governments have had their origins in superstition, in power, in deception, and in conquest — not in the expression of society's common interests and the common rights of each human being. These corrupt sources of government result in monarchies and other governmental forms based on various expressions of the principle of hereditary succession. Paine insists that there are numerous principled and practical reasons to oppose government based on any hereditary principle, but the most fundamental reason for opposing this standard is that no people and no individual can give away their rights to posterity. No collective or individual decision can preempt the legitimate choices of future generations. This principle is not only the basis for rejecting hereditary succession but directly relates to Paine's sensitivity to and rejection of all forms of prerogative and his strident attacks on the deadening authority of precedents. They are false principles, which chain the present and future to the tyranny of the past — and even that not because the past was virtuous but simply because it was. Human rights are violated and governments degenerate into greater injustice, ignorance, and remoteness from the principles of nature. This is the real precedence offered by governments and it must be broken. To break it there must be a new political beginning. Mere reform will not suffice. The political world must begin again. This is the deeper spirit of Paine's advocacy for American independence. Independence represented more than a changing of the guard, substituting rulers and laws. It was to be a new beginning based on new principles that are actually the original principles of any just political association. He concludes *Common Sense* with this call for a moral departure in an independent America.

> WHEREFORE, instead of gazing at each other with suspicious or doubtful curiosity, let each of us hold out to his neighbor the hearty hand of friendship, and unite in drawing a line, which, like an act of oblivion, shall bury in forgetfulness every former dissension. Let the names of Whig and Tory be extinct; and let none other be heard among us, than those of a good citizen; an open and resolute friend; and a virtuous supporter of the RIGHTS of MANKIND, and of the FREE AND INDEPENDENT STATES OF AMERICA.[15]

The American revolution's uniqueness was not to be a reflection of its particular characteristics — its American form — but of its universal character — its human form. This was to be the first revolution worked out the way a political revolution should be worked out: "on the great floor of a nation" and not "within the atmosphere of a court."[16] Previous governments and revolutions in governments had been acts of plunder and usurped power, which were perpetrated as if they constituted a right through claims of inheritance. The old system of government formation was based on the assumption of power for self-aggrandizement. The new

great floor of the nation — not a court

system, exemplified by America, delegates power for the benefit of society. The old was a system of war; the new is a system of peace. The old encouraged national prejudices because it absolutized particular values, experiences, and persons. The new promises a universal society because it is built upon the vital principles of humanity's common nature. Paradoxically, the new system of government is the oldest. It is the one based on the original, inherent rights of humanity in nature.

This paradox illustrates the error of reasoning by precedents drawn from the past: precedents never go the whole way into antiquity. Inevitably, they stop at some arbitrary intermediate stage even if that stage is hundreds or thousands of years ago. But even with great age, these precedents never break out of a cycle of one arbitrary authority pitted against another arbitrary authority. The only "resting place" or "home" in the search for a basis of authority is in nature. "The duty of man is not a wilderness of turnpike gates, through which he is to pass by tickets from one to the other. It is plain and simple, and consists but of two points. His duty to God, which every man must feel; and with respect to his neighbor, to do as he would be done by."[17]

Paine's arguments reassert his disdain for hereditary principles, which are the glue of unjust governance. The cohesion of a just government derives from proper principles of representation. Representative governments avoid the tyranny of hereditary arbitrariness by building from society and by using nature and reason as its guides. The beauty of a representational system is that it expresses society's virtue while at the same time compensating for society's limitations. Society's virtue is that in the whole it is wise; its limitation is that, in its parts, wisdom is continuously changing places. Representative government adapts to this reality by collecting wisdom where it can be found. In comparison, hereditary governments demand the same abject obedience to ignorance as to wisdom.

If the form of government should be representative, the purposes of government should be those of a republic. Republics are not themselves a form of government; they express the purpose or object for which governments ought to be instituted. The proper object of government is res publica — the public thing, which is the public good. The meaning and character of government should give testimony to its commitment to this interest of the public in both its individual and collective dimensions. Paine prefers the representational form to the directly democratic form of government for the American republic because a representative form will best conduct the public business of the nation when that nation has become too extensive and populous for the simple democratic form. He admires the "perpetual stamina" of a representational system because it is always working in concert with the order and laws of nature in the lives of the people. "Whatever are its excellencies or its defects, they are visible to all. It exists not by fraud and mystery; it deals not in cant and sophistry; but inspires a language, that, passing from heart to heart, is felt and understood."[18] His essential point is that the public interest is formulated by the public for itself, not just for the public by someone else. A representative system, therefore, must be a form of participation in the self-rule of communities.

To ensure the participatory character of a representational system, representation must be large and equal. It must delegate powers as a public trust. And it must be based on principles of equal rights. The right of voting for representatives is the single right by which all other rights are ensured and protected.

Paine repeatedly argues that humans did not enter civil society to have their lives become worse that they were in nature. In no respect is this more true than with regard to rights. Civil society is not an excuse for eliminating or reducing human rights. It is a necessity to better secure the full application of natural rights in society. Natural rights and civil rights are different. Natural rights belong to humans as rights of existence. Civil rights belong to citizens as rights of being members of a particular political community. More important than these differences, however, natural and civil rights must function as parts of an integral whole. We always directly retain those natural rights for which the individual's ability and power to execute the right is as perfect as is the right itself — for example, intellectual rights or rights of the mind. We do not directly retain those natural rights for which we lack a perfect power of enforcement in ourselves. Those natural rights become transformed into civil rights. Paine says, "All civil rights are natural rights exchanged."[19] The exchange is necessitated not by a deficiency in the natural right but by the defective powers of individuals to execute their rights on their own. By aggregating natural rights in society, thus creating civil rights, effective power of enforcement is achieved and must be used to protect — not invade — the original, equal, natural rights of all citizens.

The civil rights of civil society, therefore, are created not for the sake of claims contrary to nature but to equalize the enforcement of natural rights. Seen in this way, civil rights represent reciprocal duties among fellow citizens. The rights any one person claims and enjoys must be guaranteed to all others. Those who reject this duty jeopardize their own rights. When rights are fully understood in civil society, duties are understood as well: "for where the rights of men are equal, every man must finally see the necessity of protecting the rights of others as the most effectual security for his own."[20]

The equality of rights is a matter of principle. The specific manner by which government is organized and conducted is not a matter of principle but of opinion. As long as the relevant principles are steadfastly followed, even errors in opinion will not long endure. The one principle governing all matters of opinion must be that the majority opinion shall rule. Sometimes the minority will be right no matter how small, and sometimes the majority will be in error no matter how large. But as soon as practical experiences show this to be the case, as they inevitably will, the minority position will be transformed into the majority one and the majority position will become the minority one. Therefore, majority rule is the just principle not because it is errorless but because Paine assumes that it is capable of correcting its errors through the peaceful operation of free opinions and equal rights. Even when majority rule results in short-term errors, there is neither a need nor a justification for insurrection or rebellion as long as rights remain equal and opinions free.

The principle of equal rights has important implications for two other basic political issues — the role of a bill of rights and the meaning of liberty. Paine's concern about a bill of rights is that it not be misconstructed or misinterpreted. These errors arise if a bill of rights is or is seen to be a granting of rights fitted to a particular state of civil government. The only way the authentic and equal nature of rights can be ensured is if a bill of rights is fitted to persons as they are in nature. Therefore, the link between natural and civil rights must not be confused or jeopardized by the writing of a bill of rights. Paine says that a proper bill of rights "would be an Indian Bill of Rights."[21] That is, a bill of rights is not a grant of different or fewer rights than are bestowed on humans by nature. It is an explicit articulation of equal natural rights, which the civil order is bound to enforce with equal vigor in behalf of all its members.

The precise meaning of liberty is closely related to the principle of equal rights. That in which all persons have a stake, it is the duty of all to support, says Paine. The one duty that falls equally on all persons and from which all persons receive equal benefit is the duty to defend and honor the principle of equal rights. When this duty is properly executed, Paine says, liberty is perfected.[22] Thus, liberty has a shared, common meaning rather than an idiosyncratic, particular one. Liberty relates to a public, not a private, dimension of life. It expresses an authentication of the political community, not an authorization for isolated, individual members of society to chart unrelated courses of action. Freedom is achieved when human life is organized in harmony with its genuine nature. In other words, Paine gives freedom a universal foundation in the order of species life, not a particular foundation in the whims of individuals. The key to his position is the principle of all persons' equal claims and of the duty to honor the equality of these claims. "Whenever I use the words freedom or rights, I desire to be understood to mean a perfect equality of them," he reminds us.[23]

Paine called America "the land of love and liberty."[24] The dynamic force that moves persons to their duties of liberty is love. Although rationality is knowledge of nature and its principles, it is the affections that open us up to the guidance of reason. In the neighbor and the friend — through love, trust, and empathy — humans discover the equally shared principles of human life, which are the foundation of proper politics. "The Almighty hath implanted in us these unextinguishable feelings for good and wise purposes. They are the guardians of his image in our hearts. They distinguish us from the herd of common animals. The social compact would dissolve, and justice be extirpated from the earth, or have only a casual existence were we callous to the touches of affection."[25] Both in *Common Sense* and in his war letters to Washington, published as *The American Crisis,* Paine repeatedly contrasts the war efforts of the British and the Americans. The war is a battle of coercive force for the British; it is a war of natural feelings for the Americans. At times America has had no bond of union other than its common interests and affections. The American mode of power has been founded, ultimately, on eros.

Paine had a deep respect for the nonformal and noncoercive grounds of a political union. On the one hand governments will wither away and their instruments of coercion will wither with them as civilization increasingly reorders itself on natural principles. Authority will not be power contra nature but the power of nature. But on the other hand Paine still saw a need for formal governmental authority at the present stage of history. The affections were not extensively and sufficiently ripened. And when duties, affections, and interests coincide, as he believed they did regarding the union of states, it is essential that the virtue of this unity be protected with public authority as well as with love. Paine's disagreement with the form of the Articles, therefore, was based on his judgment that its structure depended on circumstances that had not been sufficiently developed and matured. It was an issue of developmental timing not of direction or principle.

Nevertheless, it is difficult to overstate Paine's noncoercive orientation. Society's understanding and consolidation of natural principles is a matter of evolution. Not everyone will change their thinking at the same time or under the same circumstances. "Time and reason must cooperate with each other to the final establishment of any principle."[26] Not only must there be wise experimentations, there must be a spirit of tolerance, which permits the advantageous interaction of time and reason. Of course, the temptation is to punish and to coerce. But this approach only has retrogressive effects. It forces people to stretch unnaturally; as a result, they misinterpret and misapply even the best of laws.

New government officials will face their greatest challenge, asserts Paine, trying to break the conventional association of governmental energy and effectiveness with coercion. Even Washington, who was deeply revered by Paine during most of his life, exhibits this old habit: "he has yet to learn that the strength of government consists in the interest the people have in supporting it."[27]

> Mere politicians of the old school may talk of alliances, but the strongest of all alliances is that which the mildness, wisdom, and justice of government form, unperceived, with the people it governs. It grows in

the mind with the secrecy and fidelity of love, and reposes on its own energy. Make it the interest of the people to live in a state of government, and they will protect that which protects them. But when they are harassed with alarms which time discovers to be false, and burdened with taxes for which they can see no cause, their confidence in such government withers away, and they laugh at the energy that attempts to restore it. Their cry then is, as in the time of the terror (not to your tents, O! Israel), but "to the NEXT ELECTION O! CITIZENS." It is thus the representative system corrects wrongs and preserves rights.[28]

The affections also guide governments in the proper methods of governing. Paine points to two directions of governing: keeping the people ignorant or making the people wise. The choice seems to concern a simple matter of knowledge — its absence or its presence. But Paine emphasizes participation in government and its place in the development of the affections rather than mere knowledge. Isolation is ignorance. It is to be out of touch with the rational principles of nature. To be in touch, to be wise, is not just to possess information but to experience the quickening of affections through participation in the shared life of a community of equals. Participation puts us in touch with one another and with the bonds of fellow feeling that make it possible for us to be rationally governed because participation ties us to the proper principles of human nature. By making people involved in the public affairs of a nation and removing the elements of mystery from the proceedings of their government, harmony can be restored and preserved among the people and confidence can be justly granted to that government.

Nature, Paine claims, provides constancy worthy of devotion. In artifice he sees the flux of experimentation. Government is an experiment, the artifice of civil society. Yet even in its most degenerate forms, it has the high obligation to serve the truths of nature. But governments, even in their most elevated forms, will never fully embody natural truths. The obligation of government is constant, but there is no single or constant form that governments will embody in their pursuit of this obligation. In fact as a human invention, governments should be encouraged to assume a variety of forms even if all of these forms are obligated to serve the same ultimate purpose. This is no less true of representative governments than of any other form of government. Representative government has no single organizational form that all must follow.

Nevertheless, some conditions that affect the structure of governments are deducible from reason and must be observed. For example, never invest any individual with extraordinary powers and never invest any powers in the hands of even a large number of individuals for a long, uninterrupted time. Yet there are still a variety of specific governmental organizations that could be fully consistent with these general principles.

Actually, Paine takes this matter a step further. Varieties of governmental forms are not just permissible and to be expected, they are potentially beneficial and should be encouraged. He argues that it is in the common interest that each state constitution should be different from the others. In principle, the American union is natural, but governmentally it is experimental. "[We] have the happy opportunity of trying variety in order to discover the best."[29] This diversification of governmental forms helps posterity choose a model according to the successes of actual political experiments. We cannot be too free in this experimentation as long as we remain anchored in the principles of nature. This relationship — with the principles of nature — not the specifics of its formal organization — is what constitutes the justice of a government. "[A] just [constitution is] that which considers mankind as they come from their maker's hands — a mere man, before it can be known what shall be his fortune or his state; and freedom being secured in this first and naked state, is forever secured through every possible change of rich and poor."[30]

That the union is natural in principle relates to another important characteristic of Paine's political views. Paine starts his analysis in nature and aspires to end there too. Thus, even the American governmental union he sought with such passion was only a preliminary goal, not an ultimate one. Ultimately, even this political union must be overcome. The fullest union must be that of all humanity. Paine never tired of identifying his true country as the world. When he heralded the American cause in the revolution as the cause of mankind, he did not mean that America's success would be the success of all or that all would find their satisfaction in the American success. He meant, simply, that the American cause was a necessary and significant step against the sword and the court. It introduced the just challenge of the natural constitution of human beings in society: "the mutual dependence and reciprocal interest which man has upon man."[31]

The contagion of this new challenge will sweep the rest of the world with it. This process reveals the one great hierarchical principle within Paine's radical egalitarianism. Justice is a constant movement from particularity to universality. The more universal are the characteristics exhibited in particular life situations, the more authoritative they will be. It is a movement to unity, the recapturing of uncontaminated human nature. This goal is at the heart of Paine's political theory and his religion as well. Government should take on different particular forms precisely because governmental forms are not themselves universals. The same perspective that encourages varieties of governmental forms eventually leads to the total transcendence of governments. As the particularities of governments are refined and the true principles of public life are clarified, particularistic institutions will become increasingly obsolete. And all the great laws of human life will be understood as laws of nature. Whether or not this condition will ever be realized in fact, there is always in Paine's theory a naturalism overwhelming even the highest achievements of positive historical politics.

Paine's contemporaries, especially those who vigorously supported the Constitution of 1787, frequently called him an Antifederalist. This was an identity he strongly rejected. His denial, although unambiguous, was always constructed on the narrowest of grounds. He defined Antifederalists only on the basis of their support for a limited number of the Article's structural characteristics. He dissociated himself from the Antifederalists by dissociating them from any larger political vision or general set of political principles. As early as 1780 he called for a continental congress to amend the Articles because he wanted a stronger central government to affirm America's common lot and because he wanted the western lands to be the common right of all Americans. Yet he simultaneously attacked the Federalists and their proposed instrument of government, the 1787 Constitution. His objections, he insisted, were not on Antifederalist grounds but on "constitutional" grounds. However, the constitutional grounds he argued were extraordinarily similar to those of many Antifederalists and related directly to the political theory reflected by the Articles and the vision of their Antifederalist supporters. The fact that Paine preferred forms associated with the Constitution of 1787 and was troubled by the Articles' forms can only be of secondary relevance when he insists that governmental forms are always matters of experimentation. The issues of real primacy are more fundamental than those of governmental organization. In this latter sense, Paine gives important expression to and support for the fundamental political vision of the Articles.

Some of his objections to the Constitution of 1787 were as particularistic as those he used to define antifederalism. He was uncomfortable with the Senate and especially disliked the length of senators' terms of office. And he did not like the form of the executive. The office had too many powers and it should not be put in the hands of a single individual. Most of his objections, however, were more theoretical. The Constitution, he charges, is an ill-advised attempt to imitate the British Constitution. Specifically, it attempts to replicate for America the British form of a mixed constitution. Mixed governments are corrupt for two primary reasons. First, their basis for justice becomes mere order, the balancing of particular interests. Nothing lifts such governments above mere order. They aspire to nothing more than to balance particularities. Many people view this as practical, but it contributes nothing to the moral progress of the people. Second, mixed governments mystify. Their elaborations and indirections confuse the people and make it more difficult for them to benefit from the direct guidance of their reason and feelings. For Paine the purpose and form of government was simple. Its purpose was to serve the defect of human moral virtue. Its form was to be as direct and simple as possible to serve that purpose: "the more simple anything is, the less liable it is to be disordered, and the easier repaired when disordered."[32]

The Federalists represent, for Paine, the worst possibility: America losing its relationship to the principles of nature. The Constitution of 1787's conception of the people is one that deprives them of both private manners and public principles. It offers a government driven by power not consent — by coercive force not the choices of its constituent members. Examples of this orientation are readily identified in its press for a standing army during peace and for the creation of a prodigal governmental revenue. Federalists live by indirection and slights of hand that serve the interests of factions. Their true intentions are always concealed; they depend solely on artifice and management; their purposes are codes for power (for example, they call for more energy in government but do not want more energy from the people — they want energy over the people not the energy of the people); they are to government what atheism is to religion — "a nominal nothing without principles";[33] and they give new relevance to a prudent warning — "he that picks your pocket always tries to make you look another way."[34]

In a letter published in the *Philadelphia Aurora,* Paine vigorously pursued his quarrel with the Federalists. An extended quotation from that letter reveals the nature and intensity of Paine's attack on Federalist principles.

> [The Federalists] advocated plans which showed that their intention and their cause were not good. They labored to provoke war. They opposed every thing which led to peace. They loaded the country with vexatious and unnecessary taxes, and then opposed the reduction of them. They opposed a reduction of useless offices that served no other purpose than to maintain their own partisans at the expense of the public. In short, they run themselves a-ground first, by their extravagance and next by their folly. Blinded by their own vanity, and though bewildered in the wildness of their own projects, they foolishly supposed themselves above detection. They had neither sense enough to know, nor logic enough to perceive, that as we can reason upward from cause to effect, so also can we reason downward from effect to cause, and discover, by the means they make use of, the motives and object of any party; for when the means are bad, the motive and the end to be obtained cannot be good.
>
> The manners also, and language of any party is another clue that leads to a discovery of their real characters. When the cause and principles of a party are good, its advocates make use of reason, argument, and good language. Truth can derive no advantage from boisterous vulgarity. But when the motives and principles of a party are bad, it is necessary to conceal them; and its abettors having principles they dare not to acknowledge and cannot defend, avoid everything of argument, and take refuge in abuse and falsehood.
>
> The federal papers are an instance of the justness of this remark. Their pages are crowded with abuse, but never with argument; for they have no principles to argue from: and as to falsehood, it is become so naturally their mother tongue, especially in New England, that they seem to have lost the power as well as the disposition, of speaking the truth. Those papers have been of great aid to the republican cause, not only by the additional disgrace they have brought on their own disgraceful faction, but by serving as a foil to set off, with greater éclat, the decency and well principled arguments of the republican papers.[35]

What is most bewildering to Paine is the extent to which ordinary Americans have lent their support to federalist interests. There is nothing unexpected about some people who want status, offices, and benefits advocating extravagances, wars, and taxes to support them. But why are they being supported by people who have no prospects beyond bearing the burdens of these ambitions? How can this thoughtlessness of the people, which is leading them to support the blackguardism of the Federalists, be accounted for? Paine is without a final explanation but not without hope.

His hope is based first on the natural wholesomeness of the people, which he believes eventually will be quickened and repulsed at such obvious vulgarities. As long as citizens retain access to their native affections and principles, reason will recover its rule and will clear away this fog of delusion. The second and more specific ground for hope is the strengthening of a counter movement: the vices of federalism have helped to shape a more virtuous republicanism. Paine describes a Federalist/Republican drama. In that drama, federalism is the protection of particularistic interests. Possession of power is their means. Masking their intended use of power is their prudence. Federalism is the creed of political particularism. Republicanism is the sovereign rule of the people. It is the search for a more perfect application of natural principles to public life through a representative system of government. Evidence of its efforts include the cultivation of peace and brotherhood at home and abroad, the refinement of civil manners, and the limiting of taxes as much as possible. "Religion and War is the cry of the Federalists; Morality and Peace the voice of Republicans."[36] The combination of morality and peace is congenial with nature. It expresses a consistency and directness that supports it as a genuine and valid commitment. However, the joining of religion and war is a contradiction that can only suggest hypocrisy and false purposes.

These perspectives are reflected in Paine's view of himself. In an 1806 letter that was written near the end of his life, Paine describes for the mayor of Philadelphia, John Inskeep, the purpose of his life and work.

My motive and object in all my political works, beginning with *Common Sense,* the first work I ever published, have been to rescue man from tyranny and false systems and false principles of government, and enable him to be free, and establish government for himself; and I have borne my share of danger in Europe and in America in every attempt I have made for this purpose. And my motive and object in all my publications on religious subjects, beginning with the first part of the *Age of Reason,* has been to bring man to a right reason that God has given him; to impress on him the great principles of divine morality, justice, mercy, and a benevolent disposition to all men and to all creatures; and to excite in him a spirit of trust[,] confidence and consolation in his creator, unshackled by the fable and fiction of books, by whatever invented name they may be called.[37]

It is symbolically significant that Paine's first public writing, *Common Sense,* with its dramatic call for American independence, was bracketed with his last known private correspondence, an 1808 letter to Thomas Jefferson. Jefferson was not only a loyal political ally and a warm, personal friend of Paine's; he embodied the republican spirit that was Paine's solace in the face of both British tyranny and federalist hypocrisy. Paine used some of his most pungent language, under the pen name of "A Spark from the Altar of '76," to defend Jefferson's political and personal integrity. Because he saw Jefferson as a man of true moral principles, Paine's defense was animated by a passion for the man and for the public teachings he represented.

One of the great pastimes of American intellectuals has been to quarrel over the pedigree of Jefferson's political ideas. Like the Bible, he has been quoted on behalf of an incredible array of political directions and possibilities. And like the Bible, the richness and variety of his own formulations have contributed significantly to this interpretive tumult. None of America's great political leaders is as elusive and, even, contradictory as Jefferson. The antitheses that form this confusion are more prominent in Jefferson than in Paine. Both were radical traditionalists: their struggle centered on the creation of a new foundation for ancient hopes. And as Vernon Parrington and Wilson Carey McWilliams have argued, it is the moralist in them that unites all their warring parts and gives them a basis for theoretical cohesion and direction.

As with Paine, the moral principles that Jefferson chose as guides to public life are those of nature, directly accessible to everyone. "The great principles of right and wrong are legible to every reader; to pursue them requires not the aid of many counselors. The whole art of government consists of being honest."[38] And for Jefferson, too, a public morality based on the order of nature required a religious perspective that affirms this world, its principles and possibilities, as the proper basis of meaning and truth. Jefferson and Paine shared a devotion to Deism, and both men targeted Christianity for special criticism precisely because it undermines a proper moral basis for life in community. Jefferson's opposition to Christianity rested on two main issues. First, he opposed Christianity because it was a form of tyranny over the human mind and he opposed every form of such tyranny. He saw Christianity as a tyranny over the mind because it rested on authority, not on self-discovery — on the power of priests and doctrines and books, not on the direct discoveries of persons through the experiences of living their own lives. Second, he opposed Christianity because, in relationship with truth, it teaches atheism. It draws humanity to the mystifications of a god of revelation and away from direct knowledge of nature's order and the creator God.

Reason, for Jefferson, was the great stimulus to the discovery and expression of moral principles. But the proper basis for reason is in the emotions, not the calculations of self-interest or the speculations of mental abstractions. Affections must guide moral reasoning. Reason without this solid base in the sentiments of benevolence, justice, sympathy, and friendship, Jefferson describes as miserable. His affective reason was in sharp contrast with the materialistic rationality of, for example, Hamilton, and it offered Americans a very different political direction for their rational choices.

Jefferson insisted that good government was the consequence of pursuing the common interest in public affairs. This quest is impossible without the fraternal bonding of equals. This bonding is the basis for a proper public life in community and the ground for genuinely common interests, which are simultaneously beneficial to the individual members of the community. Good government must understand its instrumental role of service to the people. Government must never take the place of the people but must help them "close the circle of our felicities."[39]

The material factor central to Jefferson's search for principled government was the pattern of property acquisition and holding. His writings are filled with laments about the corrupting effects of property monopolies, especially in France. The pattern is clear: the appropriation of property has been extended so far as to violate natural rights. The earth is given as a common property for all persons to live and labor on. To encourage industry it is justifiable to allow some of the commons to be personally appropriated. However, we must ensure that others are not made destitute by these permitted appropriations. Other employments and productive possibilities must be provided to those who have been excluded from the appropriations. If we do not ensure that productive opportunities are available to all, especially to those without personal property holdings, the natural right to labor the earth returns to the destitute and supersedes the permitted property acquisitions. Jefferson's standard was modest in degree but radical in scope: a small portion of productive land should be provided by every possible means for everyone.[40]

The foundation of equal opportunity for all persons to labor and be productive rested directly on access to some land holdings. This is in principle a matter of natural right and in practice a matter of good government. Societies of small landholders create the most desirable and just states. Jefferson says he would prefer to see the American states follow China's example of having small agrarian communities in which all citizens are husbanders.[41] In a letter to John Jay, Jefferson describes these cultivators of the earth as "the most vigorous, the most independent, the most virtuous, and they are tied to their country, and wedded to its liberty and interests, by the most lasting bonds."[42]

Jefferson's "hundreds" system showed just how deeply committed he was to America's agrarian communities. It was a proposal that did not differentiate between authority and liberty, rulers and ruled. By building his entire governmental system on local wards, Jefferson dramatized the degree to which his political thinking was anchored in a society of equals formed according to natural principles. Eldon Eisenach argues: "The unique feature of Jefferson's ward or hundreds system proposal is that in this hierarchy of office there is no lateral entry; to rise in power and distinction, every man must first be selected in the community of equals and prove his capacity to earn the trust of his immediate peers in an unstructured, undifferentiated environment."[43]

The holding of inherited property was of great importance to Jefferson. Inheritance represented the dictates of past generations on the present with the potential that many people would be denied the possibility of productive lives. Jefferson claimed it was a self-evident principle that the right to use and enjoy the earth belonged to the living not to the dead. The claims of particular persons cease when they cease, and the portion they claimed reverts back to society. Other particular persons get their property not as a natural right but according to the laws of their society to which they are subject, laws that must be formulated for the well-being of the whole community. Although society is superior to an individual, no generation is superior to another generation. Consequently, neither the government through the representatives of the nation nor the people themselves can validly commit debts beyond what they can reasonably be expected to repay in their own time by themselves. Jefferson estimates a generation's own time to be no longer than thirty-four years from the date on which a debt is engaged. For similar reasons, no society can impose a perpetual constitution or a perpetual law on the next generation of that society.

A just distribution of property, which provides a modest but productive basis for all citizens, must be coupled with the education of the common people. Their education must be built on respect for their intrinsic spirit and goodwill. If they err, the response should not be too severe. Harsh punishments introduce fear and distrust of the people's own best judgments. They should be reclaimed through the enlightenment of their best natures. This is one of the reasons why Jefferson argues that just, republican government should be mild in the punishment of rebellions. The people's vitality, which is needed for healthy government, and the people's trust in their intrinsic competency are vulnerable and easily can be discouraged by punitive force. Health is the first principle. If government loses the grounds for its health — citizens attentively involved in public affairs — it will become diseased and fit only for wolves.

Education is the basis for the moral transformation of a society. Change is more practical and more positive when it operates persuasively through the spirit than when it operates forcefully through the body. To Dickinson, near the end of his life, Jefferson writes of the satisfaction he has in the benevolent effects of their instructive efforts when "compared with those of the leaders on the other side, who have discountenanced all advances in science as dangerous innovations, have endeavored to render philosophy and republicanism terms of reproach, to persuade us that man cannot be governed but by the rod."[44] And to John Adams, Jefferson offers this lesson from his long life of political purposes and experiences: "Bigotry is the disease of ignorance, of morbid minds; enthusiasm of the free and buoyant. Education and free discussion are the antidotes of both."[45] Education is necessary to stimulate dreams of better futures and to build effective paths to those futures. It is not needed merely to comply with the tyrannizing authority of the past.

Given the unpalatableness of the past and Jefferson's taste for change and reform, it is not at all surprising that he strongly encouraged an ongoing process of constitutional revision. Fundamentally, he was not so much supporting transformations in government as transformations in society — the moral progress of the people. Society needed to move beyond the corruptions of history to new and more just possibilities founded on nature. Given this, what is most surprising is his general satisfaction with the Articles of Confederation and the limited nature of the reforms he proposed for it. His general view was that the Articles and the thirteen state constitutions were the best in history but that even they needed continuing refinement. In August of 1787 he wrote: "I confess, I do not go as far in the reforms thought necessary, as some of my correspondents in America. . . . My general plan would be, to make the States as one as to everything connected with foreign nations, and several as to everything purely domestic."[46] Jefferson's perspective was a commonly articulated view among Antifederalists in 1787.

Specifically, he considered adjustments to the Articles on several matters. He thought the proposal to separate executive business from the Congress was appropriate, he wanted Congress to appoint an executive committee to act during the sessions of Congress in a manner similar to the way the Committee of the States was to act during congressional recesses, and he considered adjustments for matters of commerce. In general, he never challenged any basic theoretical tenet that informed the Articles. Even the matter of the power of the purse posed no stumbling block. Although the Articles of Confederation did not grant Congress taxing powers, Congress has these powers by the law of nature, and it should exercise this power within the dynamics of nature.

When two parties make a compact, there results to each a power of compelling the other to execute it. Compulsion was never so easy as in our case, where a single frigate would soon bring on the commerce of any state the deficiency of its contributions; nor more safe than in the hands of Congress, which has always shown that it would wait, as it ought to do, to the last extremities, before it would execute any of its powers which are disagreeable.[47]

Not only was Jefferson content with the framework of the Articles, he was considerably troubled by the Constitution of 1787. A letter to John Adams illustrates his reaction.

How do you like our new constitution? I confess there are things in it which stagger all my disposition to subscribe to what such an Assembly has proposed. The house of federal representatives will not be adequate to the management of affairs, either foreign or federal. Their President seems a bad edition of a Polish King. He may be elected from four years to four years, for life. . . . Indeed, I think all the good of this new constitution might have been concluded in three or four new articles, to be added to the good, old and venerable fabric, which should have been preserved even as a religious relique.[48]

Jefferson admitted to Madison that there were things about the new constitution that he liked. He liked the principle of separating powers, the requirement that taxes be initiated in the legislative house chosen directly by the people, the compromise of equal and proportional representation schemes for Congress, the opportunity for some direct elections by the people, and the combined executive/legislative form of the veto. He also told Madison what he did not like. First of all, Jefferson was perplexed by the omission of a bill of rights. The Articles did not contain a bill of rights, but the state constitutions typically did. This was the appropriate arrangement under its ordering of formal authority. However, when the foundation of formal governmental authority was shifted to the national government, state constitutional articulations of rights were no longer sufficient. Rights must be articulated and protected by the most fundamental formal governmental authority within any particular constitutional order. Jefferson, on this occasion and on repeated occasions prior to the ratification of the Bill of Rights, supported a consistent list of items that he felt were essential for a proper bill of rights: rights on religion and press, on protection from standing armies, on restriction of monopolies, on enforcement of habeas corpus, and on jury trials. "The second feature I dislike, and strongly dislike, is the abandonment, in every instance, of the principle of rotation in office, and most particularly in the case of the President."[49] And finally, the other major complaint was about the energy of government created by this new constitutional order. "I own, I am not a friend to a very energetic government. It is always oppressive. It places the governors indeed more at their ease, at the expense of the people."[50]

Nevertheless, Jefferson in the end lent his support to the new constitution. It is clear that he did so because he was true to his own principles not because of his enthusiasm for the principles of the Constitution or of those of its chief interpreters and defenders. Jefferson spoke of his "disposition to subscribe to what such an Assembly has proposed."[51] This disposition was informed by two considerations. The primary issue always was the people, their vitality and education, not the structure of governmental apparatus.

> [The people] are the only sure reliance for the preservation of our liberty. After all, it is my principle that the will of the majority shall prevail. If they approve the proposed constitution in all its parts, I shall concur in it cheerfully, in hope they will amend it, whenever they shall find it works wrong. This reliance cannot deceive us, as long as we remain virtuous; and I think we shall be so, as long as agriculture is our principle object, which will be the case, while there remains vacant lands in any part of America.[52]

It is enough to make most Federalists dizzy. Jefferson offered his willingness to support ratification of the Constitution of 1787 because of his commitment to majority rule, reason, virtue of the people, and the continued agrarian form of American life!

The other reason for Jefferson's disposition to support ratification of the 1787 Constitution is closely related to the first. The natural "manure" of a free people must be protected. The French lack "manure" in their country life and this has affected all dimensions of their life as a people. This cannot be allowed to be America's fate. A vital rural America must feed the tree of liberty from time to time with the blood of patriots and tyrants.[53] The people must remain open and vital. Opposition to change must not be the conventional response to experimentations and innovations. If it becomes the characteristic response, the people will quickly become infertile. They will lose the guidance of their natural virtue, in which case their self-correcting capabilities will be lost, and the people will lose their taste for public affairs. In either case, the public life of democracy will lose the nourishment of natural principles. Thus, change, even when its specific forms raise serious doubts, is more a friend than an enemy to a vital people.

Jefferson's willingness to support ratification because he did not want to obstruct change did not mean that he assumed a passive or indifferent role in discussions of its merits. He conducted a vigorous and extended exchange with Madison, for example, on behalf of a bill of rights. And he prepared and supported various plans to force changes on the issues of a bill of rights and rotation in office. Specifically, his thinking was similar to that of a 1788 Massachusetts plan to change the office-holding provisions and get a bill of rights in the Constitution. The general idea was to have nine states agree to the Constitution but then have the others hold out until needed changes were secured. Jefferson's continued concerns were not fired by a rigid and well-developed set of fixed requirements about the specific form government must take. In fact, just the opposite. There was an amazing amount of experimental openness about the detailed form and arrangement of governmental structures and processes. He did not confuse particulars with universals. But given his principles, it is possible that he was more accommodating of particulars than the well-being of his higher purposes warranted.

Jefferson's personal attitude also was not marked by passivity, indifference, or satisfaction once the Constitution of 1787 received the formal support of most states. His own assumptions led him to conclude that the people had seen a need for change and wisely brought it into being. This may have been a naive version of what actually happened, but it made it possible for him to do more than personally comply with his principles — he could still fully believe in their efficacy and wisdom.

> I did not at first believe that eleven States out of thirteen would have consented to a plan of consolidating them as much into one. A change in their dispositions, which had taken place since I left them, had

rendered this consolidation necessary, that is to say, had called for a federal government which could walk upon its own legs, without leaning for support on the State legislatures. A sense of necessity, and a submission to it, is to me a new and consolatory proof that, whenever the people are well-informed, they can be trusted with their own government; that, whenever things get so far wrong as to attract their notice, they may be relied on to set them to rights.[54]

Jefferson was moved to support the consolidation of the Constitution, not by his own assessment of the need for such a change but by his full confidence that it was based on a change in the disposition of the people in the states and his faith in those people. His ultimate support for the ratification of the Constitution of 1787, therefore, was based on a majoritarian theory antithetical to the theory of majority restraint at the heart of that document.

Whether it was Paine, Madison, Jefferson, or Hamilton; the Articles of Confederation or the Constitution of 1787; Pennsylvania farmers or Boston merchants; there was a commitment to an American national union. Thus, ironically, the issue of state-centered or nation-centered sovereignty did not divide Americans at the deepest level even if it was a matter of some passion. At the deepest level Americans were united — they were committed to their political union as one people. The sovereignty issue was not the fundamental divider because supporters of both major alternatives had the same objective: an appropriate, enduring union of the American people. Supporters of the Constitution of 1787 saw the union as a feat of engineering: the union had to be constructed wisely, directly, and self-consciously or else it would become another unrealized dream. Supporters of the Articles saw it as a matter of farming: it had to be nurtured; it had to grow and ripen with time, patience, hope, and trust. Even within this radical tradition there were considerable differences as to how the union was to be nurtured, as Paine and Jefferson illustrate. Paine saw the feelings of solidarity, which would lead to a new fraternity, in the ideal of the union. To place the national life directly within the context of this ideal was imperative to him. As an Englishman he had learned to cherish the national unity he challenged governmentally. On the other hand, Jefferson and most Americans had a colonial experiential base, which suggested that feelings of solidarity grow from more localized contexts. If properly cared for, those feelings would lead to union and the new fraternity too, but the terminus was more remote from both the proximate and ultimate goals — the union and the new fraternity.

In spite of Jefferson's support for the ratification of the Constitution of 1787 (although it was rather eccentric), it was not uncommon to find him numbered among the antifederalist opponents of the new political order. Francis Hopkins asked him directly if this charge was just. Jefferson's response, at one level, was a dodge. He was neither a Federalist nor an Antifederalist he said. Their form not their arguments was his reference point. They are parties and he wanted nothing to do with these curses on moral agency. "If I could not go to heaven but with a party, I would not go there at all."[55]

After ratification, however, with the Federalists in power, Jefferson was not at all bashful about expressing his distaste for the Federalists not simply because they were a party but also because of their vision of politics and their excesses in the exercise of power. To an Italian he wrote in 1796:

> In place of that noble love of liberty and republican government which carried us triumphantly through the war, an Anglican monarchical aristocratical party has sprung up, whose avowed object is to draw over us the substance, as they have already done the forms, of the British government. The main body of our citizens, however, remain true to their republican principles; the whole landed interest is republican, and so is a great mass of talents. Against us are the Executive, the Judiciary, two out of three branches of the legislature, all the officers of government, all who want to be officers, all timid men who prefer the calm of despotism to the boisterous sea of liberty, British merchants and Americans trading on British capital, speculators and holders in the banks and public funds, a contrivance invented for the purpose of corruption, and for assimilating us in all things to the rotten as well as the sound parts of the British model. . . . In short, we are likely to preserve the liberty we have obtained only by unremitting labors and perils. But we shall preserve it; and our mass of weight and wealth on the good side is so great, as to leave no danger that force will ever be attempted against us. We have only to awake and snap the Lilliputian cords with which they have been entangling us during the first sleep which succeeded our labors.[56]

I would argue that the Articles of Confederation must be theoretically understood within the context of the following assumption: that it was purposefully designed and supported by persons who believed it would provide an appropriate and just governmental form for the American political experiment. In Paine and Jefferson these assumed perspectives are explicitly expressed, even if unwittingly. They give concrete voice to the American revolutionary spirit that asserted independence and designed the first attempt to shape the American political union. Without being the narrow partisans of a particular governmental design, they articulated the latent assumptions and purposes that made the form of the Articles intelligible and attractive to most ordinary Americans during the first decade of independent life for these united states.

Jefferson's and Paine's primary purpose was not to devise a governmental invention. They wanted to reestablish an environment in which the principles of nature would again govern human society. As with the underlying principles of the Articles, they had confidence in the ordering possibilities that were the results of the intrinsic and spontaneous patterns and dynamics of human life in community. Their political ideas emphasized community, the building of communities, the equality of persons in community, and the primacy of the natural affections in leading public life to the common good. The Articles could not be seriously supported as an instrument of national union without the effectively presented idea of a natural order accessible to all persons equally, which persuasively moved society through the educated affections of the majority to a harmony of interests wherein the good of the whole is also good for each of the members of the whole. This vision relates to the limits of the Articles and to its best possibilities as well. It was a vision well known to most Americans largely because of its eloquent articulations by patriots such as Paine and Jefferson. They gave defense and vitality to the underlying theoretical vision of the Articles of Confederation even if they never were direct and self-conscious spokesmen for its outer forms and conventions.

Ideological agreement with the Antifederalists is not a prerequisite for regretting the absence of an understanding of their positive commitments. From the beginning, the name thrust upon them by their adversaries, "Antifederalist," associated them negatively with a principle that they cherished highly in their own political talk. That label inhibited their effective advocacy of federalism as they understood it and masked the transformation of the concept of federalism in the new governmental design offered by the Constitution of 1787. Yet within the dominant tradition of the American revolution, it was the Antifederalists, paradoxically, who articulated the more familiar concept of federalism, not the Federalists with their modified theory. Antifederalists, therefore, were very much positively commited to established federal norms and perspectives, just as the dynamic thrust of the Federalists reflected their deep-seated opposition to this original federal idea.

Many interpreters of the Antifederalists since the mid-1970s have developed the case for their positive perspectives and contributions: Sheldon S. Wolin, James H. Hutson, Michael A. Gillespie, Michael Lienesch, and Wilson Carey McWilliams, for example. But no one has contributed more to making the perspectives of the Antifederalists accessible to American political discourse than Herbert J. Storing. His authoritative collection of all substantial Antifederalist writings and his introductory essay, "What the Anti-Federalists Were For," are the major components of his legacy. Nevertheless, when he characterizes Antifederalists as "the champions of a negative and losing cause," who lost primarily because "they had the weaker arguments" and because they failed to develop a systematic political alternative, the positive political message of the Antifederalists is hidden.[1] In the end Storing drives his interpretation of the Antifederalists in the direction of Cecelia Kenyon's portrait of "men of little faith."[2]

Storing and Kenyon also provide an unnecessarily narrow framework for interpreting the Antifederalists, whether they are characterized as being politically negative or positive. This narrow framework is the ratification debates and issues defined by the principles of the 1787 Constitution. In this context it is quite difficult to avoid reading the Antifederalists negatively. Not only did they lose, but their voice in this debate was unavoidably one of reaction and opposition. But these ratification issues arose within a political world that already had institutional form, theoretical direction, and standards of constitutional legitimacy. Why it is intrinsically negative and an act of little faith to be advocates of that political world, to pursue the positive principles of the Declaration of Independence and to hold on to the legitimacy of the constitutional order that grew out of those principles is not self-evident.

Michael Lienesch has argued that "though they seemed to be incompetent framers, Antifederalists were in fact only framers of a different kind who on their own terms were extremely efficient."[3] "Their own terms" can be captured through an exploration of their positive political home in the Articles of Confederation.[4] The Articles grew out of a tradition of political ideas and values expressed by the Declaration of Independence that were widely accepted in revolutionary America. And antifederalism is the extension of that tradition through the Articles and into the debates about their continuing viability.

Certainly the Antifederalists were the proponents of an overtly lost cause; the Constitution of 1787 was ratified. But beyond that specific issue of overt form, who won and who lost and what was won or lost is a considerably more complicated and ambiguous matter. And however their efforts are expressed or assessed, it is simply inaccurate not to acknowledge the Antifederalists' positive commitment to a political tradition that gave Americans principles and direction before the 1787 Constitution was drafted, a political tradition that continues to have considerable vitality two hundred years after that constitution was ratified. It is a most unfortunate interpretive habit to limit understandings of the Antifederalists to the 1787 document's definition of ratification issues when the perspectives they raised were never exclusively based on the eccentricities and oppositions of that controversy. Both the form and the substance of their issues predate the Constitution of 1787 and continue to be important in American constitutional life today. Others may not share their faith and, hence, judge it to be seriously flawed; fair enough. But that does not diminish in the slightest the positive form of their own vision. In the words of Michael Lienesch:

> it is better and truer to see the Federalist founders not as so astonishingly superior to their Antifederalist counterparts, but as simply different. Federalists and Antifederalists alike were founders. . . . But they were founders of different kinds holding different definitions of founding. In large part, their views reflected dissimilar notions of political action. They also implied divergent expectations about the future. . . . These differences would devolve into heated conceptual conflict.[5]

Three students of the American nation's earliest decades, Cecelia Kenyon, Herbert Storing, and Gordon Wood, are sources of specific interpretations that add much to understandings of this era but which also have complicated positive readings of the Antifederalists' political principles. When Cecelia Kenyon examines the Antifederalists' arguments, she too asserts that "their ideas are an essential part of the American tradition."[6] But she assumes that "the American tradition" is a relatively uniform one based on the principles of the 1787 Constitution. Thus, finding antifederalist arguments at home in American politics leads her to three related conclusions: (1) that there are no significant differences in the political theories of the Federalists and the Antifederalists; (2) that both camps can be linked to the political ideas of the 1787 Constitution; and (3) that the real difference between these two groups is one of intellectual style not one of intellectual substance.

This difference of style Kenyon calls "two underlying and opposing intellectual tendencies."[7] One tendency is toward fixed ideas. It is the doctrinaire orientation that gives people "a kind of ideological security in unstable times."[8] The other inclination is a willingness, if not a will, to experiment. It reflects the empirical or pragmatic open-mindedness that sees America as "a great political laboratory."[9] The Antifederalists show the former tendency and the Federalists the latter, we are told. The Antifederalists did not understand compromise. They exaggerated differences whereas the Federalists tried to minimize them. Exploiting what Kenyon calls the advantages of a purely negative position, the Antifederalists displayed their true temperament — "being more ideologically oriented, more inflexible, more doctrinaire in their political thinking."[10]

The difficulty with Kenyon's argument is twofold. First, all distinctions have been reduced to matters of style. This argument will be challenged in the subsequent discussion of antifederalist ideas. And second, even the matters of style are not obviously as she describes them. In fact, it is much easier to distinguish between these two camps on the basis of the substance of their conflicting political preferences than on the grounds of intellectual style. Because both exhibited ideological intransigence and both exhibited an open-minded, experimental spirit, it would be inaccurate simply to reverse Kenyon's categories, making the Federalists the doctrinaires and the Antifederalists the innovators. But the Antifederalists must be seen as more than the holders of the rigidity of vision Kenyon imposes on them just as the Federalists must be seen as more than political experimenters.

Paradoxically, one of the major impediments to the Antifederalists' effective opposition to the proposed Constitution was their unwillingness to present the issues as simple either/or choices. This was much less the case with the Federalists. They presented the issue of ratification as a matter of their document or chaos and national suicide. Further, it was to be this document untouched or nothing. At best there is something anomalous about absolutizing a document praised for its innovative relativism; it offers an intriguing example of Hartz's "irrational liberalism."[11] It was the Federalists who pressed for haste, who projected life as being on the brink of disaster, and who argued for popular support because of the renown of the document's authors. That is not the spirit of fearless, open-minded, nondoctrinaire experimentation.

The Antifederalist Brutus Jr., for example, looked at two common Federalist arguments for ratification: "1st. That the men who found it, were wise and experienced; that they were an illustrious band of patriots, and had the happiness of their country at heart; that they were four months deliberating on the subject, and therefore, it must be a perfect system. 2nd. That if the system be not received, this country will be without any government, and of consequence, will be reduced to a state of anarchy and confusion, and involved in bloodshed and carnage."[12] Brutus' reply to the first Federalist argument is straightforward: "If it is good, it is capable of being vindicated; if it is bad, it ought not to be supported. It is degrading to a freeman, and humiliating to a rational one, to pin his faith on the sleeve of any man, or body of men, in an affair of such momentous importance."[13] Brutus' argument expresses a considerably less doctrinaire approach than did the Federalists' claims for submission to mere personal reputation.

The Federalists frequently sketched their contemporary circumstances in the most dire of terms. Not accepting their system of government, they claimed, would not just make matters worse — American political life would utterly fail. However, their characterizations of the contemporary conditions are amenable to empirical testing. Antifederalists judged their opponents' representations as factually inaccurate and exaggerated, which happens to be an empirical conclusion sustained by most historical analyses today. A plebian of New York in 1788 says,

> We are told, that agriculture is without encouragement; trade is languishing; private faith and credit are disregarded, and public credit is prostrate; that the laws and magistrates are contemned and set at nought; that a spirit of licentiousness is rampant, and ready to break over every bound set to it by the government; that private embarrassments and distresses invade the house of every man of middling property, and insecurity threatens every man in affluent circumstances: in short, that we are in a state of the most grievous calamity at home, and that we are contemptible abroad, the scorn of foreign nations, and the ridicule of the world.[14]

He asks people to describe honestly their personal life conditions, to consider the consequences common to the conclusion of any war, to reflect on America's actual relationships with other nations, and to describe the patterns of interactions among the states as they know them to be through their own firsthand experiences. The Federalists, he insists, have not accurately described the everyday facts of American life and are not primarily driven by those facts.

Antifederalists challenged the Federalists' dogma of disaster, but they did not formulate an alternative dogma of contentment. Overwhelmingly, they, not the Federalists, sought what James Monroe called "some middle course."[15] In a significant sense it was precisely their willingness to change that deepened their vulnerability. The typical Antifederalist position was not built on the assumption that everything was as it should be with the political system but on the judgment that there were defects in the Articles that needed remedy — Edward Randolph: "The confederation was destitute of every energy, which a constitution of the United States ought to possess";[16] Centinel: "Experience [has] shown great defects in the present confederation" and "That the present confederation is inadequate to the objects of the union seems to be universally allowed";[17] Brutus: "We have felt the feebleness of the ties by which these United States are held together, and the want of sufficient energy in our present confederation, to manage, in some instances, our general concerns";[18] the Minority of the Pennsylvania House: "The confederation no doubt is defective and requires amendment and revision";[19] an Old Whig: "It was the misfortune of these articles of confederation that they did not by express words give to Congress power sufficient for the purposes of the union";[20] a Federal Republican: "We were taught by sad experience, the defects of the present articles of confederation, and wisely determined to alter and amend them";[21] Philadelphiensis: "The powers of Congress were certainly too limited to promote the general good of the union";[22] Cornelius describes the principle defects of the Articles;[23] Consider Arms, Malichi Maynard, and Samuel Field: "Fully convinced, ever since the late revolution, of the necessity of a firm, energetic government, we should have rejoiced in an opportunity to have given our assent to such a one";[24] George Mason: "I candidly acknowledge the inefficiency of the confederation";[25] a delegate who has "Catched Cold": "That our actual confederation is defective from a want of energy. . . . That a new government is indispensable for remedying the defects of this";[26] Melancton Smith: "The defects of the Old Confederation needed as little proof as the necessity of an Union";[27] and an "Impartial Examiner": "It seems to be agreed on all sides that in the present system of union the Congress are not invested with sufficient powers for regulating commerce, and procuring the requisite contributions for all expenses, that may be incurred for the common defense or general welfare."[28] These statements are a mere sampling of perspectives common to Antifederalists throughout the union.

Almost all Antifederalists acknowledged the need for change. Although many preferred that these changes be achieved through amendment of the Articles and some called for a new Constitutional Convention with a clear and proper charge, most Antifederalists were willing to accept and work within the proposed constitutional system if it were appropriately amended. For the most part the amendments they sought were limited in number and scope and amenable to reasonable discussions. Such positions do not describe a pattern of ideological intransigence or doctrinaire paranoia. There were fears and anxieties on both sides, both sides painted the other's fears in exaggerated forms, and there were points of rigidity and accommodation on both sides. For example, most Antifederalists were willing to live with an amended Constitution. Federalists initially refused to consider amendments but subsequently accepted the possibility of them. They, however, insisted that the changes, if any, be made after ratification whereas the Antifederalists argued that the changes must precede ratification.

Antifederalists were totally perplexed by the Federalists' moderation and openness to compromise that contributed to their ability to mold the proposed Constitution but their rigid opposition to any modifications in the face of extended evaluation and deliberations. What is the virtue of responding to the pressures of the moment and to expediency but not to the questions of reflection and principle? Is that the spirit of open-mindedness? As a New York Antifederalist noted, "If the convention, who framed this plan, were possessed of such a spirit of moderation and condescension, as to be induced to yield to each other certain points, and to accommodate themselves to each other's opinions, and even prejudices, there is reason to expect, that this same spirit will continue and prevail in a future convention, and produce an union of sentiments on the points objected to."[29]

Antifederalists could not understand the haste and rigidity of the Federalists while they — Antifederalists — sought to accommodate change and remain open to working within the new constitutional order.

They saw high stakes and sensed the benefits of some revisions. It was, at least in part, prudence and practical wisdom that led them to the position that amendments must be considered prior to ratification not after.

> The amendments contended for as necessary to be made, are of such a nature, as will tend to limit and abridge a number of the powers of government. And is it probable, that those who enjoy these powers will be so likely to surrender them after they have them in possession, as to consent to have them restricted in the act of granting them? Common sense says — they will not. When we consider the nature and operation of government, the idea of receiving a form radically defective, under the notion of making the necessary amendments, is evidently absurd.[30]

Certainly an inclination to open-mindedness should not result in empty-headedness. The Antifederalists' position was neither rigid nor foolish.

The balance, restraint, and accommodation that can be found in antifederalist arguments are all the more remarkable given the Federalists' intentional violations of law and principle. The Constitutional Convention did not execute its charge. It chose to act independent of that charge with the consequence of violating its responsibilities. And it arbitrarily proclaimed illegal and unprecedented procedures and criteria for ratification. Of course Antifederalists noted and pressed these violations. But it is remarkable that they were able to center their responses in actual engagements and accommodations of the specifics of this new governmental system and not become frozen by the indecency and lawlessness of the Federalists' usurpations.

And finally, the Antifederalists knew full well that the federalist design was not fundamentally a pragmatic response to the failures of the confederacy. Twentieth-century consciousness, which suffers from acute federalist absolutism, accepts that illusion with ease. But to Antifederalists the persons and the issues were quite familiar. They were part of the debate for independence and parts of the writing, ratification, and implementation of the Articles of Confederation. The Federalists of 1787 did not so much discover a political design in their management of events as they managed events to realize their political design. In this they were only more successful than the Antifederalists. The meaningful difference between them, however, was not style or a mental inclination toward nonideological experimentations as opposed to doctrinaire rigidity. It was their advocacy for conflicting political visions composed of variant elements and distinctive balances. If antifederalism is a part of the American political tradition, and it is, it does not mean that it substantively represents nothing more than federalism and that it stylistically limits American experimentalism with its doctrinaire manner of believing what everyone else already believed. It means that the American political tradition is considerably more complex than is commonly acknowledged and that neither experimentalism nor rigidity have a single source or manifestation within its complex sources.

In his discussion of what the Antifederalists were for, Herbert Storing designates them as "conservatives." Yes, they were the defenders of the status quo. But Storing's use of conservatism, although understandable, is largely torpid. He is not pointing to a coherent conservatism of consciousness and purpose that articulates principled standards of conservative value and behavior. It is the use of "conservatism" that simply records the accidental fact of a commitment to previously existing forms and principles. This notion of conservatism results in that famous "conservative" pantheon — Herbert Hoover, Leonid Brezhnev, Adolph Hitler, Ronald Reagan, Pope John Paul II, and American children at Christmas. Acknowledging that almost everybody has some deep attachment to previously existing forms and principles is fine, but why should it be assumed that "conservative" necessarily captures a meaningful representation of the substance of their political ideas? This is especially the case with the Antifederalists. They were, on the whole, defenders of the status quo, but historicism and mere precedence were not their authoritative principles; they preferred instead the radical transformations invited by their readings of nature. And the status quo they defended was not some ancient regime but an unprecedented political experiment less than twelve years old. They were fighting for the credibility of their political innovations. The Federalists, in large measure, were trying to protect social and political traditions, institutions, and advantages established for a considerably longer time. In fairness, Storing's discussion of their conservatism does not misrepresent Antifederalists as much as it misleads contemporary understandings of them. The narrow grounds of their "conservatism" are unlikely to be recognized in the first place or maintained in the second.

Conservative is a label that misses the same aspects of novelty and innovation that get lost whenever the Antifederalists' attempts to protect the viability of their political experiment are represented as mere ideological rigidity.

Gordon Wood offers another interpretation of the Antifederalists that complicates our ability to consider their political ideas on their own terms. Wood argues that the ratification debate was not a clash of ideas but a social crisis. "The quarrel was fundamentally one between aristocracy and democracy."[31] He describes it as a conflict between the educated, propertied class and an agrarian/small town underclass — between those who looked upon the people as unfit to hold public office and those who refused to accept this imputation of inferiority. How people read the probable success of the new constitution and how they read the actual success of the Articles depended largely on their assumptions about the social character of the government's leadership. The struggle for ratification made manifest "a broad social division between those who believed in the right of a natural aristocracy to speak for the people and those who did not."[32] In spite of the "preponderance of wealth and respectability in support of the Constitution, what remains extraordinary about 1787–1788," says Wood, "is not the weakness and disunity but the political strength of the anti-federalists."[33] The vital struggle was not between the magistracy and the people but between the few and the many.

Wood constructs a significant, insightful, and largely persuasive analysis in his well-known ratification chapter, "The Worthy Against the Licentious." His argument that there was a major social crisis at the heart of this debate is well-confirmed by his thorough and thoughtful handling of the historical evidence. The danger of his argument is that it may imply the insignificance of the conflict among political ideas. The issue of the primacy of ideas or material conditions is an important one, especially for the development of strategies of change. It is also a misleading issue. Fundamental social divisions do not exist without promoting conflicting theories of explanation, justification, and recommendation. And the antagonisms between contesting political theories sort partisans into socially identifiable groups. It is a misunderstanding of social forms to see them without theoretical rationales, just as it is a misunderstanding of political theories to see them without concrete social and economic sources and consequences.

Even Plato's Socrates offered a theory that was filled with clear partisan implications for the Athens of his day. This was not the form of his theory and not its stated intent. It was the inevitable consequence of theorizing in a world where, in absolute terms, the only true knowledge is knowing that we don't know. Under such circumstances none of our choices and meanings soar purely into realms of spiritual universality. All analytical constructions are formed to one degree or another by the particularities that differentiate specific social possibilities. Thus, when the social dimensions of a crisis are taken seriously that should never suggest that the theoretical dimensions of the crisis should be taken any less seriously, and vice versa. Wood's argument affirms and develops an essential component of this episode in American constitutional history — the social element. It does not eliminate or discredit the reality and salience of this issue's theoretical elements.

The Antifederalist voices of 1787–1788 were many and varied. Wolin characterizes their voices as "the expression of diverse local narratives."[34] They spoke with a variety of emphases and balances. Some lamented bicameralism; others praised it. Some appreciated the equal representation of the states in the Senate; others condemned the Senate as an aristocratic stronghold. Some used a Lockean-style nature; others used a more Rousseauean nature. Some attacked the Constitution because it did not protect religious liberty; others decried the Constitution's secularism and elimination of religious tests for public office holding. Regional differences were also in evidence. New Yorkers, without a Bill of Rights in their state constitution, were less troubled by the lack of one in the Constitution of 1787 than were Virginians. And of course the slave trade and the three-fifths representation formula were viewed quite differently in South Carolina and Massachusetts. Nevertheless, there was a substantial consistency and focus in their assumptions, their interpretations, and their conclusions. It is appropriate to speak of the antifederalist position not because it is without discrepencies but because, like all traditions of political meanings, it maintains a consistent and broadly shared core theory.

Further, this antifederalist theory was not just a theory of criticism. It was more fundamentally a theory of advocacy. Its critiques of the Constitution of 1787 express the interplay of its positive theory of politics with the new system of government proposed for ratification. What it opposed was a direct function of what it advocated. Its political purposes were not the consequences of its attacks. Rather, the nature and direction of its critiques were the results of its positive theoretical commitments. The important issue is to identify the positive substance of antifederalist theory, not just what it is about the Constitution of 1787 that is being opposed. Antifederalists saw themselves acting within the politics of 1776 — the politics of the Articles of Confederation, the Declaration of Independence, and the whole process of justifying and achieving American political independence. There was a framework of meanings and explanations at hand that for the most part they could assume and use to inform their political perspectives. Nevertheless, much of their writings about the Constitution's proposed ratification is based upon their own view of the theoretical dimensions of the political experiment they supported and did not want to see fail prematurely or unnecessarily.[35] Their positive theoretical position can be clarified through a discussion of their use of three basic principles: nature, republicanism, and federalism.

The Antifederalists made it clear that their first principles were derived from nature, not history — what a Democratic Federalist called "principle," not "precedent."[36] "William Penn" wanted to show his readers in the *Philadelphia Independent Gazetteer* "that in laying down a political system it is safer to rely on principles than on precedents, because the former are fixed and immutable, while the later vary with men, places, times, and circumstances."[37] Nature is both good and constant, said a farmer in the *Maryland Gazette*. It should be the consulted source for principles of government and public life. When nature is consulted in preference to and with implicit opposition to history, the association of antifederalism with conservative political theory becomes more of a problem than a clarification.[38]

Nature, in addition to being the proper source of moral and political principles, is directly knowable by all persons. The order of nature is such that common sense is equal to the task of properly guiding and regulating human conduct. Nature gives inviolable rights and direct knowledge of those natural rights to all who possess them. Any just order of society or of governance must protect humanity's enjoyment of those principles to which it has a natural and, therefore, indefeasible right.[39] Republicus insists that "government should be formed on principles of equal right; [and] also that those principles should be precisely delineated and guaranteed by the most solemn sanctions."[40]

Given that nature has provided criteria for human life applicable to all persons at all times and places and has made those criteria accessible to all, it is not a bit surprising that those who held to this view asserted humanity's natural equality and freedom. "All men considered in a state of nature, before any government formed, are equally free and independent, no one having any right or authority to exercise power over another, and this without any regard to difference in personal strength, understanding, or wealth." The law of equality must guide the principles reason chooses to rule our beloved children, says a Maryland farmer.[41]

To emphasize equality was to emphasize community — the collective bonds of human life. Equality ties human beings together and gives them a positive, intrinsic bond. They have the same essential form, are guided by the same fundamental principles, and share personal interests that are common as well. Equal liberty, so much praised by the Antifederalists, is not a principle of individualistic or particularistic departures from the fabric of the whole. It is the freedom of the community to be true to the authentic natural principles of human life. All humans are born equal and possessed of unalienable rights, which natural reason shows must be honored for the safety and happiness of the people.

It is the people as a community that is the source of all political power. "They have an incontestable right to check the creatures of their own creation, vested with certain powers to guard the life, liberty, and property of the community."[42] The authority of natural principles provides the grounds for the people's self-rule. As a community of equals they author the practical means of governance and monitor their performances. Fortunately, the people not only originate civil authority and have the right, in principle, to regulate the authority they create, they possess the intrinsic capabilities sufficient to run the governmental forms they establish. The people's self-rule is complete — they are fully capable of creating and operating their own system of authority. "Honest affection for the general good and common qualifications are sufficient. Administration has always been best managed, and the public liberty best secured, when plain honesty and common sense alone governed the public affairs."[43]

Writing to the people of Pennsylvania, Centinel explains his patriotic devotion to America. He treasures the unprecedented transformation of the American political community into one that manifests the principles of nature rather than the corruptions of history. "It is here that human nature may be viewed in all its glory; man assumes the station designed him by the creation; a happy equality and independency pervades the community; it is here the human mind, untrammeled by the restraints of arbitrary power, expands every faculty: as the field to fame and riches is open to all, it stimulates universal exertion, and exhibits a lively picture of emulation, industry, and happiness."[44] Government, properly constituted, is a human institution that should seek to comply with the principles of nature. The Massachusetts constitution expressed this specific idea in a way that Antifederalists commonly supported. Government is "a social compact by which the whole people covenants with each citizen, and each citizen with the whole people, that all shall be governed by certain laws for the common good."[45]

To Antifederalists, however, the creation of government raised issues of both moral principle and political form. The concept that best expresses what the Antifederalists sought as the moral spirit of government is that of a "republic." Politically, America was to be a republic. This idea did not define or describe particular structures or procedures that government had to possess, but it signified the moral qualities that must legitimate political authority. Antifederalists used the concept of federalism to represent their thinking about governmental forms or structures. Thus, a common formulation of antifederalist affirmation and a term that wedded the language of political form to that of public morality — America was to be a "federal republic."

When Antifederalists spoke of the American republic, they associated that idea with a number of features they assumed to be essential to republican civil life. Luther Martin of Maryland stated a familiar antifederalist view of a republic's general characteristics: "governments of a republican nature, are those best calculated to preserve the freedom and happiness of the citizens. . . . Governments of this kind, are only calculated for a territory but small in its extent."[46] Centinel expresses a similar idea but with the more radical agrarian edge that was often at the core of antifederalism. He insists that the great end of a republic is "to protect the weak from the oppression of the powerful, to put every man upon the level of equal liberty."[47] Of course if the people were the sovereigns, republican government had to be accountable and had to be framed in such a manner "that all persons who are concerned in the government, are made accountable to some superior for their conduct in office."[48] Ultimately, this responsibility rested with the people. Agrippa argued that in a republic power always returns to the people. Republican government, Antifederalists insisted, protected the people's freedom and happiness, was meant for a relatively small and coherent territorial expanse, and had to be based on a system of responsibility for all parts and members of civil society.

Republican government preserved the people's freedom and happiness not simply by intent, but because of a number of the people's and their government's essential features. Three characteristics of the people and the setting for their public life had especially important republican implications. The people must strive to be and actually become virtuous. A republic exists only, says Centinel, when the great body of the people is virtuous.[49] "A virtuous people make just laws, and good laws tend to preserve unchanged a virtuous people."[50] Or, as Philadelphiensis said, "The complexion of the governing is ever the color of the governed."[51]

Antifederalists often linked the virtue of the people to a simplicity of manners, which they saw bringing energy and health to the public body or republic.[52] The substance of the people's virtue was universal in character — unerring observation and obedience to the laws of nature. Because Antifederalists cherished the principles of nature as the grounds for virtue, they had a strong faith that this virtue could actually shape the civic life of their republic. This posture is well stated by James Monroe in his address to the Virginia Convention: "I believe firmly that the body of the people are virtuous, at least sufficiently so to bear a free government; that it was the design of their Creator in forming such an order of beings that they should enjoy it, and that it is only by a strange and unaccountable perversion of his benevolent intentions to mankind, that they are ever deprived of it."[53]

A virtuous republic will be a civil order in which there is a strong attachment to public affairs and to the good of the whole. Antifederalist spokesmen insisted repeatedly that there is no hope for a free government if the people do not exhibit a "heroic love for the public good."[54] For them the authority of the people was not relevant only in original or ultimate circumstances. It represented the continuous obligation for a broad and substantial involvement of the general citizenry in a public pursuit of the common good. The end of civil authority is the common good. The foundation upon which it is to be established is the common consent of its citizens immersed in res publica. The common good in this tradition is not the sum of particular goods but the universal, which includes all particulars. Humanity's natural equality creates the basis for this happy integration of common and individual interests wherein the authentic interest of one person is directly related to the authentic interests of all. Therefore, the only standard for public life is the common one — it must serve the well-being of the whole and its constituent parts. Republicus presents it this way: "no community can possibly have any but one common public interest, that is, the greatest good of the whole and of every individual as a part of that whole."[55]

Virtue, public affairs, and the common good come together in the life of the community. Antifederalists looked upon the collective life of a civil society as a blessing. John DeWitt, for example, writing to the citizens of the Commonwealth of Massachusetts, emphasized the contributions of "civil associations, founded upon equality, consent, and proportionate justice" to American life even from its first European settlements.[56] "The people" was both a lofty concept of legitimacy and a concrete experience of daily life. "The chief blessings of society, like individuals, are fond of association, and have a mutual dependence upon each other. They form links of one chain, and are all actuated by the same cause."[57] Antifederalists were strongly committed to the assumption that an actively involved political community, serving the good of the whole, had to be organized so that the whole was accessible and intelligible to its members. Their framework for thinking was universal — nature; their framework for action was local — small, coherent, and relatively homogeneous communities. These were to be the primary political associations that gave a meaningful and practicable basis for participation and for the formation of interests that in serving all would benefit each. Paradoxically, the universal laws of nature that transcend any particular community are given vitality in the patterns of engagement and commitment in primary communities established to affirm nature's truths.

The people's freedom and happiness also are dependent on several principles necessary to guide the formation and operation of a republic. The most frequently cited of these principles by antifederalist authors were a proper system of representation, governmental simplicity, majority rule, and the political prominence of the yeomanry. Given their strong commitment to the sovereignty and active participation of the people in communities of comprehensible scale, their willingness to commit themselves to representative institutions at all is a testimony to their political realism and their openness to reasonable experimentation. The direct rule of the people, even in their primary communities, was not practical without some structure of representation. "In a free republic, although all laws are derived from the consent of the people, yet the people do not declare their consent by themselves in person, but by representatives, chosen by them, who are supposed to know the minds of their constituents, and to be possessed of integrity to declare this mind."[58] Antifederalists used a concept of "full and equal representation" to summarize the qualities they believed were required for a legitimate representation system. When the powers vested in the people are mediately exercised by their representatives, that representation, said an "Impartial Examiner" to his fellow Virginians, must be ample and complete.[59]

Representation is ample or full when it is extensive enough to include all parts of the people even if they are widely dispersed with little communication beyond their own neighborhoods. Representation is complete and equal when it gives every type of perspective within the community a voice similar to its incidence in the whole. The principle of equal representation is also important for covenants beyond the primary community. "In forming a *confederation* of *independent* republican states," says a Federal Republican, "it hath always been esteemed a fundamental law, that each state should have an equal representation."[60]

Antifederalists' insistence on a small, coherent political community was directly related to their notion of representation. And their insistence that a republic should be built within the similar manners, sentiments, and interests of a people also reflects the nature of representation as they saw it. A true representative of the people must be like the people being represented. If the people themselves are too heterogeneous and incoherent, they cannot be properly mirrored by their representatives. "The great art, therefore, in forming a good constitution, appears to be this, so to form it, as that those to whom the power is committed shall be subject to the same feelings, and aim at the same objects as the people do, who transfer to them their authority."[61] If this is achieved, a Federal Farmer argues, a meeting of representatives will articulate the same feelings, opinions, and views as an assembling of all the people.[62] The Maryland convention heard Samuel Chase argue this point as follows: "A representative should be the image of those he represents. He should know their sentiments and their wants and desires — he should possess their feelings — he should be governed by their interests with which his own should be inseparably connected."[63] A Federal Farmer used this same argument to press the importance and impact of jury trials.

Emphasis on the sympathetic association of the represented and their representatives led the Antifederalists to insist that the conditions for this attachment were not accidental and that the means for authorizing representation — elections — must be well established, carefully designed, and properly conducted. Cincinnatus, for example, speaks of elections as a fixed, fundamental right set by the constitutions of the states, not an incidental matter left to the jurisdiction of legislatures.[64] This perspective is articulated by Melancton Smith to the New York convention. "It is a truth, capable of demonstration, that the nearer the representative is to his constituent, the more attached and dependent he will be. In the states, the elections are frequent, and the representatives are numerous: They transact business in the midst of their constituents, and every man may be called upon to account for his conduct."[65]

Representation must be equal and full. The selection of representatives must be based on direct and familiar associations through procedures protected as fundamental rights. There must be sufficient numbers of representatives frequently elected who conduct their business in open amid their constituents. And representation must be limited. It is not a prerogative to be savored by a few but a responsibility that must be broadly shared. A Federal Farmer put it this way:

> A man chosen to this important office for a limited period, and always afterwards rendered, by the constitution, ineligible, will be governed by very different considerations: he can have no rational hopes or expectations of retaining his office after the expiration of a known limited time, or of continuing the office in his family, as by the constitution there must be a constant transfer of it from one man to another, and consequently from one family to another. No man will wish to be a mere cypher at the head of government: the great object . . . then will be, to render his government a glorious period in the annals of his country. When a man constitutionally retires from office, he retires without pain; he is sensible he retires because the laws direct it, and not from the success of his rivals, nor with that public disapprobation which being left out, when eligible, implies.[66]

Antifederalists took no common, fixed position on nonsuccession in office, but they did share a strong commitment to short terms with explicit limitations on eligibility to ensure review and rotation of public office holding by the people's representatives.

A straightforward, uncomplicated governmental architecture, what Antifederalists called a simple government, was another of the crucial characteristics of their free republic. This was a feature of republican politics that discouraged primary governmental organization on a broad, continental scale. A continental scale inevitably required more intricacy and elaboration of forms and procedures than what was consistent with a standard of simplicity. Antifederalists were drawn to simplicity not only by the practical issues of scale but by their moral vision, which interpreted simplicity as a reflection of the virtue necessary for the community's freedom and as a condition necessary for the vitality of nature in common life. The arguments of Republicus and Centinel capture this aspect of antifederalist understanding. "It is a well known maxim that the simpler a machine is, it is the more perfect; the reason on which it is grounded is obvious: viz, because it is the less liable to disorder, the disorder more easily discovered, and when discovered, more easily repaired and in no instance is this maxim more applicable than in the great machine of government."[67] "The highest responsibility is to be attained, in a simple structure of government, for the great body of the people never steadily attend to the operations of government, and for want of due information are liable to be imposed on. If you complicate the plan by various orders, the people will be [so] perplexed and divided in their sentiments about the source of abuses or misconduct . . . that the imposition of the people may be rendered imperfect or perhaps wholly abortive."[68]

One of the simplest of governmental principles necessary for a free republic is that of majority rule. A community of consent and equality has only to fear the loss of the majority's voice. The majority is the civil expression of both authority and legitimacy. The value of the majority in theory led the Antifederalists to value the majority's concrete manifestation in practical American life as well. That practical manifestation was the yeomanry. This appreciation of the common people as the majority was based on the assumption of their intrinsic competency. "I believe the great body of people to be virtuous and friendly to good government, to the protection of liberty and property."[69] Having already accepted an "aristocratic" principle in the form of representation, they viewed even the best practical representation in a small state to be several degrees more aristocratic than the body of the people itself.[70] Thus, it was essential that in every other respect the yeomanry remain vital, significant, and empowered for public life.

A Maryland Farmer argued that governmental order must rest on the order of society. The proper social order for the American republic must be a dominant yeomanry. They are the only persons who deserve to be designated legislators by birth. Their characteristics — independence, mildness by nature, moderation in manners, and perseverance in all honest pursuits — nourish the spirit of a republic.[71] Placing government in the hands of the majority, the yeomanry, was a major aspect of Melancton Smith's vision of the American republic.

> A representative body, composed principally of respectable yeomanry is the best possible security to liberty. — When the interest of this part of the community is pursued, the public good is pursued; because the body of every nation consists of this class. And because the interest of both the rich and the poor are involved in that of the middling class. No burden can be laid on the poor, but what will sensibly affect the middling class. Any law rending property insecure, would be injurious to them. — When therefore this class in society pursue their own interest, they promote that of the public, for it is involved in it.[72]

The Antifederalists, in a manner similar to that of Paine and Jefferson, insisted on limited government. And as with Paine and Jefferson, this feature of their ideas has been read with a more purely Lockean cast than is merited. The Lockean sense of limited government is that of negative government — a realm of pragmatism, amoral procedures, fair rules, and competent referees. The republican tradition of the American revolution projected limited but positive government. The limitation of government was a consequence of the principle of popular sovereignty and the instrumental status of all governments. All authority, natural and civil, is in the republican tradition an expression of orderliness in law, not arbitrariness in will. A profound reverence for the law is a part of the republican spirit and the source of substantial limitations on government.

Another limitation on government relates to the purposes of civil society. Human beings enter into society and in the process surrender a part of their natural liberty for the sake of their membership in civil society and its governmental protections. If they surrendered all of their natal rights they would be no better than absolute slaves to the governor and would have a radical form of unlimited government. And if they yielded up less of their autonomy than is necessary for a well-ordered community the government would be too feeble to protect them and they would be vulnerable to becoming slaves by conquest. "To define what portion of his natural liberty, the subject shall at all times be entitled to retain, is one great end of a bill of rights."[73] A bill of rights states important limits on governmental authority. Some actions and some fields of action are closed to governmental jurisdictions. They are the protected realms of natural liberty.

Antifederalist sentiment was on the side of enumerating these retained rights. Enumeration neither creates nor destroys natural rights. The basic principle is well established, they held, that the supreme power is in the people and that in all cases "they reserve all powers not expressly delegated by them to those who govern."[74] Nevertheless, the people, "and very wisely too, like to be express and explicit about their essential rights, and not to be forced to claim them on the precarious and unascertained tenure of inferences and general principles."[75] Enumeration does not create the rights that limit government, but enumeration of the most essential reserved rights in a bill of rights is advantageous in effectively limiting the authority of governments, especially centralized, comprehensive governments.

The final limitation on government that was of special salience to the Antifederalists was restrictions on coercive force. A healthy republic lives by persuasion, not force. Force compels humans; by persuasion they are drawn. Even the freest of governments supported by the greatest degree of voluntary consent will need some recourse to force to secure full obedience to the law, but the extent of this force should be as limited as possible. "In free governments the people, or their representatives, make the laws; their execution is principally the effect of voluntary consent and aid; the people respect the magistrate, follow their private pursuits, and enjoy the fruits of their labour with very small deductions for the public use."[76]

George Clinton's assertion to his fellow New Yorkers was that the surest support for republican government was through the confidence and affections of the people. Without this, government can only be maintained by force and the coercion of the sword.[77] A free republic will never use a standing army to execute its laws. It must trust in the positive support of its citizens. And this support arises from the people knowing their representatives in government, from the responsibilities of the representatives to represent the people, and from the powers available to the people to replace their representatives if necessary. Even from a practical perspective, the greater danger is to draw the cord of power too tightly. "The opinion of power in a free government is much more efficacious than the exercise of it: it requires the maturity of time and repeated practice to give due energy and certainty to the operations of government, especially to such as affect the purse of the people."[78]

This poses a great paradox. The common assumption is that coercion is the real source of governmental energy. But Candidus argued: "we have more to expect from the affections of the people, than from an armed body of men."[79] The Antifederalists' faith always was that a free government would be able to exert power far superior to that of governments dominated by principles of authority. In a certain sense government is strengthened as it limits itself and becomes limited. Correspondingly, governance becomes more effectively comprehensive if its foundation is properly parochial.

Sheldon Wolin has read the federalist victory as a victory over the differences created by strong and protected local political venues. Federalists saw these differences as fragmentations and weaknesses. To the Antifederalists they embodied health and strength. This difference of perspectives is part of the conflict between Deism and Christianity. The monotheism of Christianity so vigorously attacked by Paine was objectionable precisely because it celebrated an abstract unity rather than a wholeness manifested through a multiplicity of distinctive particulars.

In the context of parochial pluralism the challenge for Antifederalists was to strengthen the persuasive principle, because coercion was the inevitable alternative.

> Our true object is to give full efficacy to one principle, to arm persuasion on every side, and to render force as little necessary as possible. Persuasion is never dangerous not even in despotic governments; but military force, if often applied internally, can never fail to destroy the love and confidence, and break the spirits, of the people: and to render it totally impracticable and unnatural for him or them who govern, and yield to this force against the people, to hold their places by the peoples's elections.[80]

The threat was clear and ominous: if a government of influence and effectiveness secured by the affections of the people cannot be established, a government of force cannot be avoided.

Even if it was well checked and noncoercive, the limited government of a republic was to be positive in its purposes. One of the strongest and clearest statements of the positive purposes of a republic was offered to Virginians by Denatus. "The constitution of a free people ought to be formed in the best possible manner for the happiness of them, and their posterity, it ought to contain some mode, riveted through its very essence, for the present and succeeding ages, to be educated in the principles of morality, religion, jurisprudence, and the art of war."[81] Charles Turner offered an almost identical summary of positive governmental objectives to the delegates of the Massachusetts ratifying convention in February

1788.[82] Both men point to a government of more than process: a government of positive consequences as well.

Republican government has an active, positive responsibility to nurture morality, the teachings of religion (usually assumed to be any form of Protestant Christianity), the principles of natural and civil law, the provisions of the constitution, and the art of battle for the benefit of all its citizens. Perhaps the two charges that may appear to be most incongruous are those that relate to the art of war and to religion. Antifederalists, in spite of their commitment to strengthen persuasive principles as much as possible, felt that any free government was in jeopardy when the sword, no matter how restrained initially, becomes the monopoly of the state and its standing armies. "A well regulated militia, composed of the yeomanry of the country have ever been considered as the bulwark of a free people."[83] The people's skill in the arts of war was not designed to undermine persuasion but to prevent their own military incompetence from inviting the creation of an organized, permanent military force, which too easily could be used against them. This view, not a National Rifle Association–style individual prerogative, expresses the spirit and intent of the second amendment to the 1787 Constitution.

The religion issue, although complex and quite confusing in a number of respects, also reveals the positive purposes Antifederalists commonly attributed to republican government. It reflects the public, not merely individual, character of liberty in their thinking too — what several Antifederalists explicitly called "public liberty." There is not a single position on the religion issue that fairly represents all major Antifederalist views, but for many there was no contradiction in their simultaneous calls to recognize religious liberty and to foster religion in the public life of the community. Sometimes this latter issue was expressed quite crudely — demanding the elimination of papists, Mohammedans, Jews, Turks, heathens, and atheists from political participation.[84] These views reflected nothing more than conventional, parochial hatreds. Local habits and prejudices inevitably seek refuge and legitimacy in any theory that protects and authorizes principles of local preference.

However, apart from this obviously arbitrary use of the role of primary communities, most Antifederalists did not want government to dictate specific matters of conviction and doctrine, but they did want government to be informed by and supportive of the great truths of religious faith. These truths provided a foundation for the veracity of moral obligations, the legitimate bonds of community, and the understanding of nature's laws and nature's God. (Most of these spokesmen saw themselves as Protestant Christians, not as Deists, but the deistic cast to the Christianity they expressed was considerable in many cases.) The people must be free to determine matters of religious conviction separate from the determinations of public authority. Yet the government must foster the religious life of its citizens. In the *Massachusetts Gazette* of March 7, 1788, David describes this delicate relationship as he sees it working in his home state. "Never did any people possess a more ardent love of liberty than the people of this state; yet that very love of liberty has induced them to adopt a religious test. . . . Thus religion secures our independence as a nation, and attaches the citizens to our own government."[85]

The republican spirit as the Antifederalists saw it is well charted but still leaves open questions about the actual forms of governmental structures most appropriate to its unique vitality. It was in their concept of federalism and in their view of themselves as the genuine Federalists that these detailed matters of governmental structure received the most consistent attention from the Antifederalists. Most simply put, federalism had two main features according to almost all original revolutionary-era Federalists such as the Antifederalists. It involved multiple — almost always two — levels of governmental structures. And it required the formal primacy of the local community's government and the instrumentality of the general or federal government.

> To erect a federal republic, we must first make a number of states on republican principles; each state with a government organized for the internal management of its affairs: The states, as such, must unite under a federal head, and delegate to it powers to make and execute laws in certain enumerated cases, under certain restrictions. . . . A federal republic in itself supposes state or local governments to exist, as the body or props, on which the federal head rests, and that it cannot remain a moment after they cease. In erecting the federal government, and always in its councils, each state must be known as a sovereign body; but in erecting this government, I conceive, the legislature of the state, by the

expressed or implied assent of the people, or the people of the state, under the direction of the government of it, may accede to the federal compact.[86]

Antifederalists understood that a federal system constituted an enigma — the primary governments were in a sense secondary and vice versa. State sovereignty, for example, was important for the preservation of a meaningful and dynamic interaction between local and general governments precisely because in a federal arrangement the states had surrendered important dimensions of their sovereignty. State sovereignty was similar to natural rights in Antifederalists' thinking.

> As individuals in a state of nature surrender a portion of their natural liberty to the society of which they become members, in order to receive in lieu thereof protection and conveniency; so in forming a federal republic the individual states surrender a part of their separate sovereignty to the general government or federal head, in order that, whilst they respectively enjoy internally the freedom and happiness peculiar to free republics, they may possess all that external protection, security, and weight by their confederated resources, that can possibly be obtained in the most extended, absolute monarchies.[87]

To form free republics some sovereignty must be surrendered as well, but a bill of rights is needed to protect the most significant rights that have been retained. To form a federal government some of the sovereignty of free republics must be surrendered, but the principle of state sovereignty must be declared to protect the most significant powers that have been retained. The Antifederalists had their own struggles with important issues of political balance; they had to determine the right equilibrium between liberty and authority and the right equilibrium among the levels of governmental authority.

In addition to this issue of principle, federalism was important to the Antifederalists as a practical way of joining together their love of free republics bound to small territories of unified purpose with the reality of America's extensiveness and diversity, which they also recognized and valued. A confederation of republics, or federalism, united these two realities in a way that they saw as both effective and principled. As a matter of precept and practicality, the Antifederalists' concept of federalism involved a strong commitment to each state republic and to the union of republics. Their commitment to either one of these governmental forms did not detract from their commitment to the other. It was their unique understanding of federalism that joined their localism and nationalism into a political whole.

The union was not an issue for Antifederalists. They were committed to preserving the union just as they had been committed to creating the union in the first place, and they wanted to establish a government equal to the purposes of that union. Overwhelmingly, they sought to strengthen the general government in relation to the states. But they had a distinctive view of the nature and role of the states within the union. Melancton Smith's speech, delivered during the ratification debate in New York during June 1788, succinctly captures the spirit of Antifederalists on this matter. He argued that he was as strongly impressed with the necessity of a union of the states as anyone could be. Further, he was prepared to make every reasonable concession and change to strengthen the general government, willingly sacrificing anything for the union except the liberties of the people.[88] The union had to be efficient enough to serve the people, but proper service to the people required that it also had to be limited.

The most common distinction used by the Antifederalists to differentiate the roles of state governments from those of the common government was that of internal and local affairs assigned to the states and external and national affairs assigned to the general government. "The perfection of a federal republic consists in drawing the proper line between those objects of sovereignty which are of a general nature, and which ought to be vested in the federal government, and those which are of a more local nature and ought to remain with the particular governments."[89] In all cases the Antifederalists held that the state governments were the better judges of the specific circumstances and dispositions of their citizens.

The internal-local/external-national distinction typically meant that military affairs, diplomacy, and continental and international commerce were seen as the substance of the external-national dimension, although there was some variety of thinking about specific kinds of direct taxes for designated purposes. Everything else was to be retained as an internal-local matter of primary community concern. As is true of similar political distinctions of this sort (for example, separation of powers), we are presented with a differentiation considerably clearer on paper than in practical affairs of governance. Nevertheless, it guided Antifederalists' thinking and evaluations of balancing arrangements within the federal system.

Another concept used to work through the balancing of the federal system raised the issue of the union's authority. Did the union, the federal head, have the authority to operate directly upon citizens as well as upon states? Increasingly, Antifederalists answered "yes." "It is admitted that the powers of the general government ought to operate upon individuals to a certain degree. How far the powers should extend, and in what areas to individuals is the question."[90]

In general, Antifederalists' sensitivity to the protection of state governments in the federal system was not an expression of their opposition to the union or even to the strengthening of the political center of the union. They were the initial advocates of the union and actively parented its political independence. And their support for the states did not take on a doctrinaire character. They assumed the need for constitutional adjustments and were working on a variety of ways to accomplish them and to reinterpret the details of the federal association to make it more effective.

Their desire to affirm and protect state governments within federalism was directly related to their willingness to redraw the line between the primary community and the secondary community, between local and general government. They supported a more energetic government. They were willing to expand general authority and constrict local authority. They accepted the idea of direct relationships between citizens and the federal government. In the face of these changes, a strong line of defense for the state republics was equally unavoidable if the fundamental principles and characteristics of any federal equilibrium were to be preserved in a form recognizable to their principles and habits. Stripping the states of their sole political protection could only be interpreted by them as an attack on federalism in both theory and fact. Protecting the form of Article 2 was necessary to maintain a structure of decentralized power without which the Federalists' dream of a unified society governed by a strong state would prevail.

A detailed inventory of Antifederalists' complaints and criticisms of the Constitution of 1787 is exceedingly long and varied but remarkably coherent. This coherence is uncommon not only because of the variety of issues pursued but because the Antifederalists were never a coordinated national movement with a recognized common leadership. For the most part the Antifederalists communicated through the speech of undistinguished men in thirteen different state locales. Their unity of voices is in some senses an artifact of contemporary scholarship more than a feature of their own literal speaking. Nevertheless, it is unlikely that mere negativism or a doctrinaire temperament of opposition to change could have achieved such an integration of perspectives under these conditions of radical fragmentation.

The cohesiveness of their criticism of and opposition to the ratification of an unamended constitution is a consequence of a reasonably well-developed, positive political theory that also was the tacit paradigm for the majority of ordinary citizens in most states of the union. Their organization and communication was fragmented and isolated, yet their arguments cohere because they are informed by a set of positive political ideas that were familiar to and strongly supported by large numbers of Americans. The issue is not the adequacy or propriety of their views. It is a matter of a fair reading — of knowing what they opposed or questioned and how this related to who they were and what they were for. In this respect they are no different than the Federalists. The Constitution of 1787 must be read and has been read on the basis of what its authors and supporters were for, not what they were against. Analogously, the Antifederalists knew what it meant to stand in the political tradition of 1776 and how that tradition differentiated itself from the one associated with the events and the document of 1787. They deserve to be read accordingly.

The illegitimacy of the Constitutional Convention's ignoring its charge in both substance and process was a fundamental affront to the sovereignty of the people. Even if it used the name of the people, the convention was not authorized by the people to do what it did. Governmental authority reverts to the people, not to a convention organized by the authority of the very government to be overturned. "The right of originating a system for consolidating the union, belonged only to the people, but the federal Convention have taken possession of it, when called for a different purpose, and can any one say their proceedings are not founded in usurpation?"[91]

Neither virtue nor the general welfare were evidenced or honored by the new system when examined by the Antifederalists. When they studied the schemes for representation, examined the tools for coercion, analyzed the limitations on the states, and pondered the absence of enumerated rights, they saw the operation of ambition, power, reputation, status, and wealth. The common good, public virtue, and natural liberty had no discernible place. The Federalists, for example, when they argued that the new constitution should be supported because of the stature of its authors, did nothing to diminish the Antifederalists' fear that they were being confronted primarily by individual ambition, not an alternative route to the good of the whole. "Whether it be calculated to promote the great ends of civil society, viz. the happiness and prosperity of the community; it behoves you well to consider, uninfluenced by the authority of names."[92]

The absence of a bill of rights was a deep concern for Antifederalists. Federalist resistance to adding a bill of rights, after they failed originally to include one, was even more alarming. It was essential that the most important retained natural rights be enumerated in the house of sovereign political authority. Article 6 of the proposed constitution changed that house, making it imperative that these rights be articulated within the new setting of sovereignty — the federal government. Meaningful state protections within the system of the Articles were at best of unsure standing in this new order. Antifederalist commitment to free republics required that this issue of public liberty be resolved without mystery or ambiguity. "It is evident, that the general government would necessarily annihilate the particular governments, and that the security of the personal rights of the people by the state constitutions is superseded and destroyed; hence results the necessity of such security being provided for by a bill of rights to be inserted in the new plan of federal government."[93] This is a reasonable and principled position. If governmental arrangements that have protected basic values are changed, then an alternate means to ensure these values must be found. Federalists had great difficulty engaging this issue even on these benign grounds.

Other issues also troubled antifederalist sensibilities. The secrecy of the Philadelphia convention and the absence of a record of deliberations did not suggest either a government or a group of leaders who knew their place or who genuinely believed in an effective sovereignty of the people or in the political competency of common people. Slavery and the slave trade, although not the same issues for all Antifederalists, were deeply disturbing issues for Antifederalists in the nonslave states. Whether slavery could be eliminated in the short term was doubtful, but it was not just another practice to be included and bargained over within the shared affirmations of political union. Slavery was an inappropriate ground for a just alliance. It is "inconsistent with the genius of republicanism, and has a tendency to destroy those principles on which it is supported, as it lessens the sense of the equal rights of mankind, and habituates us to tyranny and oppression."[94]

Other antifederalist criticisms were centered around four issues of great significance to their theory of politics: the status of the states, the nature of representation, the complexity of the constitutional design, and the balance of persuasion and force in the new political plan. Antifederalists interpreted the federalism of the new constitution as a pretense. The Constitution would effectively abolish or trivialize state governments, making a genuine federal arrangement impossible. "It is beyond a doubt that the new federal constitution, if adopted, will in a great measure destroy, if it do not totally annihilate, the separate governments of the several states. We shall, in effect, become one great Republic.... From the moment we become one great Republic, either in form or substance, the period is very shortly removed, when we shall sink first into monarchy, and then into despotism."[95] The problem was reconfiguring the relationship of state governments and the general government. The new constitution was, as they saw it, the complete abandonment of the federal principle and the adoption in its place of a consolidated national plan of government.

The states' only effective ground for limiting the encroachments of consolidated power — their formal sovereignty — had been taken from them. Further, the national sovereignty of the constitutional order is expressed as a compact of all the people not as an association of the states. Thus, it not so much establishes a supreme power over the states as it eliminates their relevance. The supreme power is established over the individuals within the states. Thus, to the Antifederalists the Constitution of 1787 did not offer a form of federalism. It proposed a consolidated government unfriendly to the direct and concrete expression of the people in their local communities and threatened to undermine and eventually corrupt the peoples' liberties. In this basic respect, and in many other related areas ranging from provisions for civil trials to the creation of a splendid Federal City, the Constitution of 1787 was interpreted as an expensive and ambitious scheme that would undermine federalism, threaten liberties, and depress the general public's knowledge of and enthusiasm for public affairs.

If federalism was lost, could republicanism be saved? Antifederalists saw few grounds for encouragement. The 1787 Constitution's representation system was a dramatic departure from the principles and practices of free republics as they had been previously articulated by Americans. Republican principles of representation required a sufficiently ample representation, specifically defined terms of office (most commonly for one year), limitations on the number of consecutive terms of office for which any person was eligible (thus guaranteeing the rotation of public office holding), and means of recall from office. On every count, the Constitution of 1787 violated these standards. Two persons would represent whole states in the Senate; a single executive would not have the counsel of a committee of the states; presidents would serve for four years, senators for six, and nonelected judges for life; all elected officials were continuously eligible for reelection; no provisions for popular recall were authorized; only the impeachment of executive and judicial officers was possible, and that by the legislative body most remote from the people; juries, the representatives of the people in court proceedings, were not secured in civil cases; and treaties could be ratified without the approval of the peoples' representatives in Congress or in the states.

Brutus called this governmental pattern a system of nominal representation.[96] And the inclusion of slaves in the calculus of representation made it worse than nominal — it was false and corrupt. Slaves were not granted three-fifths of the regular standing and benefits of representation. Rather, slave owners were offered greater representation; they were politically rewarded. The morality of slavery per se was not the only issue.

Antifederalists found it no easier to justify this built-in inequality of representation. To add insult to injury the 1787 Constitution was seen as defective regarding the conduct of elections. The control given to Congress over the time, place, and manner of holding elections threatened the integrity of suffrage itself, thought Patrick Henry.[97] Under the pretense of regulation, free elections could be annihilated. If free elections were jeopardized, the practical mechanism for achieving proper representation would be lost.

Antifederalist eyes could not examine this pattern and avoid seeing a social agenda as well as a governmental one. This was an aristocratic scheme to dissociate, isolate, and immobilize the yeomanry. Government was made to be remote and privileged. The 1787 Constitution, they suspiciously charged,

> has no provision for securing the eligibility of good men. If good members without much property should oppose the wealthy but unprincipled ones in Congress, and prevent their passing oppressive acts, such as revenue-acts, calculated to promote speculation — to protect defaulters — and to plunder the people, (as this system undoubtedly will of all their property) will not those unprincipled members exert themselves to pass an act, requiring for senators and representatives so high a qualification of property, as to exclude for ever from Congress, the good men who have not great estates? Surely they will.[98]

Nothing in the Constitution's governmental design could contain their suspicions when every precept of ample and complete representation appeared to be abandoned — purposively abandoned.

The complexity of the 1787 Constitution's governmental design offered no countervailing solace. Its lack of simplicity was discussed on three grounds. First, it was seen as too complex — as a "labyrinth of innovation."[99] Antifederalists saw an intricate contrivance too mysterious to be observed much less understood by mere common sense. Second, its complexity invited the development and pursuit of secret ambitions. It was a system, a Columbian Patriot found, "marked on the one side with the dark, secret and profound intrigues, of the statesman, long practiced in the purlieus of despotism; and on the other, with the ideal projects of young ambition, with its wings just expanded to soar to a summit."[100] And third, its dark complexity was deepened by its purposeful ambiguities.

"The ambiguity of the whole, is its greatest fault. I remember, in a public court yard, to have heard a baptist preacher make three score and sixteen objections to it, and grunt and condemn it from end to end — and within five minutes a practitioner of the law, to defend it most vociferously from end to end. A blacksmith at my elbow, pitied them both — I really thought then, what I still think, that we all knew very little about it."[101] Separating powers and then mixing together the very powers that were just separated cannot avoid introducing ambiguity. What does a vice president do? How will the Congress define the federal judiciary? Will presidents pardon persons who have not been convicted? (They never dreamed that there might be questions about presidents pardoning persons who have not been charged!) Simplicity — and with it, intelligibility and accessibility to the common people was lost — or such was the antifederalist perception of the 1787 Constitution.

Antifederalists were unable to find patience or a positive place for persuasion in the Constitution of 1787. Charles Turner said he could not adopt a government that wears the face of power without giving it especially close scrutiny.[102] When government does not have and, more importantly, does not seek the confidence of the people, it can only be expected to be executed by force.[103] The instruments of coercion are in clear view. Military power no longer has the civilian control it had under the Articles. And, most ominously, the possibility of a standing army during peace time is now permitted. To many Antifederalists the Constitution of 1787 "substitutes fear for virtue, and reduces men from rational beings to the level of brutes." If Americans "submit their necks to the yoke, they must expect to be governed by the whip and goad."[104] The dilemma posed by the 1787 Constitution went full circle for the Antifederalists. Government designed by the "harpies of power" cannot honor the people, expect their virtue, or protect their liberties.[105]

Antifederalists as a whole were more accommodating than they have been given credit for being and more accommodating than one might have expected them to have been had their own positive tradition of political ideas been acknowledged. Their opposition to the ratification of an unamended constitution does not in itself reveal who they were and it does not define their importance to future generations. Their import and identity both precede and succeed the drafting and ratification of the

Constitution of 1787. It was their vision of politics that pressed for and structured American independence, shaped America's first constitutional plan, and transformed America's second constitutional order beyond its native intentions and possibilities. The spirit of their political ideas, in American constitutional terms, was central to the theoretical vitality of the Articles of Confederation. Confidence in the underlying and informing principles of the original American revolution permitted them to accept considerable modifications of political process and structure. Consequently, the expression of Antifederalists's criticisms of the 1787 Constitution was always animated by a positive sense of their own distinctive political values and purposes.

The Articles in a Tradition of 8
Conflicting Democratic Ideas

Louis Hartz, in his benchmark study, *The Liberal Tradition in America,* describes the setting for American political ideas this way:

> American political thought ... is a veritable maze of polar contradictions, winding in and out of each other hopelessly: pragmatism and absolutism, historicism and rationalism, optimism and pessimism, materialism and idealism, individualism and conformism. But, after all, the human mind works by polar contradictions; and when we have evolved an interpretation of it which leads clearly in a single direction, we may be sure that we have missed a lot. The task of the cultural analyst is not to discover simplicity, or even to discover unity, for simplicity and unity do not exist, but to drive a wedge of rationality through the pathetic indecisions of social thought. In the American case that wedge is not hard to find. It is not hidden in an obscure place. We find it in what the West as a whole has always recognized to be the distinctive element in American civilization: its social freedom; its social equality.[1]

In this statement Hartz describes the primary objective of this study — the articulation of a "wedge of rationality" within American political ideas — and summarizes the circumstances under which this objective must be pursued — "a veritable maze of ... contradictions, winding in and out of each other hopelessly." I have centered my interpretation of American political life and thought in its broadly democratic context, a context without canon and feudal law but shaped by persistent patterns of conflict for which no singly dimensioned explanation suffices. This is a political environment marked by the tensions between its two great democratic values — the love of liberty and the love of equality. My focus, therefore, has been on the paradoxical character of a hybrid tradition of democratic assumptions, values, and purposes. Viewed within the tensions of their composite setting, American democratic ideas are simultaneously consensual and divisive — a source of considerable continuity and stability, and a source of conflict and change.

For example, most Americans today embrace a similar variety of political perspectives. They commonly embrace elements such as a participatory understanding of politics; a decentralization of power; a significant measure of social equality; a respect for majoritarian preferences; a commitment to freedom for individuals and capital; an orientation to politics shaped by operational and economic efficiencies; a centralization of initiative and authority; and a preference for activist, rational leadership. Although all of these values and perspectives creep into the political thinking of most Americans, this commonality is misleading. First, these elements have heterogeneous sources and point to heterogeneous consequences. They do not form an easily integrated whole. And, second, these and other similarly heterogeneous views are combined and expressed in an incredible variety of ways, which differentiate individuals and groups from other individuals and groups, from themselves on other issues, and from themselves on the same issue at other times. As a result, even though the theoretical elements are broadly shared, controversies and conflicts result that hide an awareness of the shared commonalities among adversaries and, equally, hide an awareness of the intrinsic conflicts threatening allies and alliances.

In prominent "liberal" and "conservative" positions, for example, there is a similar tension — a willingness to strengthen the control of central, state power for the purpose of getting government off our backs. Liberals who desire private choice and cultural diversity typically focus their efforts on strengthening the authority of the national government, expecting it to be the agent of change and protection. And conservatives may offer protections from taxes but not from deficits; may prefer the private sector for economics but not for matters of moral and aesthetic choice; may celebrate the free marketplace but are virtual statists on defense, an aggressive foreign policy, and law and order. And one must feel a certain amount of compassion for as well as irritation with persons in corporate America, regardless of their ideology, who five to six days a week foster an intensification and centralization of power in the name of a rationalistic, technological creed that is directly contrary to their simultaneous nostalgia for traditional notions of morality, piety, and family.

I have argued that the most basic constitutional tradition of American politics — that by which American public life is constituted — is a hybrid tradition or a compound of competing democratic ideals. In fact, it is this hybrid tradition of democratic tensions that Americans use to interpret the meaning of the Constitution of 1787, rather than the more literal meanings of the Constitution of 1787, which define the limits and forms of American democracy. Ironically, this circumstance reenforces the impression of the 1787 document's great practical wisdom because the document has been able to succeed even when its own assumptions and purposes have been denied, discredited, displaced, or transformed.

For example, one of the strongest arguments for the writing and ratification of the U.S. Constitution was that a stronger and more vigorous central government was needed to promote commercial development and success. In addition to promoting this intention, the 1787 document grants Congress the principles by which this purpose can be pursued and achieved — power over "interstate commerce" coupled with a "supremacy clause," for example. Nevertheless, throughout the greater portion of American history the functional framework in which American commercial successes were achieved is hauntingly similar to the one "repudiated" by the Constitution.

American capitalism developed primarily through state laws and the legal interpretations of state courts. Property laws and corporation laws are state laws. And in the nineteenth century virtually all significant banking laws were state laws, as were legal standards relating to markets, contracts, credit, and insurance. Furthermore, when Congress was not self-limiting in executing its commerce powers, the Supreme Court was busy defining "interstate commerce" so restrictively and "intrastate commerce" so broadly that local conditions and control were protected from the actions of Congress. Clearly, something considerably more complex than what is stated in the 1787 Constitution was at work. The American constitutional tradition again manifests itself as more complex than is suggested by the specific rationales and forms of the second constitutional document. Yet there is an apparent satisfaction with the sufficiency of the

U.S. Constitution as the basis for political understandings, even though
what has "worked" is sometimes remarkably dissimilar to its best known
rationales. Furthermore, there is no clear awareness that the principles
central to the tradition of the Articles have any practical relevance to
American political understandings even though there are striking manifestations of norms and practices directly related to that tradition.

Interpretations of the original intentions and specifications of the Bill
of Rights provide another significant example of this muddled constitutional orthodoxy. The most common "story" about the Bill of Rights
implies that it is a grand federalist document, integral to the original
principles of the 1787 Constitution, designed to offer special protections
for the freely competitive individuals of Madison's and Locke's political
theories. However, this formula distorts both the historical and the
theoretical origins of the Bill of Rights and in the process makes it more
difficult to understand the issues that have been central to the evolution
of its meaning. The Bill of Rights is the great, enduring legacy of the
Antifederalists. Its addition to the constitutional form was insisted upon
as a remedy to perceived deficiencies, ambiguities, and errors in the 1787
Constitution. And its positive purpose was to protect the choices and
established traditions of popular majorities — the people — in the more
localized political settings of the states. What the Bill of Rights has become
for many Americans today should not be casually read back into 1791.

The First Amendment does not offer protections for individual
citizens against government, only against Congress. By only limiting
Congress, state and local community preferences are protected. The
current Miller pornography standard permitting limitations of speech
based on local community standards makes no sense in terms of the rights
of individuals qua individuals in their relationships with government. It is
quite intelligible, however, in terms of an intent to protect the choices of
local communities in their relationships with national governmental
authority. Similarly, the Second Amendment does not assert a National
Rifle Association–style right of individual gun possession. It claims the
right of the people (not individual citizens) to protect their society (not
their private intentions and purposes) through the formation of a "well
regulated militia" (not through hunting, recreation, and criminal attacks).
Antifederalists believed that in the original Constitution a peoples' army

had been displaced by a professional military establishment. Therefore, they felt the need to reassert the principle of a citizens' defense force and to assert protections against the possible excesses of a centralized and professionalized coercive authority. These citizens' protections were extended in the Third and Fourth Amendments. The Third Amendment addresses the quartering of soldiers, and the Fourth Amendment specifies security against unwarrantable searches and seizures.

Amendments Five, Six, Seven, and Eight explicitly apply familiar standards of state and local criminal procedures to the new national authority. In the Ninth Amendment the people, in effect, insist that the process of creating civil rights — enumerating their natural rights in the civil context — shall not jeopardize the full range of their natural rights, specifically the rights retained by the people separate from any enumeration. And finally, Amendment Ten specifically claims for the states or the people all powers not specifically assigned to the national government or prohibited to the states.

Even after the Fourteenth Amendment applied the "privileges and immunities" of citizenship, "due process of law," and the "equal protection of the laws" to the states in 1868, there was little change in either the interpretation or application of the Bill of Rights. Deference to the states, not to individuals, was still the rule. The Slaughterhouse Cases, for example, recognized no obligation to protect individual citizens against abusive actions of state governments. And when the Supreme Court protected state segregation practices in *Plessy v. Ferguson* in 1896 there was further evidence that the civil liberties of the Bill of Rights were not soon to be applied to the states. Consequently, the Bill of Rights functioned more consistently as a protection for the states and their more localized majoritarian preferences than as a protection for individual citizens.

It was not until 134 years after the Bill of Rights was ratified that the first of its specific provisions was applied to the states. In 1925 the First Amendment's protection for free speech was applied to state jurisdictions. This launched the slow, fifty-year process of modifying the meaning of the Bill of Rights. To understand both the historical and contemporary issues relating to the Bill of Rights' role, a homogenized federalist ideology will not do. There has been a mixed tradition fed by divergent sources. The explanatory framework used to analyze political life in the

United States must make it possible to access this mixture, with its unique tensions, and make it intelligible. It must explain why the Bill of Rights has been and continues to be the ground for protecting both individual and communal claims, minoritarian and majoritarian principles.

The political fate of the Antifederalists, as Jefferson made clear in his First Inaugural Address, was not determined by their conversion to the principles of the Constitution of 1787. Instead, political circumstances gave them a grand opportunity to animate the forms of government created by the 1787 Constitution with a new political vision and spirit — the old political vision and spirit of America's founding. The legacy has been a composite political tradition.

There are obvious and immediate difficulties faced by a mixed constitutional tradition that is represented by a document conceptually homogeneous in its specific articulations. Under these circumstances the compound character of the constituting order becomes more difficult to identify and discuss because, however much its characteristics are exhibited in national life, they are not reflected in the explanatory document. The challenge created by these circumstances is to find a way of expressing the tacit or implicit features of the constitutional tradition more overtly and explicitly. American democracy has been constituted by the theoretical elements directly represented in the formalized structures of its political institutions and by the explicit argumentation of its constitutional document. In addition, alternative theoretical elements — indirectly, informally, implicitly, and functionally present — have contributed to the shaping of American democracy. The challenge for interpreting and understanding American democracy, then, is to provide a framework that examines these alternative tacit elements more clearly and systematically so that their interactions with the overt tradition are more fully articulated.

It is in the context of struggling with this question that I have turned to the Articles of Confederation — both as a document defining specific governmental forms and as a political metaphor representing a distinctive set of democratic perspectives. Just as the Constitution of 1787 means so much more to American politics than its denotative forms specify, so too the meaning of the Articles is deeper than its most specific purposes and forms. It represents — sometimes concretely, sometimes symbolically —

the tacit tradition that has been incorporated into the constituting of American democratic life. It is significant not as an end in itself but as an essential ingredient of the whole. It is significant not as an alternative to the Constitution of 1787 but as its thinking has become incorporated into the meaning of that document. It is significant not as a conscious, isolated rallying point for Americans but as an implicit source of alternative perspectives within their acknowledged heritage. In short it is significant because it gives concrete representation to many of the tacit dimensions of America's hybrid democratic theory.

Although this study asserts a composite democratic tradition in America, it has focused its attention on only one part that mixture. This imbalance is not a reflection of either personal theoretical preferences or judgments of relative significance. In a genuinely mixed tradition all components of its interactions must be taken seriously and the compound must be appreciated as it finally eclipses its distinct sources. In the American case there is a significant impediment to appreciating the mixed character of its political thinking: the hidden role of a tacit tradition. Therefore, this study used the Articles of Confederation as both a form and a symbol by which the tacit order constituting American politics can be brought into overt interactions with the more familiar, because overt, aspects of America's constitution.

The assumptions, values, and purposes of the Articles of Confederation did not die in 1789. They are still part of the dialogue that expresses the political energies of the American people. They represent a democratic tradition that builds from the primacy of the people rather than from the formal organization of authority in government. The politics that tradition proposes not only originates in its popular base, it can only be practical if its operations come from that base. Power is not the foundation of its politics but a by-product of political life. Its politics does not define power or merely impose it. It achieves it through the activities of a public-spirited, virtuous people. Government as well is not sustained by its architecture but by the qualities of its constituent people. These are assumptions Americans used to overthrow colonialism and to design indigenous political authority. And they are assumptions and perspectives that Americans continue to use as they deal with the political controversies of the 1990s.

The Articles' political vision, not only the ideology of market econ-
omies, has fed the American search for political cohesion without coercive
power at the center or the top of governmental structures. The power of
a whole and healthy people has been frequently assumed and, perhaps,
even more frequently preferred. It is not merely the Articles' losing the
battles of 1787–1789 that accounts for its tacit place in America's constitutional order. Even in 1776 and in 1781 it projected the power of a tacit
order; that is, even as the overt authority, it made authority covert. It was
to be the character of the people not institutional forms that would
determine the success of America's perpetual union. For example, its
understanding of republicanism was not based on overt structural forms
and procedures. It depended upon implicit conditions: the moral foundation of a good people. Consequently, government was not primarily a
tool of coercion necessary for the purposes of stability and order but a
means by which an elevated people could express and realize their high
aspirations.

Sovereign power — which is at the heart of coercive power — was
centered in more localized contexts precisely because there it could be
watched, checked, and even transformed. It could be transformed by being
tied to the purposes of a community of equals. Processes of consent could
limit government abuse and encourage the transformation of power
according to the intrinsic principles of nature. Thus, not only did the
Articles offer an organic/developmental model for American politics in
its own time, it continues to offer implicit alternatives to the mechanistic
politics of the 1787 model in our time.

Wendell Berry, a twentieth-century antifederalist poet, essayist, and
farmer, adheres to a relatively direct and pure form of the Articles' model.
Berry speaks to culture, the places where humans live and are nurtured.
Politics, on the other hand, embodies the places and processes of coercion,
control, and manipulation. The contemporary preference for control has
led to formal organizations of artifice that increasingly violate the informal order of nature. Berry hopes to raise the implicit principles of nature
to self-conscious prominence to save them from destruction, not just from
misunderstanding or neglect. He points to an America and a way of
viewing life in America very much related to that offered by the Articles
of Confederation and the tacit tradition it symbolizes.

Berry's essay, "A Defense of the Family Farm," is especially exemplary of this pattern. For him, a family farm is both a particular place and a metaphor for the general conditions necessary for a good life. It is a place of familiarity — a place small enough to be known and cared for by a single family, where there is a long connection between the family and the farm, where the family members are the workers who are also in charge, and where intimate knowledge, attention, and care protect against abuse. In the long run, this familiarity repays the family and the whole nation, giving both a present and future ground for health and satisfaction. It is Berry's view that

> the justifications of the family farm are not merely agricultural; they are political and cultural as well. The question of the survival of the family farm and the farm family is one version of the question of who will own the country, which is, ultimately, the question of who will own the people? Shall the usable property of our country be democratically divided, or not? Shall the power of property be a democratic power, or not? If many people do not own the usable property, then they must submit to the few who do own it. They cannot eat or be sheltered or clothed except in submission. They will find themselves entirely dependent on money; they will find costs always higher, and money always harder to get. To renounce the principle of democratic property, which is the only basis of democratic liberty, in exchange for specious notions of efficiency or the economics of the so-called free market is a tragic folly.[2]

Berry's special lament is that the family farm is failing because it belongs to a set of values that are failing. There is no saving the family farm apart from saving the values, traditions, and way of life to which it is attached. It is in jeopardy because of the increasing power of alternate beliefs that reduce value to quantity, that transform relationships into specialized and mechanical interactions, and that define communities as nothing more than settings for competition. The only standard becomes money and both personal and communal life become increasingly dissociated from morality and religion. In a nutshell, "we are not very religious and not very democratic, and THAT is why we have been destroying the family farm for the last forty years — along with other small local enterprises of all kinds."[3] This failure of values is something we have done to ourselves.

> One could argue that the great breakthrough of industrial agriculture occurred when most farmers became convinced that it would be better to own a neighbor's farm than to have a neighbor, and when they became willing, necessarily at the same time, to borrow extravagant amounts of money. They thus violated the two fundamental laws of domestic or community economy: You must be thrifty and you must be generous; or, to put it in a more practical way, you must be (within reason) independent, and you must be neighborly.[4]

If Americans have failed themselves, then they must find ways to renew themselves. They must concentrate on redemption, not on salvation. Government, for example, cannot be expected to bail them out. They must look to themselves and to their tradition to become reinvigorated. If they do this they will remake rural communities in which they will trust each other and help each other and in which they will expand their competencies and limit their dependencies. Berry ends his discussion of family farms with an endorsement of what he calls "Amish principles" as distinct from Amish forms. These principles call for Americans to anchor their lives in family and local communities, to practice neighborliness, to maintain the domestic arts, to use technology without displacing humans or nature, to establish a comprehensible scale to life, to foster deep bonds with our children, and to esteem life both as a practical art and a spiritual discipline. This has been the creed of the American yeomanry and it reflects principles significant to the vitality of America's tacit forms. Just as one imagines that these principles have been overwhelmed, they resurface, finding novel and unexpected ways to reassert themselves. Americans must find ways to recognize more straightforwardly the subtle but powerful aspects of America's tacit tradition within the larger story of American national life.

Berry's view is helpful in this respect because he gives a strong contemporary voice to these tacit ideals. At the same time, he may be too easily dismissed as a quaint, exotic agrarian. Most Americans are unlikely to be convinced that it is their lot to return to small-scale, local structures of life. Nevertheless, Berry and the tacit tradition he reflects can have considerable value. America faces complex difficulties and challenges. It also possesses a complex democratic tradition that it can draw upon in shaping its responses. The more aware Americans are of the constitutional tradition's possibilities, the more potential tools they will have available with which to tackle the problems.

Sheldon Wolin characterizes the mixture of democratic principles in American political life as its unique complexity, a complexity from which it benefits. Without this complexity, America suffers. "It's a complication of centralization, in terms of decentralizing things, and it's a complication of decentralization, in realizing the centralized things that have to be done. Clearly, you need both. The problem is the movement away from a federal, decentralized system to an increasingly, almost hopelessly, overcentralized system, so that the whole emphasis has fallen in the one direction."[5]

This complex, hybrid tradition of American democracy has been largely unidentified, even if continually experienced, not only because of its tacit elements but because the mixture does not represent anyone's design or intention. In this sense it is profoundly irrational. Perhaps Americans are not more reflective about their political ideas because they sense the distress that could come with a more thoughtful attentiveness. How can one make sense of the intellectual basis for choices when (1) the movement most associated with private sector primacy and maximal liberty for the individual defines pornography according to local community standards and finds it objectionable to establish a constitutional principle of equal opportunity under the law for both male and female citizens and when (2) the movement associated with stronger and more active government and majoritarianism is less willing to support the military capabilities of government and more insistent on particular protections for homosexuals and persons accused of crimes and on choices for pregnant women?

The more carefully we look, the more American democracy appears to be closer to a surrealist's collage than an intelligible order. Our tendency — both intellectually and intuitively — is to want American democracy to fit together, make sense, and be of whole cloth. Thus, we either address only part of the American democratic order and speak of it as a pure tradition or we perceive American democracy's dual tendencies and, typically, press for a devolution of it into a purer, if not pure, single tradition. This study has argued that these perceptions are inaccurate and inadequate. The tradition of American political ideas does not express a single pattern of democratic life. There clearly are broad and deep patterns of competing impulses that are as central to the fundamental shape of American political debates today as they were to the American political founding more than two centuries ago. Furthermore, as American politics has evolved, these competing impulses have become increasingly bonded together within a mixed tradition and decreasingly available for differentiated study and pure, principled choice.

Nothing symbolizes this compound of assumptions, argumentations, and purposes better than the Reagan-Bush decade, which allowed Americans to commit themselves simultaneously to the classical principles of entrepreneurial capitalism and negative government and to the imposition of majoritarian habits and prejudices without experiencing the slightest sense of discontinuity. Consequently, the political alternatives that engage the attention of most Americans today are not consistent and clear alternatives such as those offered by Wendell Berry. Instead, today's political issues and choices are shaped by the diversity of ways in which the elements of a compound tradition can be arranged and rearranged. This creates a politics that looks like nonideological experimentalism, but the appearance is deceiving. The experimentation is a direct consequence of the unique character and power of America's dominant political ideas, not of their absence.

Even if the American democratic tradition does pattern itself in a way similar to what is claimed here, there are bound to be considerable differences in the evaluation of this pattern. My view is that, on balance, the tensions of this mixed democratic tradition have been beneficial for American political life. Let me explain the basis for this judgment. America's hybrid theory of democracy has been salutary, first, because its complexity provides an ample foundation for richly varied combinations of political ideas pointing to a considerable range of political purposes and implications. Within these various combinations, nevertheless, the specific elements tend to function with a patterned consistency. The variety is primarily a consequence of which elements are combined and how they are combined. The functional patterning within these varied combinations of the diverse elements of American democracy can be summarized as follows.

The political ideas most directly associated with individual liberty and the governmental structures of the Constitution of 1787 make up the part of the mixture that is most easily identified and, thus, most frequently emphasized and discussed. Obviously, the ease of identifying these elements is directly related to their overt status. They are most prominent in shaping the formal structure of America's basic governmental institutions and processes. Because of the overt authority of the Constitution of 1787, its ideas are especially powerful in shaping political consciousness and in expressing explicit intentions. Consequently, this part of the hybrid has dominated the definition of formal political life and given form to the conventional understandings of authority in democratic America. Americans have relied most on these ideas when their reading of an issue or a circumstance suggests to them the primary need for order and/or continuity.

On the other hand, the political ideas associated with the egalitarianism of purposeful communities and the decentralized governmental system of the Articles of Confederation constitute the part of the hybrid frequently unrecognized and seldom explicitly emphasized. The neglect of these ideas is a function of their covert status, not of their absence or lack of vitality. The primary manifestations of their vitality have been cultural rather than governmental. They are embedded in habits, norms, and prejudices more than in rules; they are expressed through the subconscious intentions of a people rather than in their conscious definitions; and they are associated with inherent images of nature instead of the mechanistic intricacies of human artifacts. This tacit side of the mix of democratic ideas has been especially important when Americans have searched for and asserted the grounds for political legitimacy. The ideas central to America's tacit political life are more commonly those to which Americans turn when their primary objectives are motivational more than order-centered and when they seek grounds for reform, protest, and reaction rather than the continuity of known and established institutions and principles.

These patterns reflect balances, not categorical differentiations. It is the variety of interactions among these elements that has been healthy for

American politics. Yet these interactions would be impossible without a framework for political theorizing that was both differentiated and unified. The ideas of the Articles have given vitality and direction to the governmental forms of the Constitution of 1787 just as the ideas of the Constitution of 1787 have given practical stability and unity to the perpetual union declared in 1776. Americans have not had to reject their principles of legitimation to protect functional authority, nor have they had to abandon their notions of order to become politically mobilized. The same mixed tradition that is the source of their political consensus and continuity is the source of their political conflicts and change. In short, Americans experience both the frustrations and satisfactions of a theory of democracy that soothes the wounds of conflict by placing differences within a setting of agreements and that confronts the power of conformity by placing consensus within a setting of diversity.

This strangely unique pattern of political ideas is especially valuable to a people isolated by fate, by fact, and by inclination. America was a different world, a new world, and most Americans even today have cherished a sense of their separateness or uniqueness. Furthermore, Americans have no common basis for national identity apart from their politics. The immediate, pressing implication of the absence of canon and feudal law in America is not, as Louis Hartz asserts, the inevitability of purely Lockean politics. It is instead more likely that America will become victimized either by the antagonisms generated among competing democratic theories or by the conformity created by a purified democratic theory. America was especially vulnerable to the destructive threats from both conflict and consensus because in both cases it had to fashion the core of its political meaning and national identity without the benefit of any alternative, internal political tradition with which it could interact and without interest in any external political tradition to which it could relate. It already was isolated and without canon and feudal law. If in addition it had been without the tensions of a hybridized tradition of democratic ideas, America would have been a prime candidate for the ravages of conflict or for the incapacitation of agreement. By incorporating opposing ideas of democracy into a shared national creed, American politics has been saved from the twin extremes of its unique circumstances and attitudes. An isolated consensual society, lacking the diversity of alternative traditions and identities, has remained vital, in part, because of the complex and irrational tensions of its consensus. And a society continually at odds with itself, yet seldom willing to reach beyond itself, has found cohesion because of the inclusiveness of its theoretical base.

America's intellectual challenge is not to "resolve" the conflicts within the consensus of American politics either by denying the reality of its conflicting parts or by becoming the champion of a single part of the consensual mix. In other words the challenge is not to make America's democratic consensus — its constitutional order — internally consistent. It is quite unlikely that such an enterprise could succeed. Generations of such attempts have failed. Moreover, the price of mere consistency could be devastating for America. Physically and psychically isolated and devoid of any alternative political and cultural identity, America would be left with only the deadening power of a unified set of uncontested ideas. It would be stripped of any intrinsic source of positive tensions necessary for the vitality of a people.

The unique form of America's political tradition, however, must be better and more self-consciously understood. This requires, especially, an attentiveness to the paradoxical association of conflict and agreement in American democracy. Perhaps the greatest impediment to the study of this tradition and its paradoxes is the largely tacit status of one of its major elements. Before the uniqueness of the hybrid can be explored effectively there must be greater recognition given to its differentiated constituent parts. This has been the preoccupation of this study. It has used the Articles of Confederation as both a literal and metaphorical representation of the tacit component. Thus, the theory of the Articles must become a part of explicit political understandings, not to supersede the literal and meta-phorical content of the Constitution of 1787 but to make it possible to see the remarkable variety of ways these two traditions can and have been mixed together in expressing American politics.

The contemporary concepts Americans use to make sense of their politics, concepts such as "liberal" and "conservative," make too little sense. They do not clarify the real theoretical issues or the theoretical basis of these issues. Americans are not faced with the choice between two different, reasonably consistent, theoretical traditions. Most typically, their differences with one another represent the diversity of choices possible

Shared but mixed traditions

when a people is exploring the various ways to configure the elements of a shared but mixed tradition. If that is so, it is necessary to understand better the intricate possibilities of a hybrid tradition, to identify the patterns of specific combinations that structure contemporary political debates and alternatives; to anticipate the recombinant political possibilities or, at least, accept the likelihood of a constantly modulating politics; to develop analyses of the unique theoretical meanings and implications of these various compositions; and to develop analyses of the relationship between these particularistic formulations and the fuller forms of the hybrid.

Even at the time of America's founding in the 1770s and 1780s, a unique blend of democratic ideas exhibited itself. A mixed democratic tradition has persisted, along with its unique tensions. In fact, American democracy has become increasingly varied and complex in the process. For example, the simultaneous affirmation of forms of localism and forms of nationalism has been a recurring American practice. Similarly, Americans have had special difficulties differentiating the Declaration's claim that all are created equal from the Constitution's standard of equal opportunity under the law. An important reason for this difficulty is that Americans generally value both liberty and equality but possess little self-consciousness of the tensions between them. Also, in American political theory it has been the tradition of individualism and negative government that has been most responsible for making the case for a stronger and more formal central authority. The greatest pressure for substantially reduced government, decentralization, and localism has come from the communal side of American democratic thinking. This is why the Bill of Rights' limits on governmental power, and especially national governmental power, have been difficult to interpret: they are the legacy of the more communal Antifederalists rather than of the individualistic Federalists. And finally, America has always had to deal with the enigma of a minoritarian tradition that has fed conformism and a majoritarian tradition that has fostered diversity.

This may be a most propitious time for a new American self-consciousness. Suddenly, the seemingly irrational impulses of mixed political enterprises and the tensions they express can be seen in many prominent places. The European Economic Community is moving to a differentiated but integrated Western Europe. The former Soviet Union is now struggling to create a new political form based on sovereignties within a sovereignty, unsure how to build commonwealth and independence simultaneously. Environmentalists encourage us to think globally and to act locally. Even Mikhail Gorbachev's vision of a "common European home," embraced with great hopefulness by many Western Europeans, has a surprisingly familiar ring to popular American sentiments, which have always had an attraction to "one sovereign nation with fifty sovereign states." One of the important paradoxes of contemporary politics is central to the political founding of the United States: the complex interplay between a comprehensive union and vital parochial traditions. Perhaps we have arrived at a special moment in time — a time when taking America's puzzling uniqueness and complexity seriously may lead to something more than American separatism. Today an exploration of the unique mixture of elements at the center of American democracy may broaden Americans' political understandings and kinships.

Am. has always had to deal with the tension of a minoritarian tradition that has fed conformism & a majoritarian trad. that has fostered diversity

Appendix

THE ARTICLES OF CONFEDERATION AND PERPETUAL UNION

BETWEEN THE STATES OF NEW HAMPSHIRE, MASSACHUSETTS BAY, RHODE ISLAND AND PROVIDENCE PLANTATIONS, CONNECTICUT, NEW YORK, NEW JERSEY, PENNSYLVANIA, DELAWARE, MARYLAND, VIRGINIA, NORTH CAROLINA, SOUTH CAROLINA, GEORGIA.

ARTICLE 1. The stile of this confederacy shall be "The United States of America."

ART. 2. Each State retains its sovereignty, freedom and independence, and every power, jurisdiction, and right, which is not by this confederation expressly delegated to the United States, in Congress assembled.

ART. 3. The said states hereby severally enter into a firm league of friendship with each other for their common defense, the security of their liberties and their mutual and general welfare; binding themselves to assist each other against all force offered to, or attacks made upon them, or any of them, on account of religion, sovereignty, trade, or any other pretense whatever.

ART. 4. The better to secure and perpetuate mutual friendship and intercourse among the people of the different states in this union, the free inhabitants of each of these states, paupers, vagabonds, and fugitives from justice excepted, shall be entitled to all privileges and immunities of free citizens in the several states; and the people of each State shall have free ingress and regress to and from any other State, and shall enjoy therein all the privileges of trade and commerce, subject to the same duties, impositions, and restrictions, as the inhabitants thereof respectively; provided, that such restrictions shall not extend so far as to prevent the removal of property, imported into any State, to any other State of which the owner is an inhabitant; provided also, that no imposition, duties, or restriction,

This copy of the final draft of the Articles of Confederation and Perpetual Union is as found in the *Journals,* November 15, 1777, 9:907–925.

shall be laid by any State on the property of the United States, or either of them.

If any person guilty of, or charged with treason, felony, or other high misdemeanor in any State, shall flee from justice and be found in any of the United States, he shall, upon demand of the governor or executive power of the State from which he fled, be delivered up and removed to the State having jurisdiction of his offense.

Full faith and credit shall be given in each of these states to the records, acts, and judicial proceedings of the courts and magistrates of every other State.

ART. 5. For the more convenient management of the general interests of the United States, delegates shall be annually appointed, in such manner as the legislature of each State shall direct, to meet in Congress, on the 1st Monday in November in every year, with a power reserved to each State to recal its delegates, or any of them, at any time within the year, and to send others in their stead for the remainder of the year.

No State shall be represented in Congress by less than two, nor by more than seven members; and no person shall be capable of being a delegate for more than three years in any term of six years; nor shall any person, being a delegate, be capable of holding any office under the United States, for which he, or any other for his benefit, receives any salary, fees, or emolument of any kind.

Each State shall maintain its own delegates in a meeting of the states, and while they act as members of the committee of the states.

In determining questions in the United States, in Congress assembled, each State shall have one vote.

Freedom of speech and debate in Congress shall not be impeached or questioned in any court or place out of Congress: and the members of Congress shall be protected in their persons from arrests and imprisonments, during the time of their going to and from, and attendance on Congress, *except for treason,* felony, or breach of the peace.

ART. 6. No State, without the consent of the United States, in Congress assembled, shall send any embassay to, or receive any embassy from, or enter into any conference, agreement, alliance, or treaty with any king, prince, or state; nor shall any person, holding any office of profit or trust under the United States, or any of them, accept of any present, emolument, office or title, of any kind whatever, from any king, prince, or foreign state; nor shall the United States, in Congress assembled, or any of them, grant any title of nobility.

No two or more states shall enter into any treaty, confederation, or alliance, whatever, between them, without the consent of the United States, in Congress assembled, specifying accurately the purposes for which the same is to be entered into, and how long it shall continue.

No state shall lay any imposts or duties which may interfere with any stipulations in treaties entered into by the United States, in Congress assembled, with any king, prince, or states, in pursuance of any treaties already proposed by Congress to the courts of France and Spain.

No vessels of war shall be kept up in time of peace by any State, except such number only as shall be deemed necessary by the United States, in Congress assembled, for the defence of such State or its trade; nor shall any body of forces be kept up by any State, in time of peace, except such number only as, in the judgment of the United States, in Congress assembled, shall be deemed requisite to garrison the forts necessary for the defence of such State; but every State shall always keep up a well regulated and disciplined militia, sufficiently armed and accoutred, and shall provide, and constantly have ready for use, in public stores, a due number of field pieces and tents, and a proper quantity of arms, ammunition and camp equipage.

No State shall engage in any war without the consent of the United States, in Congress assembled, unless such State be actually invaded by enemies, or shall have received certain advice of a resolution being formed by some nation of Indians to invade such State, and the danger is so imminent as not to admit of a delay till the United States, in Congress assembled, can be consulted; nor shall any State grant commissions to any ships or vessels of war, nor letters of marque or reprisal, except it be after a declaration of war by the United States, in Congress assembled, and then only against the kingdom or state, and the subjects thereof, against which war has been so declared, and under such regulations as shall be established by the United States, in Congress assembled, unless such State be infested by pirates, in which case vessels of war may be fitted out for that occasion, and kept so long as the danger shall continue, or until the United States, in Congress assembled, shall determine otherwise.

ART. 7. When land forces are raised by any State for the common defence, all officers of or under the rank of colonel, shall be appointed by the legislature of each State respectively, by whom such forces shall be raised, or in such manner as such State shall direct; and all vacancies shall be filled up by the State which first made the appointment.

ART. 8. All charges of war and all other expenses, that shall be incurred for the common defence or general welfare, and allowed by the United States, in Congress assembled, shall be defrayed out of a common treasury, which shall be supplied by the several states, in proportion to the value of all land within each State, granted to or surveyed for any person, as such land and the buildings and improvements thereon shall be estimated according to such mode as the United States, in Congress assembled, shall, from time to time, direct and appoint.

The taxes for paying the proportion shall be laid and levied by the authority and direction of the legislatures of the several states, within the time agreed upon by the United States, in Congress assembled.

ART. 9. The United States in Congress assembled, shall have the sole and exclusive right and power of determining on peace and war, except in the cases mentioned in the 6th article; of sending and receiving ambassadors; entering into treaties and alliances, provided that no treaty of commerce shall be made, whereby the legislative power of the respective states shall be restrained from imposing such imposts and duties on foreigners as their own people are subjected to, or from prohibiting the exportation or importation of any species of goods or commodities whatsoever; of establishing rules for deciding, in all cases, what captures on land or water shall be legal, and in what manner prizes, taken by land or naval forces in the service of the United States, shall be divided or appropriated; of granting letters of marque and reprisal in times of peace; appointing courts for the trial of piracies and felonies committed on the high seas, and establishing courts for receiving and determining, finally, appeals in all cases of captures; provided, that no member of Congress shall be appointed a judge of any of the said courts.

The United States, in Congress assembled, shall also be the last resort on appeal in all disputes and differences now subsisting, or that hereafter may arise between two or more states concerning boundary, jurisdiction or any other cause whatever; which authority shall always be exercised in the manner following: whenever the legislative or executive authority, or lawful agent of any State, in controversy with another, shall present a petition to Congress, stating the matter in question, and praying for a hearing, notice thereof shall be given, by order of Congress, to the legislative or executive authority of the other State in controversy, and a day assigned for the appearance of the parties by their lawful agents, who shall then be directed to appoint, by joint consent, commissioners or judges to constitute a court for hearing and determining the matter in question; but, if they cannot agree, Congress shall name three persons out of each of the United States, and from the list of such persons each party shall alternately strike out one, the petitioners beginning, until the number shall be reduced to thirteen; and from that number not less than seven, nor more than nine names, as Congress shall direct, shall, in the presence of Congress, be drawn out by lot; and the persons whose names shall be so drawn, or any five of them, shall be commissioners or judges to hear and finally determine the controversy, so always as a major part of the judges who shall hear the cause shall agree in the determination, and if either party shall neglect to attend at the day appointed, without shewing reasons which Congress shall judge sufficient, or, being present, shall refuse to strike, the Congress shall proceed to nominate three persons out of each State, and the secretary of Congress shall strike in behalf of such party absent or refusing; and the judgment and sentence of the court to be appointed, in the manner before prescribed, shall be final and conclusive; and if any of the parties shall refuse to submit to the authority of such court, or to appear or defend their claim or cause, the court shall nevertheless proceed to pronounce sentence or judgment, which shall, in like manner, be final and decisive, the judgment or sentence and other proceedings being, in either case, transmitted to Congress, and lodged among the acts of Congress for the security of the parties concerned; provided, that every commissioner, before he sits in judgment, shall take an oath, to be administered by one of the judges of the supreme or superior court of the State where the cause shall be tried, "well and truly to hear and determine the matter in question, according to the best of his judgment, without favour, affection, or hope of reward:" provided, also, that no State shall be deprived of territory for the benefit of the United States.

All controversies concerning the private right of soil, claimed under different grants of two or more states, whose jurisdictions, as they may respect such lands and the states which passed such grants, are adjusted, the said grants, or either of them, being at the same time claimed to have originated antecedent to such settlement of jurisdiction, shall, on the petition of either party to the Congress of the United States, be finally determined, as near as may be, in the same manner as is before prescribed for deciding disputes respecting territorial jurisdiction between different states.

The United States, in Congress assembled, shall also have the sole and exclusive right and power of regulating the alloy and value of coin struck by their own authority, or by that of the respective states; fixing the standard of weights and measures throughout the United States; regulating the trade and managing all affairs with the Indians not members of any of the states; provided that the legislative right of any State within its own limits be not infringed or violated, establishing and regulating post offices from one State to another throughout all the United States, and exacting such postage on the papers passing through the same as may be requisite to defray the expences of the said office; appointing all officers of the land forces in the service of the United States, excepting regimental officers; appointing all the officers of the naval forces, and commissioning all officers whatever in the service of the United States; making rules for the government and regulation of the said land and naval forces, and directing their operations.

The United States, in Congress assembled, shall have authority to appoint a committee to sit in the recess of Congress, to be denominated "a Committee of the States," and to consist of one delegate from each State, and to appoint such other committees and civil officers as may be necessary for managing the general affairs of the United States, under their direction; to appoint one of their number to preside; provided that no person be allowed to serve in the office of president more than one year in any term of three years; to ascertain the necessary sums of money to be raised for the service of the United States, and to appropriate and apply the same for defraying the public expenses; to borrow money or emit bills on the credit of the United States, transmitting, every half year, to the respective states, an account of the sums of money so borrowed or emitted;

to build and equip a navy; to agree upon the number of land forces, and to make requisitions from each State for its quota, in proportion to the number of white inhabitants in such State; which requisitions shall be binding; and, thereupon, the legislature of each State shall appoint the regimental officers, raise the men, and cloathe, arm, and equip them in a soldier-like manner, at the expense of the United States; and the officers and men so cloathed, armed, and equipped, shall march to the place appointed and within the time agreed on by the United States, in Congress assembled; but if the United States, in Congress assembled, shall, on consideration of circumstances, judge proper that any State should not raise men, or should raise a smaller number than its quota, and that any other State should raise a greater number of men than the quota thereof, such extra number shall be raised, officered, cloathed, armed, and equipped in the same manner as the quota of such State, unless the legislature of such State shall judge that such extra number cannot be safely spared out of the same, in which case they shall raise, officer, cloathe, arm, and equip as many of such extra number as they judge can be safely spared. And the officers and men so cloathed, armed, and equipped, shall march to the place appointed and within the time agreed on by the United States, in Congress assembled.

The United States, in Congress assembled, shall never engage in a war, nor grant letters of marque and reprisal in time of peace, nor enter into any treaties or alliances, nor coin money, nor regulate the value thereof, nor ascertain the sums and expences necessary for the defence and welfare of the United States, or any of them; nor emit bills, nor borrow money on the credit of the United States, nor appropriate money, nor agree upon the number of vessels of war to be built or purchased, or the number of land or sea forces to be raised, nor appoint a commander in chief of the army or navy, unless nine states assent to the same; nor shall a question on any other point, except for adjourning from day to day, be determined, unless by the votes of a majority of the United States, in Congress assembled.

The Congress of the United States shall have power to adjourn to any time within the year, and to any place within the United States, so that no period of adjournment be for a longer duration than the space of six months, and shall publish the journal of their proceedings monthly, except such parts thereof, relating to treaties, alliances or military operations, as, in their judgment, require secrecy; and the yeas and nays of the delegates of each State on any question shall be entered on the journal, when it is desired by any delegate; and the delegates of a State, or any of them, at his, or their request, shall be furnished with a transcript of the said journal, except such parts as are above excepted, to lay before the legislatures of the several states.

ART. 10. The committee of the states, or any nine of them, shall be authorized to execute, in the recess of Congress, such of the powers of Congress as the United States, in Congress assembled, by the consent of nine states, shall, from time to time, think expedient to vest them with; provided, that no power be delegated to the said committee, for the exercise of which, by the articles of confederation, the voice of nine states, in the Congress of the United States assembled, is requisite.

ART. 11. Canada acceding to this confederation, and joining in the measures of the United States, shall be admitted into and entitled to all the advantages of this union; but no other colony shall be admitted into the same, unless such admission be agreed to by nine states.

ART. 12. All bills of credit emitted, monies borrowed and debts contracted by, or under the authority of Congress before the assembling of the United States in pursuance of the present confederation, shall be deemed and considered as a charge against the United States, for payment and satisfaction whereof the said United States and the public faith are hereby solemnly pledged.

ART. 13. Every State shall abide by the determinations of the United States, in Congress assembled, on all questions which, by this confederation, are submitted to them. And the articles of this confederation shall be inviolably observed by every State, and the union shall be perpetual; nor shall any alteration at any time hereafter be made in any of them, unless such alteration be agreed to in a Congress of the United States, and be afterwards confirmed by the legislatures of every State.

These articles shall be proposed to the legislatures of all the United States, to be considered, and if approved of by them, they are advised to authorize their delegates to ratify the same in the Congress of the United States; which being done, the same shall become conclusive.

Notes

CHAPTER 1

1. This, I believe, is the spirit of Judith Shklar's attempt to "redeem" American political theory in "Redeeming American Political Theory."
2. Rousseau, *The Social Contract*, 2.
3. Lawrence, *Studies in Classic American Literature*, 173.
4. *Ibid.*
5. Eldon Eisenach explores two coexisting and interacting forms of American political history and American politics with special emphasis on the manifestations of this dual pattern relative to issues of religion, law, and constitutionalism in "The American Revolution Made and Remembered."
6. Dworkin, *Law's Empire*, Chapters 4 and 5.
7. *Ibid.*, 227–228.

CHAPTER 3

1. Bailyn, *The Ideological Origins of the American Revolution*, vi.
2. *Ibid.*, 51–52.
3. *Ibid.*, 56.
4. *Ibid.*, 93.
5. McIlwain and Nichols, *Federalism as a Democratic Process*, 35.
6. Bailyn, *op. cit.*, 230.
7. Murrin, "The Great Inversion, or Court versus Country." 379–380.
8. Pocock, *The Machiavellian Moment*, 78.
9. *Ibid.*, 545.
10. Wood, *The Creation of the American Republic*, 45.
11. Lee, *Lee Papers*, III, 323ff.
12. Wood, *op. cit.*, 31n, 61.
13. Witherspoon, *The Works of the Rev. John Witherspoon*, 3: 39.
14. Wood, *op. cit.*, 42n, 110–111.
15. *Ibid.*, 138–139.
16. *Ibid.*, 155.
17. *Ibid.*, 44n, 286.
18. Eisenach, "The American Revolution Made and Remembered," 79–82.
19. *Journals of the Continental Congress*, I:66–67, October, 14.
20. Jensen, *The Articles of Confederation*, 87.

CHAPTER 4

1. Sutherland, *Constitutionalism in America,* 142.
2. Diggins, *The Lost Soul of American Politics,* 5.
3. Jefferson, Koch and Peden, *The Life and Selected Writings of Thomas Jefferson,* 372.
4. *Ibid.,* 400.
5. *Ibid.,* 390.
6. *Ibid.,* 377.
7. Jefferson, "First Inaugural Address," in Adler, *Annals of America,* 4: 144.
8. Zuchert, "Self-Evident Truth and the Declaration of Independence," 3ff.
9. Wills, *Inventing America,* 228.
10. *Ibid.,* 214–217.
11. Lipscomb and Bergh, *Writings of Thomas Jefferson,* 14: 140.
12. Hutcheson, *Collected Works of Francis Hutcheson,* I: 256.
13. *Ibid.,* 5: 294.
14. *Ibid.,* 4: 295.
15. Jefferson, in Koch and Peden, *op. cit.,* 390.
16. *Ibid.*
17. Wills, *op. cit.,* 246.
18. *Ibid.,* 240–247.
19. Ferguson, *Civil Society,* 103–106.
20. Wills, *op. cit.,* 375.
21. Boyd, et al., *The Papers of Thomas Jefferson,* 1: 420–422.
22. Wills, *op. cit.,* 313.
23. *Ibid.,* 318.

CHAPTER 5

1. Jensen, *The Articles of Confederation,* 254.
2. Burnett, *Letters of Members of the Continental Congress,* 1: 345–346.
3. *Journals of the Continental Congress,* 9: 932–933.
4. Niles, *Principles and Acts of the Revolution in America,* 98.
5. Burnett, *op. cit.,* 4: 63.
6. *Ibid.,* 60.
7. Jensen, *op. cit.,* 245.
8. Collier and Collier, *Decision in Philadelphia,* 195.
9. Wood, *The Creation of the American Republic,* 359.
10. Jensen, *The New Nation,* 218.
11. *Ibid.,* 247.
12. *Ibid.,* 342.
13. Niebuhr, *The Irony of American History,* viii.
14. Parrington, *Main Currents in American Thought,* 1: 295.
15. Wood, *op. cit.,* 362.

16. *Ibid.*, 383.
17. Wood, "Interests and Disinterestedness in the Making of the Constitution," 76.
18. Madison, et al., *The Federalist Papers,* No. 10, 49.

CHAPTER 6

1. Foner, *The Complete Writings of Thomas Paine,* 1: 44.
2. *Ibid.*, 234.
3. *Ibid.*, 466.
4. *Ibid.*, 467.
5. *Ibid.*, 482.
6. *Ibid.*, 506.
7. *Ibid.*, 497.
8. *Ibid.*, 600.
9. *Ibid.*, 596.
10. *Ibid.*, 612.
11. *Ibid.*, 619.
12. *Ibid.*, 357.
13. *Ibid.*, 357–358.
14. *Ibid.*, 359.
15. *Ibid.*, 46.
16. *Ibid.*, 360.
17. *Ibid.*, 295.
18. *Ibid.*, 373.
19. *Ibid.*, 276.
20. *Ibid.*, 2: 583.
21. *Ibid.*, 1: 274.
22. *Ibid.*, 127.
23. *Ibid.*, 287.
24. *Ibid.*, 2: 1095.
25. *Ibid.*, 1: 30.
26. *Ibid.*, 2: 587.
27. *Ibid.*, 960.
28. *Ibid.*, 962
29. *Ibid.*, 281.
30. *Ibid.*, 285.
31. *Ibid.*, 1: 357.
32. *Ibid.*, 6.
33. *Ibid.*, 2: 949.
34. *Ibid.*, 924.
35. *Ibid.*, 950.
36. *Ibid.*, 931.
37. *Ibid.*, 1480.

38. Jefferson, in Koch and Peden, *op. cit.,* 310.

39. Parrington, *Main Currents in American Thought,* 1: 361.

40. Jefferson, in Koch and Peden, *op. cit.,* 390.

41. *Ibid.,* 384.

42. *Ibid.,* 377.

43. Eisenach, "The American Revolution Made and Remembered," 89.

44. Jefferson, in Koch and Peden, *op. cit.,* 501.

45. *Ibid.,* 676.

46. *Ibid.,* 427.

47. *Ibid.*

48. *Ibid.,* 435, 436.

49. *Ibid.,* 438.

50. *Ibid.,* 440.

51. *Ibid.,* 435.

52. *Ibid.,* 440–441.

53. *Ibid.,* 436.

54. *Ibid.,* 453.

55. *Ibid.,* 460.

56. *Ibid.,* 537–538.

CHAPTER 7

1. Storing, *The Complete Antifederalist,* 1:3, 71.

2. Kenyon, *The Antifederalists,* xxv.

3. Lienesch, *New Order of the Ages,* 150.

4. Jackson Turner Main places the Antifederalists in this theoretical context in his study of their works, *The Antifederalists,* 17.

5. Lienesch, *op. cit.,* 139–140.

6. Kenyon, *op. cit.,* xxxviii.

7. *Ibid.,* xxxii.

8. *Ibid.,* xxxiii.

9. *Ibid.*

10. *Ibid.,* xcix.

11. Hartz, *The Liberal Tradition in America,* 208.

12. Storing, *op. cit.,* 6.3.1, 37.

13. *Ibid.,* 6. 3. 8, 39.

14. *Ibid.,* 6. 11. 5, 131.

15. *Ibid.,* 5. 21. 15, 290.

16. *Ibid.,* 2. 5. 3, 87.

17. *Ibid.,* 2. 7. 66, 156, 161.

18. *Ibid.,* 2. 9. 2, 363–364.

19. *Ibid.,* 3. 2. 7, 15.

20. *Ibid.,* 3. 3. 8, 23.

21. *Ibid.,* 3. 6. 2, 67.
22. *Ibid.,* 3. 9. 48, 123.
23. *Ibid.,* 4. 10. 16, 145.
24. *Ibid.,* 4. 26. 2, 255.
25. *Ibid.,* 5. 17. 1, 257.
26. *Ibid.,* 5. 19. 1, 268–269.
27. *Ibid.,* 6. 12. 3, 150.
28. *Ibid.,* 5. 14. 48, 199.
29. *Ibid.,* 6. 11. 13, 135.
30. *Ibid.,* 6. 11. 1 and 6. 11. 2, 129.
31. Wood, *The Creation of the American Republic,* 485.
32. *Ibid.,* 495.
33. *Ibid.,* 498.
34. Wolin, *The Presence of the Past,* 88.
35. Wolin argues that we have difficulty grasping the Antifederalists' theory of politics because of our assumptions about what a theory is and does: a theory is to provide the basis for a reduction of differences by containing individual cases within general rules and, thereby, protect us from anomalies. Therefore, if the Antifederalists used political ideas to protect differences, we will only see atheoretical immaturity. *Ibid.,* 135–136.
36. Storing, *The Complete Antifederalist,* 3. 5. 12, 62.
37. *Ibid.,* 3. 12. 19, 175.
38. *Ibid.,* 5. 1. 68, 40 and 5. 1. 92, 55
39. *Ibid.,* 4. 26. 8, 259–260.
40. *Ibid.,* 5. 13. 2, 162.
41. *Ibid.,* 5. 1. 93, 55.
42. *Ibid.,* 4. 28. 3, 274
43. *Ibid.,* 4. 23. 8, 244.
44. *Ibid.,* 2. 7. 118, 176.
45. *Ibid.,* 3. 12. 3, 169.
46. *Ibid.,* 2. 4. 44, 48.
47. *Ibid.,* 2. 7. 107, 172–173.
48. *Ibid.,* 2. 9. 197, 442.
49. *Ibid.,* 2. 7. 9, 138.
50. *Ibid.,* 2. 8. 97, 266.
51. *Ibid.,* 3. 9. 9, 106.
52. For example, *Ibid.,* 3. 6. 21, 76.
53. *Ibid.,* 5. 21. 3, 281.
54. *Ibid.,* 4. 28. 2, 272.
55. *Ibid.,* 5. 13. 7, 164.
56. *Ibid.,* 4. 3. 1, 16.
57. *Ibid.,* 4. 3. 24, 34.
58. *Ibid.,* 2. 9. 14, 369.

59. *Ibid.*, 5. 14. 28, 192.
60. *Ibid.*, 3. 6. 12, 71.
61. *Ibid.*, 2. 9. 45, 382–383.
62. *Ibid.*, 2. 8. 96, 265.
63. *Ibid.*, 5. 3. 20, 89.
64. *Ibid.*, 6. 1. 54, 31.
65. *Ibid.*, 6. 12. 35, 168–169.
66. *Ibid.*, 2. 8. 179, 312.
67. *Ibid.*, 5. 13. 7, 164.
68. *Ibid.*, 2. 7. 9, 139.
69. *Ibid.*, 2. 8. 62, 254.
70. *Ibid.*, 2. 8. 113, 275.
71. *Ibid.*, 5. 1. 72, 43 and 5. 1. 81, 49–50
72. *Ibid.*, 6. 12. 18, 159.
73. *Ibid.*, 3. 3. 22, 33.
74. *Ibid.*, 2. 8. 196, 323.
75. *Ibid.*, 2. 8. 196, 324.
76. *Ibid.*, 2. 8. 93, 264.
77. *Ibid.*, 6. 13. 13, 181.
78. *Ibid.*, 2. 7. 80, 162.
79. *Ibid.*, 4. 9. 15, 128.
80. *Ibid.*, 2. 8. 93, 264.
81. *Ibid.*, 5. 18. 9, 264.
82. *Ibid.*, 4. 18. 2, 219ff.
83. *Ibid.*, 4. 3. 28, 37.
84. For example, *Ibid.*, 4. 22. 4, 232 and 4. 23. 3, 242.
85. *Ibid.*, 4. 24. 4, 247–248.
86. *Ibid.*, 2. 8. 205, 331.
87. *Ibid.*, 3. 14. 6, 183–184.
88. *Ibid.*, 6. 12. 2, 150.
89. *Ibid.*, 3. 14. 8, 184.
90. *Ibid.*, 6. 12. 11, 155.
91. *Ibid.*, 4. 13. 16, 175.
92. *Ibid.*, 2. 7. 3, 136.
93. *Ibid.*, 2. 7. 54, 152.
94. *Ibid.*, 2. 4. 70, 62.
95. *Ibid.*, 3. 3. 20, 31–32.
96. *Ibid.*, 2. 9. 44, 381.
97. *Ibid.*, 5. 16. 8, 225.
98. *Ibid.*, 4. 13. 28, 187.
99. *Ibid.*, 4. 14. 10, 196.
100. *Ibid.*, 4. 28. 3, 274.
101. *Ibid.*, 5. 18. 14, 266.

102. *Ibid.,* 4. 18. 1, 219.
103. *Ibid.,* 3. 11. 55, 165.
104. *Ibid.,* 4. 13. 21, 178.
105. *Ibid.,* 4. 18. 1, 219.

CHAPTER 8

1. Hartz, *The Liberal Tradition in America,* 63.
2. Berry, *Home Economics,* 165.
3. *Ibid.,* 169.
4. *Ibid.,* 173.
5. Moyers, *A World of Ideas,* 105.

Bibliography

Adams, Willi Paul. *The First American Constitutions.* Chapel Hill: University of North Carolina Press, 1980.

Adler, Mortimer J., ed. *The Annals of America.* 18 vols. Chicago: Encyclopaedia Britannica, 1976.

Allen, W. B., and Gordon Lloyd, eds. *The Essential Antifederalist.* Lanham, Md.: University Press of America, 1985.

Bailyn, Bernard. *The Ideological Origins of the American Revolution.* Cambridge: Harvard University Press, 1967.

Ball, Terence, and J.G.A. Pocock, eds. *Conceptual Change and the Constitution.* Lawrence: University Press of Kansas, 1988.

Beard, Charles. *An Economic Interpretation of the Constitution.* New York: Free Press, 1935.

Beeman, Richard, Stephen Botein, and Edward C. Carter II, eds. *Beyond Confederation.* Chapel Hill: University of North Carolina Press, 1987.

Berry, Wendell. *Home Economics.* San Francisco: North Point Press, 1987.

———. *The Unsettling of America: Culture and Agriculture.* New York: Avon Books, 1977.

Borden, Morton, ed. *The Antifederalist Papers.* Lansing: Michigan State University Press, 1965.

Boyd, Julian P., ed. *The Papers of Thomas Jefferson.* 22 vols. Princeton: Princeton University Press, 1950.

Burnett, Edmund C., ed. *Letters of Members of the Continental Congress.* 8 vols. Washington, D.C.: Carnegie Institution of Washington, 1921–1936.

Collier, Christopher, and James L. Collier. *Decision in Philadelphia: The Constitutional Convention of 1787.* New York: Random House, 1968.

Dealey, James Q. *Growth of American State Constitutions.* New York: DeCapo Press, 1972.

Diggins, John P. *The Lost Soul of American Politics.* New York: Basic Books, 1984.

Dworkin, Ronald. *Law's Empire.* Cambridge: Harvard University Press, 1986.

Eisenach, Eldon J. "The American Revolution Made and Remembered." *American Studies* 13 (Spring 1979): 71–97.

———. *Two Worlds of Liberalism.* Chicago: University of Chicago Press, 1981.

Ferguson, Adam. *Civil Society.* Edinburgh: Edinburgh University Press, 1966.

Foner, Philip S., ed. *The Complete Writings of Thomas Paine.* 2 vols. New York: The Citadel Press, 1969.

Gillespie, Michael A., and Michael Lienesch. *Ratifying the Constitution.* Lawrence: University Press of Kansas, 1989.

Hamilton, Alexander, James Madison, and John Jay. *The Federalist Papers.* New York: Bantam Books, 1982.

Hartz, Louis. *The Liberal Tradition in America.* New York: Harcourt, Brace & World, 1955.

Havard, William C., and Joseph L. Bernd. *200 Years of the Republic in Retrospect.* Charlottesville: University Press of Virginia, 1976.

Hofstadter, Richard. *The American Political Tradition.* New York: Alfred A. Knopf, 1948.

Hume, David. *The Philosophical Works.* 4 vols. Edited by Thomas Hill Green and Thomas Hodge Grose. Darmstadt, Germany: Scientia Verlag Aalen, 1964.

Hutcheson, Francis. *Collected Works of Francis Hutcheson.* 7 vols. Edited by Georg Olms. Hildesheim, 1971.

Hutson, James H. "Country, Court, and Constitution: Antifederalism and the Historians." *William and Mary Quarterly* 38 (July 1981): 337–366.

———. "Riddles of the Federal Constitutional Convention." *William and Mary Quarterly* 44 (July 1987): 411–423.

Hyneman, Charles S., and Donald S. Lutz. *American Political Writing During the Founding Era: 1760–1805.* 2 vols. Indianapolis, Ind.: Liberty Press, 1983.

Jensen, Merrill. *The Articles of Confederation.* Madison: University of Wisconsin Press, 1940.

———. *The Founding of a Nation.* New York: Oxford University Press, 1968.

———. *The New Nation.* New York: Alfred A. Knopf, 1950.

———, ed. *Regionalism in America.* Madison: University of Wisconsin Press, 1965.

Journals of the Continental Congress, 1774–1789. 34 vols. Washington, D.C.: Library of Congress, 1904–1937.

Kenyon, Cecelia M. *The Antifederalists.* Indianapolis, Ind.: Bobbs-Merrill Co., 1966.

———. "Men of Little Faith: The Antifederalists on the Nature of Representative Government." *William and Mary Quarterly* 12 (January 1955): 3–43.

Koch, Adrienne, and William Peden, eds. *The Life and Selected Writings of Thomas Jefferson.* New York: Random House, 1944.

Lawrence, D. H. *Studies in Classic American Literature.* New York: Viking Press, 1923.

Lee, Charles. *Lee Papers.* 4 vols. New York: New York Historical Society, 1872–1875.

Lewis, John D., ed. *Antifederalists versus Federalists.* San Francisco: Chandler Publishing Co., 1967.

Lienesch, Michael. *New Order of the Ages.* Princeton: Princeton University Press, 1988.

Lipscomb, Andrew A., and Albert Ellery Bergh. *The Writings of Thomas Jefferson.* 20 vols. Washington, D.C.: The Thomas Jefferson Memorial Association, 1903.

Main, Jackson Turner. *The Antifederalists: Critics of the Constitution, 1781–1788.* Chapel Hill: University of North Carolina Press, 1961.

Mason, Alpheus T. *The States Rights Debate: Antifederalism and the Constitution.* Englewood Cliffs, N.J.: Prentice-Hall, 1964.

McDonald, Forrest. *We the People: The Economic Origins of the Constitution.* Chicago: University of Chicago Press, 1958.

McIlwain, Charles H., and Roy F. Nichols, eds. *Federalism as a Democratic Process.* New Brunswick, N.J.: Rutgers University Press, 1942.

McWilliams, Wilson Carey. *The Idea of Fraternity in America.* Berkeley and Los Angeles: University of California Press, 1973.

Moyers, Bill. *A World of Ideas.* New York: Doubleday, 1989.

Murrin, John M. "The Great Inversion, or Court versus Country," in J.G.A. Pockock, ed. *Three British Revolutions,* 368–429.

Niebuhr, Reinhold. *The Irony of American History.* New York: Charles Scribner's Sons, 1952.

Niles, Hezekiah. *Principles and Acts of the Revolution in America.* New York: Barns Co., 1876.

Parrington, Vernon L. *Main Currents in American Thought.* 2 vols. New York: Harcourt, Brace & World, 1927.

Pocock, J.G.A. *The Machiavellian Moment.* Princeton: Princeton University Press, 1975.

———. *Politics, Language, and Time.* New York: Atheneum, 1971.

———, ed. *Three British Revolutions: 1641, 1688, and 1776.* Princeton: Princeton University Press, 1980.

Rousseau, Jean-Jacques. *The Social Contract.* Chicago: Henry Regnery Co., 1954.

Rutland, Robert A. *The Birth of the Bill of Rights: 1776–1791.* Chapel Hill: University of North Carolina Press, 1955.

———. *The Ordeal of the Constitution.* Norman: University of Oklahoma Press, 1966.

Schechter, Stephen L., and Richard B. Bernstein, eds. *Contexts of the Bill of Rights.* Madison, Wis.: Madison House Publishers, 1990.

Shklar, Judith N. "Redeeming American Political Theory." *American Political Science Review.* 85 (March 1991): 3–15.

Storing, Herbert J., ed. *The Complete Antifederalist.* 7 vols. Chicago: University of Chicago Press, 1981.

Sutherland, Arthur E. *Constitutionalism in America.* New York: Blaisdell Publishing Co., 1965.

White, Morton. *The Philosophy of the American Revolution.* New York: Oxford University Press, 1978.

Wills, Garry. *Explaining America: The Federalist.* New York: Penguin Books, 1981.

———. *Inventing America: Jefferson's Declaration of Independence.* New York: Doubleday and Co., 1978.

Witherspoon, John. *The Works of the Rev. John Witherspoon.* 4 vols. Philadelphia, 1802.

Wolin, Sheldon S. *The Presence of the Past.* Baltimore, Md.: The Johns Hopkins University Press, 1989.

Wood, Gordon S. *The Creation of the American Republic, 1776–1787.* Chapel Hill: University of North Carolina Press, 1969.

Zuchert, Michael. "Self-Evident Truth and the Declaration of Independence." *Review of Politics* 49 (Summer 1987): 319–339.

Index